BEYOND NORMS:
IT FOR BUSINESS EXCELLENCE

BEYOND NORMS: IT FOR BUSINESS EXCELLENCE

Editors
JAYANTHI RANJAN
SANDEEP PURI
RAKESH CHOPRA

BLOOMSBURY
LONDON • NEW DELHI • NEW YORK • SYDNEY

First Published, 2013

BLOOMSBURY PUBLISHING INDIA PVT. LTD.
London New Delhi New York Sydney

ISBN: 978-93-82563-43-3

Published by Bloomsbury Publishing India Pvt. Ltd.
VISHRUT Building, DDA Complex, Building No. 3, Pocket C-6 & 7
Vasant Kunj, New Delhi 110 070

Laser Typeset by FORTUNE GRAPHICS
WZ-911/2, Shankarlal Street, Naraina, New Delhi

Printed at Anvi Composers
1 DDA Market, Block A-1B, Pachim Vihar, New Delhi 110 063

Acknowledgements

The editors are grateful to the management and Dr. Bibek Banerjee (Director) of IMT, Ghaziabad, India without whose support it would not have been possible to bring out this volume. We would like to thank Dr. Rajendra Nargundkar (Sr. Dean) and Dr. Suresh Bedi (Dean) for their guidance and help in numerous activities to organize FOBE 2012. We specially thank our knowledge partners Mazagon Dock Limited, for their support in making FOBE 2012 a big success.

Research is a painstaking business and we cannot overemphasize the importance of carefully researched papers in contributing to a volume of this type. A large number of distinguished authors from academia and practicing managers from industry have shown a keen interest in the subject area and have contributed well researched papers. Thanks to their interest that this volume has been possible. We would like to thank our colleagues from academia for their valuable time, support and guidance. The support came in many forms: review and re-review, suggestions and modifications and observations to make this volume more focused and relevant.

Our thanks are also due to Bloomsbury Publishing, their editors, production experts and their entire staff for their cooperation in bringing out this volume. We would also like to thank all the faculty colleagues, officers and staff members at IMT, Ghaziabad in extending their support for FOBE 2012. Special thanks are due to Mr. Krishna Murari Sinha for his contribution in the progress of this volume.

We value your feedback and suggestions on this volume. We look forward to your comments on emails: jranjan@imt.edu; rchopra@imt.edu; spuri@imt.edu in order to bring out a better innovative volume in future.

Finally, deep thanks go to our family members for their understanding, patience and support for this endeavor.

Jayanthi Ranjan
Sandeep Puri
Rakesh Chopra

Preface

Thinking that moves away in diverging directions to involve a variety of aspects using new developments in information technologies lead to novel ideas and solutions; associated with creativity "Thinking beyond norms with Information and Communication Technologies" provides an authoritative review of the concepts of new approaches to information and communication technologies management in the age of knowledge economy.

FOBE 2012 – International Conference Facets of Business Excellence – Thinking beyond the Box is organized by IMT Ghaziabad after the successful FOBE 2011 – International Conference Facets of Business Excellence – Leveraging Information Technology for Strategic Advantage.

The primary goal of the FOBE 2012 is to bring together creative academic and industrial experts in the field of Business Administration to discuss, exchange views and experiences on thinking beyond the box to help today's business organizations to exceed their goals and expectations while pursuing their full growth and earning potential. This conference is a platform for discussing contemporary issues in Strategy, IT, Management and Marketing and for exchanging views and experiences on various issues related to out of box thinking in business management.

It contains rich resources from the vast experiences of researchers, academicians, and practitioners in the industry. This premier reference source contains a very comprehensive knowledge on beyond norms management practices and provides an all-encompassing perspective on the importance of innovation in management practices.

Hope this volume finds space in the minds of the practicing world of business and IT and draws new landscapes in future.

Jayanthi Ranjan
Sandeep Puri
Rakesh Chopra

The Editors

DR JAYANTHI RANJAN

Jayanthi Ranjan is a Professor in IT Management area at IMT, Ghaziabad. She is also Associate Dean-International Relations, IMT Ghaziabad. She has more than 19 years of teaching experience. She has published various papers on Data clustering, Data Mining, Database security, business intelligence, educational technologies that appeared in various international refereed journals. She has over 110 publications till date. She has over 53 publications in various International Journals, 15 national conference proceedings and 10 International conference Proceedings till date. She has published 14 edited books. She has published research papers with refereed publications like in World Scientific, Emerald, Indersceince, ANSINET, GIFT society. She is the recipient of 'Best Teacher Award' from AIMA-Ghaziabad Management Association, India for her contribution to teaching and research. She is also the recipient of Best Management Researcher award, from Association of Management Scholars AIMS.

She is serving on the editorial board for the international journal "Information Technology Journal", Asian Network for Scientific Information. She is also the editorial member of "Indersceince-International Journal of E-CRM". She is the Editorial member of "Inter disciplinary journal of information knowledge and management", Informing Science Institute, UK. She is the associate editor of "Journal of Applied and Theoretical Information Technology". Her Teaching and Research interests include Data Mining & Building Data Warehouses, Information Systems Design, Information Agents Building and Business Intelligence. She can be reached at jranjan@imt.edu;

PROF SANDEEP PURI

Sandeep Puri is working as a faculty in Marketing at IMT, Ghaziabad. He is pursuing his Ph. D on Private labels. He is Gold Medalist during B. Pharmacy. He has over 19 years of experience in Industry & academics. He has held senior level positions in Marketing and Sales Management in Trident & Novartis. He has 24 publications till date. He has 5 publications in various International Journals and 9 in magazines and newspapers. He is also having 2 publications in International conference proceedings and 2 in national conference proceedings. He is also a visiting faculty at prestigious business schools like S P Jain, Singapore, Fachhochschule Vorarlberg, Austria and Great Lakes His teaching, research and training interests include Customer Relationship Management, Sales Management & Service Marketing. He has published six edited books He can be reached at spuri@imt.edu.

PROF. RAKESH CHOPRA

Dr. Rakesh Chopra is a professor in the area of Economic Environment & Strategy. He is a Ph. D and M.Phil from Mumbai University in Strategic Studies & International Relations focusing on Energy Security, M.Sc. from Madras University, and an MBA from JBIMS, Mumbai. He was Senior Visiting Research Fellow with the "Oxford Leverhulme Programme on the Changing Character of War" at Oxford University. He is an alumnus of the Harvard Kennedy School. Prior to joining IMT, he was a Professor of Strategy at XLRI Jamshedpur. He served in the Indian Navy for 38 years. He has commanded three ships including a ship in the 1971 Indo Pak war in the Eastern Theatre, and has held various operational appointments. He is an alumnus of the National Defense Academy, and the Defense Services Staff College, Wellington, where he has been on the Directing Staff. He was the Chief Instructor and Dean of the College of Naval Warfare at Karanja, Mumbai, and Chief Instructor of the Navigation & Direction School where officers specialize in the planning and conduct of maritime operations. He was mentioned in 'Mention in Dispatches' for gallantry during military operations in Sri Lanka and was awarded the Vishisht Seva Medal by the President of India for exemplary service.

Contents

Acknowledgements v
Preface vii
The Editors ix

1. A Conceptual Framework for Efficient Data Warehouse Design 1
Naveen Dahiya, Vishal Bhatnagar and Manjit Singh
2. A Secure Prospect for Unplanned Wireless Networks Request 14
Kavita M. Rathi and S.D. Sawarkar
3. Analysis of Factors Inhibiting e-Tailing in NCR Region 24
Sandeep Puri, Mayank Sahajwani, Aabhas Rastogi and Paras Arora
4. Authenticity Check of Professional Degrees through Cloud Computing in India 34
Prashanta K. Bhuyan, Susmi Routray and Suvalaxmi Singh
5. Big Data Analytics: Need of Present Era 45
Sapna Sinha and Vishal Bhatnagar
6. Building Institutional Intelligence in Higher Educational Institutions using Knowledge Management and Data Mining Techniques 54
Mamta Bhusry and Jayanthi Ranjan
7. Business Intelligence Application in Financial Sector – Credit Scoring of Retail Loans using a Hybrid Modeling Approach 65
S. Chandrasekhar
8. Eliminating the Need for Multiple Layer-2 Network for Better Traffic Management 74
Prabhjot Kaur
9. ICT Enabled Technologies 81
Neeraj Awasthy and Sukriti Tayal
10. Integrating Layered Approach with CRF to Build More Efficient Intrusion Detection System 90
Vaishali T. Deshmukh and Shubhangi Vaikole
11. National Knowledge Management Framework 101
Vinay Kumar Ahlawat and Jayanthi Ranjan

12. New Trends in Security Solution Architectures and Risk Assessment Strategies 110
Nirmalya Chakraborty, Jayanthi Ranjan and Vandna Sharma

13. On Mobile Payment Technology Adoption Issues in India: Case of Airtel Money 120
Parijat Upadhyay, Saikat Ghosh Roy and Abhishek Sharma

14. Performance Management System and Multisource Feedback: A Comparative Study of Software Organizations 130
Geeta Mishra

15. Problems in Existing RFID Systems: User-Centered Design Methods 138
Manjeet

16. Refined Coefficient Fixed Effects 144
Subrato Banerjee

17. Steganography: An Approach for Invisible Communication 151
Nidhi Gupta, Rashmi Upadhyay and Thirunavukkarasu K.

18. To Be or Not to Be: Challenges and Planning for Embracing Cloud Computing 163
Sanjiva Shankar Dubey

19. Use of VSAT Technology for Supplemental Education at School Level for Wider Accessibility 171
Nishal Joseph Thaikattil

20. Web Data Mining: Emerging Challenges of a Technique and Its Significance 183
Nudrat Fatima, Iffat Ara Khanam and Thirunavukkarasu K.

Author Index 193

A Conceptual Framework for Efficient Data Warehouse Design

Naveen Dahiya, Vishal Bhatnagar[1] and Manjit Singh[2]

Department of CSE, MSIT, Janakpuri, New Delhi
[1] Department of CSE, AIACT & R, Geeta Colony, Delhi
[2] YMCAUST, Sector-6, Faridabad, Haryana

ABSTRACT

Data Warehouses are playing an important role nowadays in providing a competitive advantage to companies, as the information extracted from data warehouses is helpful in making strategic decisions. The strategic decisions help in analyzing the past, relating it to present and forecasting of future trends. The quality of data warehouses depends on the quality of information stored. In this paper, we have presented a conceptual framework for design of an efficient data warehouse system. The Conceptual framework follows a layered approach. Layer 1 presents the factors governing information quality. Layer 2 presents the creation and validation of quality factors affecting data warehouse and Layer 3 shows the design of data warehouse system based on quality factors.

INTRODUCTION

A data warehouse (Perez et al., 2005) is a storehouse that integrates data from diverse platforms, transforms the data into information suitable for strategic decision making and loads the information into memory repositories. The data warehouse system is made open to complex queries and various data mining tools for making strategic decisions. A data warehouse system enables to analyze data along multiple dimensions at a time. An efficient data warehouse system provides quality information based on the market trends of current scenario.

The conceptual design (Kamble et al., 2008) phase is the first step in data warehouse development. It stores requirements as collected from users, managers and business analysts. It provides a complete, formal way of storing users requirements and is independent of implementation issues. The conceptual phase leads to the development of next logical design phase. The logical design (Mishra et al., 2008) phase defines data structures, data types and memory space for all the entities defined in conceptual design phase. This phase paves the way for next successive physical design phase in data warehouse development. The physical design phase is the actual implementation of data warehouse system in run time environment where the data warehouse is open to multiple clients for information extraction.

The quality of information (Calero et al., 2001)stored during each of the data warehouse design phases affects the quality of data warehouse system. The quality of conceptual design phase affects the quality of successive design phases as it is the initial phase in data warehouse development. The quality of conceptual data warehouse schema depends on quality factors called quality metrics. The quality metrics are based on the size and structural properties of conceptual data warehouse schemas. These quality metrics (Serrano et al., 2007)measure the quality of conceptual schemas in terms of understandability, efficiency and effectiveness. The quality metrics are proposed based on size and structure of conceptual data warehouse schema. The metrics proposed and created are theoretically as well as empirically validated to prove their correctness and relevance. For adapting with the changing dynamic environment redundant metrics can be removed or redefined. The conceptual model built in consideration with the quality metrics lays the foundation of a good quality conceptual schema. A good quality conceptual schema leads to the development of an efficient data warehouse system. We, in this paper have proposed a conceptual framework that starts with the regulation of quality information in the conceptual phase based on quality metrics which leads to the development of quality product.

This paper is organized as follows: Section II presents the motivation and related research. Section III outlines the research methodology. Section IV presents anintroduction to layered conceptual framework for design of an efficient data warehouse system. Section V discusses in detail the proposed conceptual framework. Section VI presents an empirical case study based on the conceptual framework. Section VII provides research implication and discussions of the proposed work. Section VIII presents limitations related to the proposedconceptualframework. Section IX concludes the paper along with enumeration of the research domains for conducting future research.

RELATED RESEARCH AND MOTIVATION

The motivation behind the creation of proposed conceptual framework for design of an efficient data warehouse system is based on the growing importance of data warehouse domain and the role played by data warehousing in strategic decision making. The right decisions made at right times is the crux of time which is made possible by means of data warehouses. An efficient data warehouse system should possess following characteristics:

(a) Integrated data from diverse applications

(b) User friendly

(c) Content includes current as well as historical data

(d) Ability to run complex queries and generate results online

(e) Ability to initiate reports

(f) View data against multiple angles

(g) Time efficient

Our present review is broadly categorized into the study of design techniques leading to the development of conceptual data warehouse schemas, quality factors affecting the quality of conceptual schemas and the approaches for creation and validation of quality factors leading towards development of efficient data warehouse system.

Some of the techniques for design of conceptual multidimensional models are as follows: starER Model (Tryfona et al., 1999), Multidimensional/ER (M/ER) Model (Sapia et al., 1998), CGMD Model (Kamble, 2008), DWDCM (Franconi and Sattler, 1999), REMDM Model (Perez et al., 2005), GOLD Model (Trujillo, 1999), EGOLD Model (Gamel et al., 2005), OOMD Model (Trujillo and Palomar, 1998),Yet Another Multidimensional Model (YAM2) (Abello et al., 2006), The Dimensional Fact (DF) Model (Golfarelli et al., 1998), MAC Model (Tsois et al., 2001).

A number of quality metrics have been proposed by various authors (Genero et al., 2008; Kpodjedo et al., 2011; Moody, 2005; Calero et al., 2001; Piattini et al., 2001; Schuff et al., 2011) based on the size and structure of conceptual data warehouse schema. Serrano et al. (2007) discussed eleven metrics. Singh et al. (2010a, b) discussed several software quality metrics, their fault proneness along with their empirical validation. The motivation behind the research is the study related to quality factors or metrics that provides basis of measurement of size and structural complexities of conceptual schemas which further affects their understandability, efficiency and effectiveness.

RESEARCH METHODOLOGY

The authors made an in depth study of various factors leading to the design of an efficient data warehouse system. The roadmap leading towards the development of conceptual framework for development of an efficient data warehouse system is shown in Figure 1. As can be seen from Figure 1, a step wise approach is followed. The methodology aims at making the existing data warehouse system more efficient in terms of information delivery. Open queries and other data extraction techniques are applied to the data warehouse system. The quality of information extracted is measured in terms of quality evaluation parameters like correctness of results to queries, response time. If the system does not make up to evaluation parameters then there exists scope of improvement in existing data warehouse system. A analysis of data warehouse design needs to be made starting from conceptual phase. Based on the structural complexity of data warehouse schema the system can be redesigned in consideration with existing quality metrics along with the newly created and validated metrics if any. The quality of newly redesigned conceptual schema can now be measured in terms of understanding time, efficiency and effectiveness. The next successive logical and physical design can be made based on the redesigned conceptual schema. The output is a data warehouse system which is more efficient in comparison to the data warehouse system we started with. Asa analogy we can state that a strong foundation paves the way for everlasting building erected on it.

CONCEPTUAL FRAMEWORK TOWARDS DEVELOPMENT OF AN EFFICIENT DATA WAREHOUSE SYSTEM

In this section, we have proposed and discussed a conceptualframework for development of an efficient data warehouse system. An efficient data warehouse that plays a major role in strategic decision making is need of time. For building an efficient data warehouse system a layered approach is proposed. The framework starts with design of conceptual schema in Layer 1 followed by creation and validation of quality metrics based on structural properties of conceptual model in Layer 2 and finally redesign of conceptual schema taking in consideration quality metrics in Layer 3. The proposed framework lays emphasis on the creation and validation of quality factors affecting quality of conceptual schema, as shown by highlighted Layer 2. This layer is the most important phase of our layered approach which is not emphasized in existing approaches. The conceptual schema can be redesigned based on the quality metrics. The redesigned conceptual schema will lead to an efficient data warehouse system when further extended to logical and physical design phases. If the quality of information is maintained at base levels then a high quality yield can be obtained at successive levels.

The design of efficient data warehouse system follows a layered approach as shown in Figure 2.

(a) Layer 1 presents the importance of information quality in the design of conceptual models of data warehouse. The output of layer 1 is a conceptual schema built using object oriented dimensional modeling technique. The schema does not take into consideration the quality factors based on size and structural complexity of conceptual schema.

(b) Layer 2 describes the whole process starting from the proposal and creation of quality metrics till their application to real dynamic environment. The quality metrics measure the quality of data warehouse conceptual schema in terms of understandability, efficiency and effectiveness based on the structural properties of schema. The output of layer 2 is a set of valid metrics defined and validated based on the structural properties of conceptual schema that provide a quality measurement of schema in terms of efficiency, effectiveness and understandability.

(c) Layer 3 shows that a good quality conceptual schema built by taking into consideration quality metrics, leading to the development of an efficient data warehouse system because conceptual phase lays the foundation of development of data warehouse. The conceptual schema built in layer 1 is redesigned taking into consideration the valid quality metrics defined and validated in layer 2.

The data warehouse conceptual schema provides a way for storing user requirements formally. The entity to be analyzed is known as fact which has numerical attributes. The fact is analyzed along multiple entities known as dimensions. The dimensions contain mostly non-numerical attributes. The facts and dimensions are related to each other using relationships of multiple cardinalities. The dimensions can form hierarchies starting from upper to fine granular levels. Various operations can be applied to conceptual schemas like rolls up, drill down, drill across, aggregation.

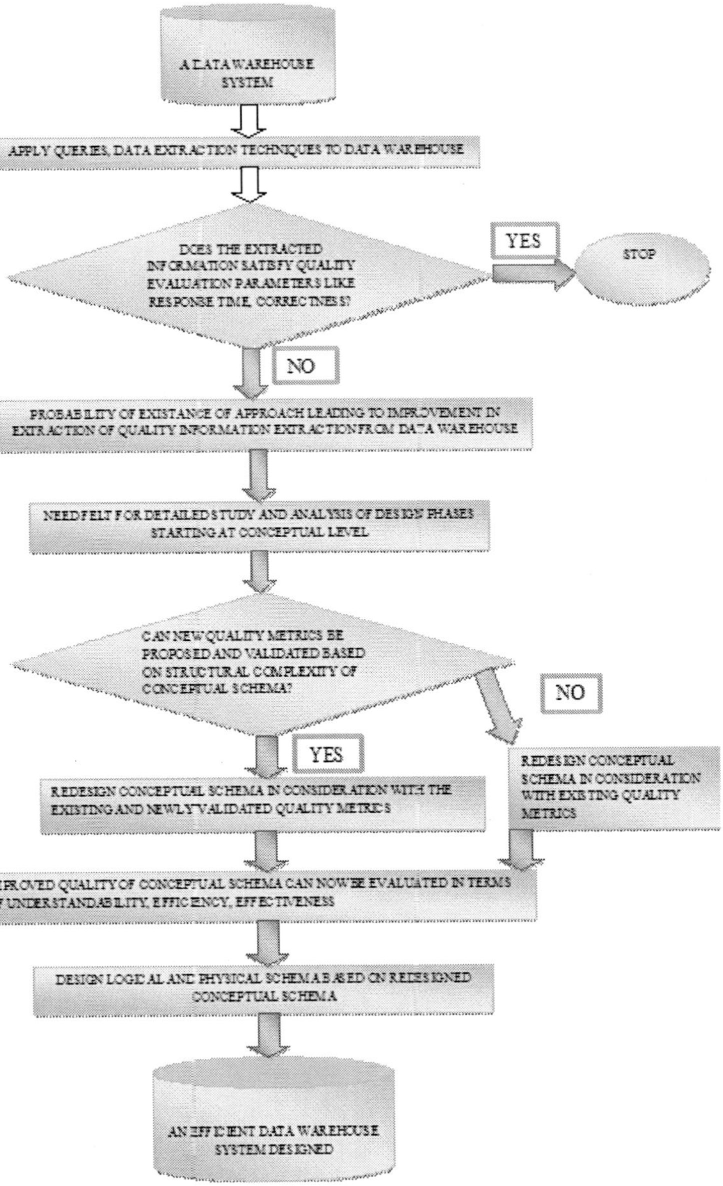

Fig. 1. Research Roadmap Leading to Development of Efficient Data Warehouse System

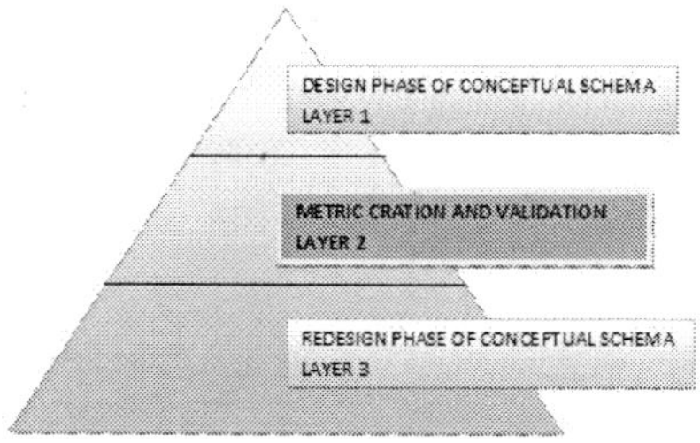

Fig. 2. Layered Approach for Development of an Efficient Data Warehouse System

DETAILED FRAMEWORK FOR DEVELOPMENT OF AN EFFICIENT DATA WAREHOUSE SYSTEM

As can be seen from Figure 3, the development of efficient data warehouse system follows a layered approach.

- **Layer 1** forms the initial phase in the data warehouse development. As seen from Figure 3, the information quality depends on data quality and data presentation quality. The data warehouse quality depends on Data quality, Data model quality and Data Base Management System quality (Serrano et al., 2007 and Serrano et al., 2008). In this paper we have discussed only the factors affecting data model quality. The data model quality depends on Conceptual model quality, Logical model quality and Physical model quality. The conceptual design phase is the initial design phase in data warehouse development, so its quality will affect the overall design quality of successive phases in data warehouse development. The conceptual model can be designed using various techniques and hence the quality of conceptual model depends on the models built using conceptual design techniques namely:
  - **Star ER conceptual model**: It consists of a single fact set around which dimension sets are arranged using relationship sets (one to many relationship between fact and dimensions). The fact, dimensions and relationship sets consist of respective attributes showing their properties as discussed by Mishra et al. (2008).
  - **Dimension Fact model**: The dimension fact (Mishra et al., 2008) modeling approach is suitable for representing hierarchies. It consist of a structure in the form of a tree whose elements are facts, dimensions, attributes and hierarchy relationships.
  - **Multidimensional ER model**: This modeling approach is an extension of entity relationship model. It shows hierarchy in dimensions and operation 'rolls up' that can be applied to dimension hierarchy levels as specified in Mishra et al. (2008).
  - **Object Oriented Dimensional model**: The technique uses object oriented features such as specialization/generalization and the concept of objects, classes to show dimension/ facts. Languages such as XML, UML (Genero et al., 2007; Lujan-Mora, 2002 and Medina et al., 2007) which support object oriented features are used for modeling approach.

The object oriented dimensional modeling approach is widely used to make conceptual schemas because it is user friendly, implementation independent, provides a formal and complete way of storing users requirements and also it supports object oriented features that represent real world objects. The object oriented dimensional model quality depends on the size and structural complexities of schema. The size and structural properties of schemas are measured in terms of size and structural metrics. The complexity of conceptual schema is measured in terms of understandability, efficiency and effectiveness using these quality metrics.

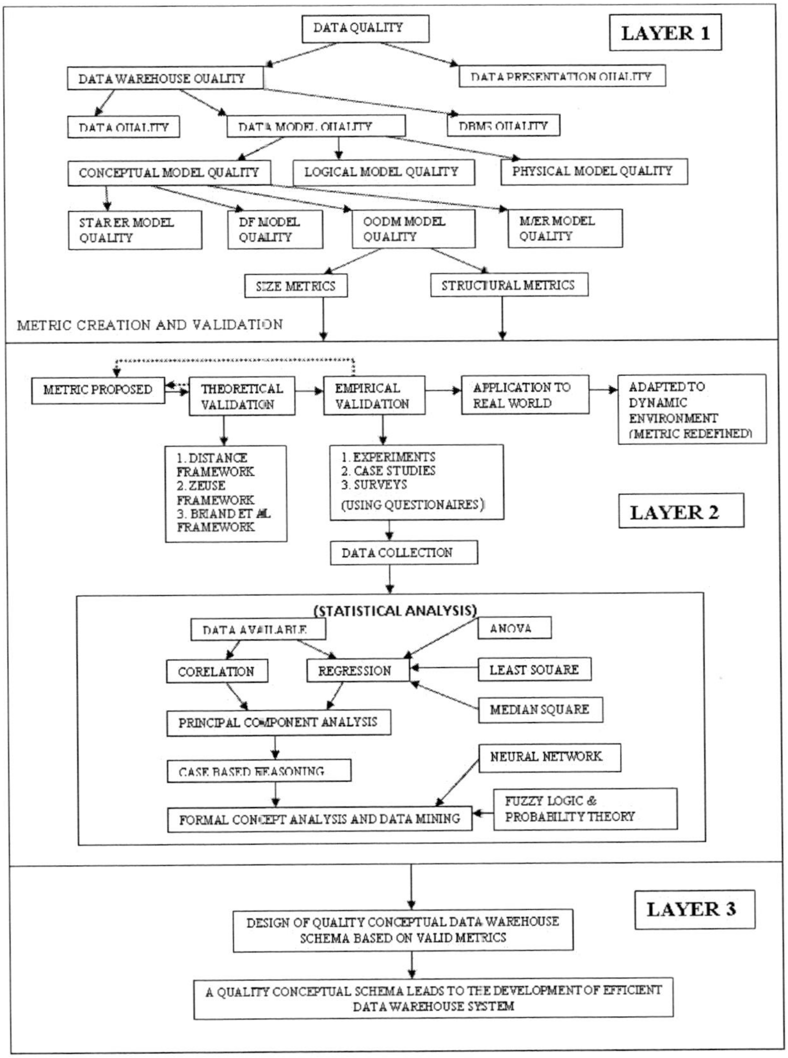

Fig. 3. Proposed Conceptual Framework for Development of Efficient Data Warehouse System

- **Layer 2** defines the complete process of quality metrics creation and validation. Based on the structural properties of conceptual data warehouse schema quality metric is proposed. The proposed metric is then **theoretically validated** (Serrano et al., 2007)to test its correctness. Broadly theoretical validation follows two approaches:
  - **Framework based on axiomatic approach**: In this approach a set of formal properties is defined for a domain. The metrics thus created are based on these properties and are used for further classification. Briand et al. framework is based on axiomatic approach.
  - **Framework based on measurement theory**: This approach is based on ratio scale and this information can be used to define the transformations that can be applied to proposed metrics. DISTANCE and Zeuse framework are based on measurement theory.

After theoretically validating the proposed metric it is subjected to **empirical validation**(Serrano et al., 2007 and Serrano et al., 2008) to prove its utility and relevance. This process is iterative as the proposed metric can be discarded or redefined depending on the results of empirical validation. Empirical validation is carried out using **experiments, case studies and surveys.** The data collected from the above mentioned techniques is applied to **statistical analysis**. The various techniques for carrying out statistical analysis are following:

1. **Correlation***:* is used to check whether there exists a relationship between independent and dependent variables.
2. **Regression***:* After correlation, the following step is to determine whether the relationship is linear or not. The various regression techniques are ANOVA, least square, median square analysis.
3. **Principal Component Analysis**: This technique finds only the principal components that can be used for data analysis and helps in reduction of redundant data.
4. **Case Base Reasoning**: is used to find the most similar cases in order to solve the new problem.
5. **Formal Concept Analysis:**It forms the subsets of the structural metrics that could be the best indicators of the understandability of the schemas.
6. **Data Mining:** This technique enables to form rules and patterns from collected data and thus help in forecasting future trends. Data mining is carried out using neural network, fuzzy or probability theory approach. There also exist many efficient data mining algorithms.

The empirical validation gives valid set of metrics which are then applied to real world applications. The redundant metrics can be discarded at this stage. The valid metrics can be redefined for adapting to the changing dynamic environment of real world projects.

- **Layer 3** takes as input the valid metrics obtained from Layer 2. Taking into consideration these valid set of metrics the conceptual schema can be redesigned. The quality of conceptual schema can be measured in terms of understanding time, efficiency and effectiveness. A good quality conceptual data warehouse schema leads to the development of a good logical schema and physical schema. In this way regulating the quality of conceptual schema leads to development of an efficient data warehouse system.

EMPIRICAL CASE STUDY

An automobile company wants to predict the sales of a car model. Based on the prediction it will decide whether to launch a new model of car in market or not. The problem faced by business executives and managers is that the organization possess large amounts of data regarding sales of car model such as customer profile including his age, sex, profession, income, demography, buying capacity, car models already bought and reasons for buying the new model. All this data resides in discrete files with different formats, on various multiple platforms and is overall in a scattered form. This kind of data is not in a form suitable for querying, analyzing past trends or prediction of futuristic sales. The managers and executives discussed the problem faced and reached to the point that the only viable solution is to build an efficient data warehouse system for analysis of car sales.

To start development of data warehouse for analysis of car sales the executives and managers laid emphasis on improving the information quality at conceptual phase itself as they knew that it is 100 times more costly to correct a defect post-implementation than during early phases of data warehouse development. For achieving best information quality, executives and managers introduced metrics (structural and size) in order to evaluate the quality of conceptual model build so far.

The conceptual model was theoretically and empirically validated to incorporate only the relevant metrics towards development of conceptual model for sales analysis of car. Several conceptual schemas were built for sales analysis of car based on valid metrics generated. Only that conceptual schema, out of the many existing schemas, was selected that gave the best possible results in terms of understandability, efficiency and effectiveness. The data warehouse build from the conceptual model when applied to online queries from business executives, managers and users resulted in near real prediction of sales of car in the past and generated future trends for sales. This enabled the forecasting of sales along multiple dimensions which was not possible without building of efficient data warehouse.

As the data is analyzed through multiple dimensions, the detailed or hidden information revealed through application of analytical queries is immense and of utmost importance. The approach enabled to select the best possible conceptual schema from many existing conceptual schemas for same domain. The conceptual schema leads to the development of a good and efficient logical and physical data warehouse system, which when subjected to queries lead to generation of accurate results.

RESEARCH IMPLICATIONS AND DISCUSSION

The implications of research work are as follows:

(a) **Framework leading to the development of efficient data warehouse system**: In the paper, we have presented a framework that will prove very fruitful in developing a efficient data warehouse system. It begins with the quality improvement of initial conceptual phase taking into consideration quality metrics and leads to the development of efficient data warehouse system.

(b) **Quality of conceptual design improved**: The framework enhances the quality of conceptual model by introduction of quality metrics that provides a measurement of conceptual schema in terms of understandability, efficiency and effectiveness.

(c) **Improved quality of final product**: The framework tends to make improvement in quality of initial design phases in data warehouse development. The quality of final product will be good if quality is maintained in the initial phases of its development.

(d) **Clear flow for design of data warehouse will be available:**The proposed approach defines a clear sequence of steps to be followed in order to achieve an efficient data warehouse system starting from the initial conceptual phase till the final design of system.

LIMITATIONS

The proposed conceptual framework is based on the study made by authors in relevance with quality improvement of data warehouse system. The framework represents mostly all the factors affecting the quality at conceptual phase, still the scope of limitations could not be ruled out:

(a) **Extensive nature of the subject**: The very expandable nature of the data warehouse domain put a limit on the amount of study made related to research domain.

(b) **Journals Accessibility**: A sincere effort has been made by authors to access the relevant matter required for the study of data warehouse development from various international journals. There exists a possibility that some papers are not included, as many of the journals do not have open access.

(c) **Issues related to quality improvement of logical and physical design phases**: In the paper, the authors have discussed only the quality factors affecting the quality of conceptual design phase.

(d) **No real data implementation for validating the framework:**The proposed conceptual framework in the paper shows an approach towards achievement of efficient data warehouse system but it lacks the practical implementation with real time data.

(e) **New elements or layer feasible with specific domain/sector data:**The approach presented in the paper is shown as a sequence of layers. Still the possibility of alternative approach with different number of layers with specific domain data could not be ruled.

CONCLUSION AND FUTURE RESEARCH

The strategic decision making in companies is based on quality of data stored and extracted from data warehouse. To assure the quality of data stored in a data warehouse, a conceptual framework is proposed. The proposed framework aims to provide an efficient data warehouse system by improving the quality at conceptual level using quality metrics. The extensible nature of data warehouse domain provides multiple research domains across which research work can be carried on further. Few of the research domains for extension of the current proposed work are following:

(a) More work may be carried out on improving the quality of logical and physical design phases by discovering the quality factors affecting the data quality at these levels.

(b) The process of transformation from conceptual to logical phase and then to physical phase may be carried out in detail for future research work.

REFERENCES

[1] Abello, A., Samos, J. and Saltor, F. (2006), 'Yam2: A multidimensional conceptual model extending uml', *Information Systems*, Volume: 31, Issue: 6.

[2] Calero, C., Piattini, M., Pascual, C. and Serrano, M. (2001), 'Towards Data warehouse Quality Metrics', *International Workshop on Design and Management of Data Warehouses (DMDW'01).*

[3] Franconi, E. and Sattler, U. (1999), 'A data warehouse conceptual data model for multidimensional aggregation', *Proc. of the Workshop on Design and Management of Data Warehouses (DMDW-99).*

[4] Gamal, N., Galal-Edeen, G. and Bastawissy, E. (2005), 'Towards a generic conceptual model for data warehouses' *Proceedings of 5th international business information management association (IBIMA)*, Egypt.

[5] Golfarelli, M., Maio, D. and Rizzi, S. (1998), 'The dimensional fact model: a conceptual model for data warehouses', *IJCIS*, Volume: 7, Issue: 2, pp: 215-247.

[6] Genero, M., Manso, E., Visaggio, A., Canfora, G. and Piattini, M. (2007), 'Building measure based prediction models for UML class diagram maintainability', *Journal of Empirical Software Engineering,* Volume: 12, pp: 517-549.

[7] Genero, M., Poels, G. and Piattini, M. (2008), 'Defining and validating metrics for assessing the understandability of entity–relationship diagrams', *Data & Knowledge Engineering,* Volume: 64, Issue: 03, pp: 534–557.

[8] Lujan –Mora, S. (2002), 'Extending UML for Multidimensional Modeling UML '02', *Proceedings of the 5th International Conference on the Unified Modeling Language,* London, UK.

[9] Kamble, A. (2008), 'A Conceptual Model for Multidimensional Data', *Fifth Asia-Pacific Conference on Conceptual Modelling (APCCM 2008),* Wollongong, NSW, Australia.

[10] Kpodjedo, S., Ricca, F., Galinier, F., Gueheneuc, Y. and Antoniol, G. (2011), 'Design evolution metrics for defect prediction in object oriented systems', *Empirical Software Engineering*, Volume: 16, Issue: 01, pp: 141–175.

[11] Medina, E., Trujillo, J., Villarroel, R. and Piattini, M. (2007), 'Developing secure data warehouses with a UML extension', *Information Systems*, Volume: 32, Issue: 6, pp: 826-856.

[12] Mishra, D., Yazici, A. and Basaran, B. (2008), 'A casestudy of data models in data warehousing', *IEEE conference*, Volume: 9, pp: 314-319.

[12] Moody, D. (2005) 'Theoretical and practical issues in evaluating the quality of conceptual models: current state and future directions' *Data & Knowledge Engineering*, Volume: 55, pp: 243–276.

[13] Perez, J., Berlanga, R. and Pedersen, T. (2005), 'A relevence-extended multi-dimensional model for a data warehouse contextualized with documents', *Proc. 8th ACM International Workshop on Data Warehousing and OLAP (DOLAP'05).*

[14] Piattini, M., Genero, M., and Jimenez, L. (2001), 'Metrics Based Approach for Predicting Conceptual Data Model Maintainability', *International Journal of Software Engineering and Knowledge Engineering*, volume: 11, pp: 703-729.

[15] Sapia, C., Blaschka, M., Hofling, G. and Dinter, B. (1998), 'Extending the er model for the multidimensional paradigm', *Springer Verlag*.

[16] Schuff, D., Corral, K. and Turetken, O. (2011), 'Comparing the understandability of alternative data warehouse schemas: An empirical study', *Decision Support Systems,* Volume: 52, Issue: 01, pp: 9–20.

[17] Serrano, M., Trujillo, J., Calero, C. and Piattini, M. (2007), 'Metrics for data warehouse conceptual models understandability', *Information and Software Technology, Volume:* 49, Issue: 08, pp: 851–879.

[18] Serrano, M., Calero, C., Sahraoui, H. and Piattini, M. (2008), 'Empirical studies to access the understandability of data warehouse schemas using structural metrics', *Software Quality Journal*, Volume: 16, Issue: 01, pp: 79-106.

[19] Singh, Y., Kaur, A. and Malhotra, R. (2010a), 'Empirical validation of object oriented metrics for predicting fault proneness models', *Software Quality Journal*, Volume: 18, pp: 3-35.

[20] Singh, Y., Kaur, A. and Malhotra, R. (2010b), 'Empirical validation of object oriented metrics for predicting fault proneness models at different severity levels using support vector machines', International journal of system assurance and engineering management, Volume : 01, Issue:03, pp:269-281.

[21] Trujillo, J. (1999), 'The GOLD model: An Object Oriented multidimensional data model for multidimensional databases', *Proc. of the ECOOP.*

[22] Trujillo, J. and Palomar, M. (1998), 'An Object Oriented Approach to Multidimensional Database Conceptual Modeling (OOMD)', *DOLAP '98 Proceedings of the 1st ACM international workshop on Data warehousing and OLAP*, New York,USA.

[23] Tryfona, N., Busborg, F. and Christainsen, J. (1999), 'StarER:AConceptual Model For Data Warehouse Design', *DOLAP'99 Proceedings of the 2nd ACM international workshop on Data warehousing and OLAP*, New York, USA .

[24] Tsois, A., Karayiannidis, N. and Sellis, T. (2001), 'MAC: Conceptual data modeling for OLAP', *Proc. of the International Workshop on Design and Management of Data Warehouses (DMDW-2001).*

A Secure Prospect for Unplanned Wireless Networks Request

Kavita M. Rathi and S.D. Sawarkar

Datta Meghe College of Engg., Airoli, Navi Mumbai

ABSTRACT

MOBILE ad hoc networks (MANETs) have gained a great deal of attention because of its significant advantages brought about by multihop, infrastructure-less transmission. Security in wireless network is becoming more and more important while the using of mobile.

Equipments such as cellular phones or laptops are tremendously increasing. This paper presents a secure prospect for unplanned wireless networks request which uses a hybrid Symmetric/asymmetric scheme and the trust between users in order to exchange the initial data and to exchange the secret keys that will be used to encrypt the data. Trust is based on the first visual contact between users. This paper is a complete self-configured secure protocol that is able to create the network and share secure services without any infrastructure. This prospect includes all functions needed to operate without any external support.

INTRODUCTION

Wireless networks [1] consist of a number of nodes which communicate with each other over a wireless channel which have various types of networks: sensor network, ad hoc mobile networks, cellular networks and satellite networks. The exponential growth in the development and acceptance of mobile communications in recent years is especially observed in the fields of wireless local area networks, mobile systems, and ubiquitous computing. This growth is mainly due to the mobility offered to users, providing access to information anywhere, user friendliness, and easy deployment. Furthermore, the scalability and flexibility of mobile communications increase users' productivity and efficiency.

A mobile ad-hoc network is a group of mobile and wireless nodes that cooperatively set up a network without the support of any centralized infrastructure. Spontaneous ad hoc networks are formed by a set of mobile terminals placed in a close location that communicate with each other, sharing resources, services or computing time during a limited period of time and in a limited space [2, 3]. Spontaneous networks can be wired or wireless. Their objective is the integration of services and devices in the same environment, enabling the user to have instant service without any external infrastructure. Because these networks are implemented in devices such as laptops, PDAs or mobile phones, with limited capacities, they must use a lightweight protocol, and new methods to control, manage and integrate them. Applications of MANETs include the battlefield applications, rescue work, as well as civilian applications like an outdoor meeting, or an ad-hoc classroom. With the increasing number of applications to harness the advantages of Ad Hoc Networks, more concerns arise for security issues in MANETs.

SECURITY REQUIREMENTS

The nature of ad hoc networks poses a great challenge to system security designers due to the following reasons:

1. **Absence of Infrastructure**: Ad-hoc network operate independently of any infrastructure which makes the, the lack of an online CA.
2. **Limited Physical security**: The wireless network is more susceptible to physical attacks ranging from passive eavesdropping to active interfering. Existing link security techniques are often applied within w ireless network to reduce security threat. as well as the small size of mobile wireless devices means they can easily be stolen and possibly modified. Consequently, the relation with the owner node is not stable, the node may be subverted.
3. **Cooperative Algorithms:** Trusted Third Party adds the difficulty to deploy security mechanisms. The routing algorithms require mutual trust between nodes which violates the principles of network security.
4. **Restricted power supply:** Mobile devices generally operate on battery power, which is exhaustible and the amount of energy available for each device mobile devices tend to have limited power consumption and computation capabilities which makes it more vulnerable to Denial of Service attacks and incapable to execute computation-heavy algorithms like public key algorithms.
5. **Dynamically changing network topology:** There is no fixed topology, the devices are mobile and may move around freely in and out of each other's range. Each node is a router. Nodes are free to move arbitrarily. Node mobility enforces frequent networking which in turn gives rise to both directional as well as unidirectional links between nodes.
6. **Lack of centralized monitoring:** Absence of any centralized monitoring makes the detection of attacks a very difficult problem because it is not easy to monitor the traffic in a highly and large scale ad-hoc network [4].

SECURITY GOALS IN AD-HOC NETWORK

The goal of security services in WSN is to protect the information and resources from attacks and misbehavior. The security requirements in WSN include:

(a) **Availability:** Ensures that the desired network services are available even in the presence of denial of service attacks.

(b) **Authorization:** Ensures that only authorized sensors can be involved in providing information to network services. Authorization is generally used to assign different access rights to different level of user.

(c) **Authentication:** Ensures that the communication from one node to another node is genuine. That is, a malicious node cannot masquerade as a trusted network node. In infrastructure –based wireless network it is possible to implement a central authority at a point such as base access point .But in MANET no central administration so it is difficult to authenticate an entity.

(d) **Confidentiality:** Ensures that a given message cannot be understood by anyone other than the desired recipients.

(e) **Integrity:** Ensures that a message sent from one node to another is not modified by malicious intermediate nodes.

(f) **Non-repudiation:** Denotes that a node cannot deny sending a message it has previously sent. This is useful when for detection and isolation of compromised nodes.

(g) **Data Freshness:** Implies that the data is recent and ensures that no adversary can replay old messages.

(h) **Robustness:** When some nodes are compromised the entire network should not be compromised.

(i) **Self-organization**: Nodes should be flexible enough to be self-organizing (autonomous) and self-healing (failure tolerant).

(j) **Time Synchronization:** These protocols should not be manipulated to produce incorrect data.

ATTACKS ON MANET

The attacks on the MANETs can be broadly classified into two categories: passive and active attacks. Both passive and active attacks can be made on any layer of the network protocol stack [5]. Malicious and selfish nodes are the ones that fabricate attacks [6] against physical, data link, network, and application-layer functionality.

Active Attacks

Active attacks can be either internal or external [7]. External attacks are carried out by mobile nodes that do not fit into the network. These attacks are launched by adversaries who are not initially authorized to participate in the network operations and access the resources without authorization. Internal attacks are from cooperative mobile nodes that are part of the network.

Compared with external attacks, internal attacks are more serious and hard to detect because the attackers know valuable and secret information from compromised or hijacked nodes and possess privileged access rights to the network resources. Active attacks involve actions such as impersonation (masquerading or spoofing), modification, fabrication and replication.

Passive Attacks

A passive attack attempts to retrieve valuable information by listening to traffic channel without proper authorization, but does not affect system resources and the normal functioning of the network. Passive attacks are very hard to detect because they do not involve any alteration of the data. Figure 1 shows a schematic description of a passive attacker C, eavesdropping on the communication channel between A and B. The active attacks are classified into different types as shown in Figure 3.

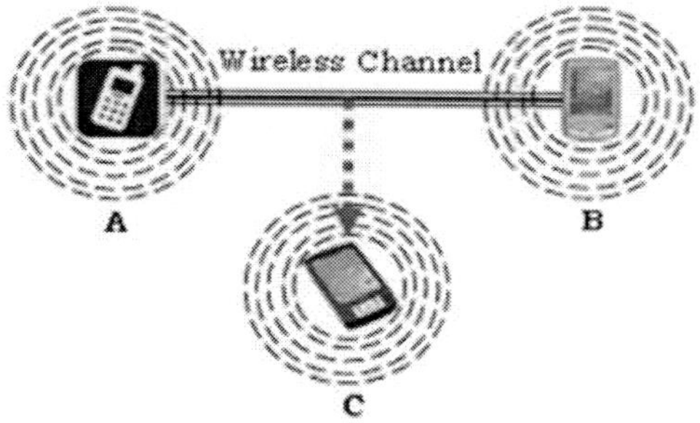

Fig. 1. A Passive Attack

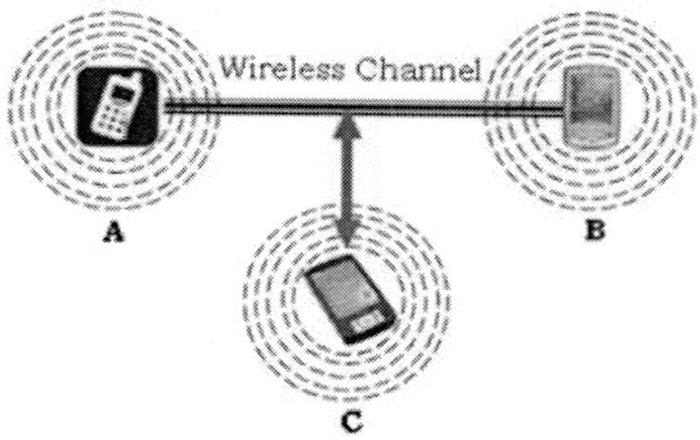

Fig. 2. An Active Attack

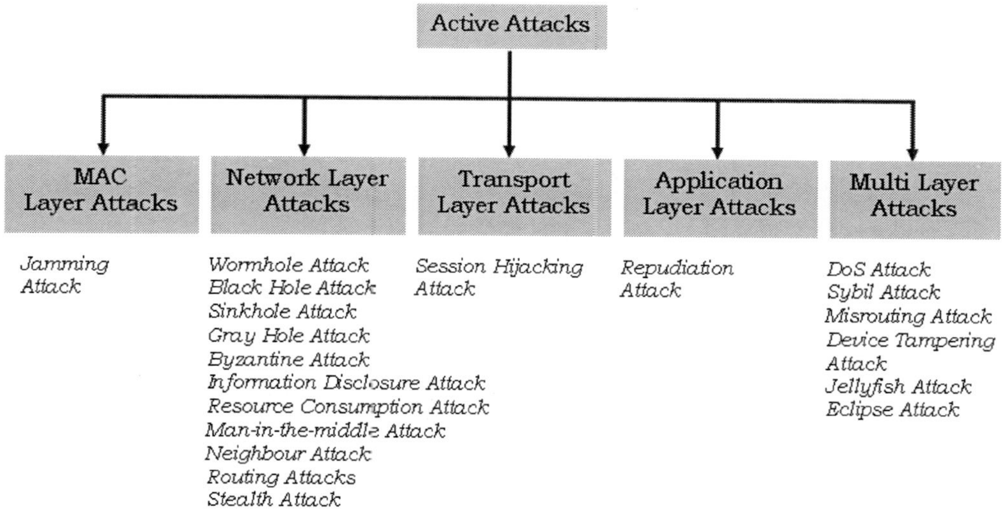

Fig. 3. Classification of Security Attacks

Jamming Attack: In this attack, the attacker primarily keeps examining the wireless medium to find out the frequency at which the receiver node is receiving signals from the dispatcher. It, then, transmits signals on that particular frequency so that free reception at the receiver is hindered without error [5].

Wormhole Attack: In this attack, a malicious node captures packets from one location in the network and "tunnels" these packets to the other malicious node at another location. The second malicious node is then expected to replay the "tunneled" packets locally. The tunnel between two colluding attackers is considered as a wormhole. The wormhole can drop packets by short-circuiting the regular flow of routing packets or it can carefully forward packets to avoid detection [8].

Black Hole Attack: This attack is a kind of denial of service where a malicious node attracts all packets by falsely claiming (advertising) a shortest path to the destination node whose packets it wants to intercept and, then, absorb them without forwarding to the destination [9].

Sinkhole Attack: In this attack, the adversary's goal is to attract all the virtual traffic from a specific area through a compromised node, creating a symbolic sinkhole with the opponent at the center as nodes on or near the path those packets follow have many opportunities to interfere with data [10].

Gray Hole Attack: A gray hole attack is a variation of the black hole attack, where the malicious node is not initially malicious, it turns malicious sometime later. In this attack, an attacker drops all data packets but it lets control messages to route through it [11].

Byzantine Attack: In this attack, a set of cooperative intermediate nodes works in combined and collectively performs attacks such as creating routing loops, routing packets on worst paths, and selectively dropping packets [16].

Information Disclosure Attack: In this, a compromised node attempts to reveal confidential or important information regarding the network topology, geographic locations of nodes, or optimal routes to unauthorized nodes in the network [8].

Resource Consumption Attack: In this attack, a malicious node intentionally tries to consume or misuse of the resources (battery power, bandwidth, and computational power) of other nodes' exist in the network by requesting excessive route discovery (unnecessary route request control messages), very frequent generation of beacon packets, or by forwarding unnecessary packets (stale information) to that node [5].

Man-In-The-Middle Attack: In this attack, the attacker exists as a neighbor to any one node in the routing path and alters data that is being transmitted and injects modified packet into network [14].

Neighbor Attack: The goal of neighbor attackers is to disrupt multicast routes by making two nodes that are in fact out of communication range believe that they can communicate directly with each other [8].

Routing Attacks: In this attack, attackers try to alter the routing information and data in the routing control packet. There are several types of routing attacks mounted on the routing protocol which are intended for disturbing the operation of the network [3].

Stealth Attacks: Stealth attacks are classified into two classes. The first class of attacks attempts to perform traffic analysis on filtered traffic to and from victim nodes. The second class partitions the network and reduces good put by disconnecting victim nodes in several ways. The methods are referred to as stealth attacks since they minimize the cost of launching the attacks [17].

Session Hijacking Attack: This attack is the major transport layer attack. Here, an adversary between two nodes takes control over a session. Once the session gets known between two nodes, the misbehaving node covers up as one of the end nodes of the session and takes control over the session [3].

Repudiation Attack: Repudiation attack is the main application layer level attack. Repudiation refers to the rejection or attempted denial by a node involved in a communication of having contributed in a part or the entire communication 3]. Non-repudiation is one of the key requirements for a security protocol in any communication network and assures that a node cannot later deny the data was sent by it.

Denial of Service Attack: In this attack, an adversary always attempts to avoid legitimate and authorized users of network services from accessing those services, where legitimate traffic cannot reach the target nodes [18].

Sybil Attack: This attack is also known as masquerade or impersonation or spoofing attack. In this attack, a single malicious node attempts to take out the identity of other nodes' in the network by advertising false/fake routes. It then attempts to send packets over network with identity of other nodes making the destination believe that the packet is from original source [15].

Misrouting Attack: This attack is also known as manipulation of network traffic attack. This is a very simple way for a node to disturb the protocol operation by announcing that it has better route than the existing one. In the misrouting attack, a on-legitimate node redirects the routing message and transfers data packet to the wrong target [16].

Device Tampering Attack: MANET nodes are generally compact, soft, and hand-held in nature. They might be broken or lost or stolen easily and misused by an opponent.

Jellyfish Attack. A jellyfish attacker first needs to intrude into the multicast forwarding group. It then interrupts data packets unreasonably for some time before forwarding them. This results high end-to-end delays and, thus, degrades the real-time applications performance [17].

Eclipse Attack: A pattern of misbehavior called an eclipse attack, which consists of the gradual poisoning of good (uncompromised) nodes' routing tables with links to a conspiracy of adversarial nodes (compromised nodes).

SECURITY ARCHITECTURE FOR MANET

Although some work has been done to increase the security of MANETs. A MANET provides its network connectivity mainly through link-layer protocols and network-layer protocols. Link-layer protocols are used to ensure one-hop connectivity while network-layer protocols extend this connectivity to multiple hops. Thus in order to achieve MANET security there are accordingly two solutions, link-layer security and network-layer security. Link-layer security is to protect the one-hop connectivity between two adjacent nodes that are within each other's communication range through secure protocols. The network-layer security is concerned with securely delivering packets between mobile nodes through multihop ad hoc forwarding. So it tries to ensure that the routing message exchange within the packages between nodes is consistent with the protocol specification and the packet forwarding of each node is consistent with its routing states. a layered secure architecture for MANETs in Figure 4. The figure depicts five-layer security architecture for MANETs, and the functionalities of each layer are illustrated as below:

SL_5	End-to-End Security
SL_4	Network Security
SL_3	Routing Security
SL_2	Communications Security
SL_1	Trust Infras tructure

Fig. 4. Security Architecture of MANETs

SL1: Trust Infrastructure Layer

Refers to the basic trust relationship between nodes, for example, like a well deployed PKI environment. Since in MANETs, there is no centralized authority to help establish the trust relationship between communicating nodes, the security mechanisms in this layer are expected to be constructed in a distributed manner and are the basic building block of the whole security system. Thus, SL1 poses a great challenge to system security designers. The security association established in trust infrastructure layer must serve for the upper layer security mechanisms.

SL2: Communications Security Layer

Refers to the security mechanisms applied in transmitting data frames in a node-to-node manner, such as security protocol WEP working in data link layer in OSI model, or physical protection mechanisms like frequency hopping. Security Mechanisms deployed in this layer may keep data frame from eavesdropping, interception, alteration, or dropping from unauthorized party along the route from the source to the destination.

SL3: Routing Security Layer

Refers to security mechanisms applied to routing protocols. In MANET, nodes exchange information about their knowledge of neighborhood connectivity and construct a view of the network topology so that they can route the data packets to the correct destinations. Every node is required to participate in the routing activity and routing is an important part to keep the network connected. Hence, SL3 is of particular significance in MANETs. In fact, the routing security layer involves two aspects: secure routing and secure data forwarding. In secure routing aspect, nodes are required to cooperate to share correct routing information to keep the network connected efficiently; in secure data forwarding aspect, data packets on the fly should be protected from tampering, dropping, and altering by any unauthorized party.

SL4: Network Security Layer

Refers to the security mechanisms used by the network protocols which performs sub-network access operations from end system to end system. For example, we can achieve the security services like peer entity authentication, confidentiality and integrity as the network layer security protocol IPSec provides, another example is the SMT mechanism from [18].

SL5: End-to-End Security Layer

Refers to end system security, such as SSL, SSH, and any application-specific security protocol. The security protocols in this layer is independent of the underlying networking technology since the related security mechanisms are restricted to only intended parties. The provision of any security service in this layer is highly dependent upon security requirements related to specific applications.

CONCLUSION

In this paper we have study the Mobile ad hoc Network have the ability to setup networks in a harsh environment. Due to mobility and open media nature, the mobile ad hoc networks are much more prone to all kinds of security risks, such as information disclosure, intrusion, or even denial of service. As a result, the security needs in the mobile ad hoc networks are much higher than those in the traditional wires networks. We have focused on designing security architecture in tackling security challenges mobile ad hoc networks are facing. We present security architecture in a layered view and analyze the reasoning for such security architecture.

REFERENCES

[1] R. Shiva Kumaran, Rama Shankar Yadav, Karan Singh "Multihop wireless LAN " HIT haldia March 2007.

[2] L. M. Feeney, B. Ahlgren, A. Westerlund. Spontaneous Networking: An Application-oriented Approach to Ad-hoc Networking. IEEE Communications Magazine. Volume 39, Issue 6, pp. 176-181. 2001.

[3] J. Lloret, L. Shu, R. Lacuesta, M. Chen, User-Oriented and Service-oriented Spontaneous Ad Hoc and Sensor Wireless Networks, Ad Hoc & Sensor Wireless Networks, Vol. 14, No. 1.

[4] Preuß S: CH Cap, Overview of spontaneous networking-evolving concepts and technologies, in Rostocker Informatik-Berichte, Volume 24. Rostock: Fachbereich Informatik der Universit; 2000 : 113–123.

[5] C. Siva Ram Murthy and B.S Manoj, "Ad Hoc Wireless Networks: Architectures and Protocols", Pearson Education, ISBN: 978-81-317-0688-6, 2006.

[6] Yang, H., Luo, H., Ye, F., Lu, S., and Zhang, L. Security in mobile ad hoc networks Challenge and solution. IEEE wireless communication, 11, 1, (2004), 38-47.

[7] Prasant Mohapatra and Srikanth V. Krishnamurthy, "Ad Hoc Networks: Technologies and Protocols", Springer International Edition, 2005.

[8] Yi-Chun Hu, A. Perrig, and D. B. Johnson, "Wormhole Attacks in Wireless Networks", IEEE Journal on Selected Areas in Communications, pp. 370-380, Vol. 24, No. 2, 2006.

[9] Yi-Chun Hu and Adrian Perrig, "A Survey of Secure Wireless Ad Hoc Routing", IEEE Security and Privacy, pp.28-39, Vol. 2, No. 3, 2004.

[10] Yih-Chun Hu, Adrian Perrig, and David B. Johnson, "Ariadne: A Secure On-Demand Routing Protocol for Ad Hoc Networks", Proceedings of 8th ACM International Conference on Mobile Computing and Networking (MobiCom-2002), ISBN: 1-58113- 486-X, pp.12-23, Atlanta, GA, USA, 2002.

[11] Jaydip Sen, M. Girish Chandra, Harihara S.G., Harish Reddy and P. Balamuralidhar, "A Mechanism for Detection of Gray Hole Attack in Mobile Ad Hoc Networks", Proceedings of IEEE 6th International Conference on Information, Communications and Signal Processing, pp. 1-5, 2007.

[12] B. Awerbuch, D. Holmer, C. Nita-Rotaru, and H. Rubens, "An On-Demand Secure Routing Protocol Resilient to Byzantine failures", Proceedings of 1st ACM Workshop on Wireless Security (WiSe'02), ISBN: 1-58113-585-8, p. 10, NY, USA, 2002.

[13] S. Basagni, M. Conti, S. Giordono and I. Stojmenovic, "Mobile Ad Hoc Networking", IEEE Press, John Wiley & Sons, New York, 2004.

[14] C. Gandhi and M. Dave, "A Review of Security in Mobile Ad Hoc Networks", IETE Technical Review, ISSN: 02564602, pp. 335-344, Vol. 23, No. 6, 2006.

[15] J. Douceur, "The Sybil Attack", Proceedings of the 1st International Workshop on Peer-to-Peer Systems (IPTPS'02), pp.251-260, Cambridge, MA, 2002.

[16] K. Sanzgiri, B. Dahill, B.N. Levine, C. Shields and E.M. Belding-Royer, "A Secure Routing Protocol for Ad hoc Networks", Proceedings of 10th IEEE International Conference on Network Protocols(ICNP2002), pp. 78-87, Paris, France, November 2002.

[17] I. Aad, J.P. Hubaux, and E.W. Knightly, "Denial of Service Resilience in Ad Hoc Networks", Proceedings of the ACM 10th Annual International Conference (MobiCom-2004), Philadelphia, PA, 2004.

[18] P. Papadimitratos, Z. Haas, Secure Data Transmission in Mobile Ad Hoc Networks, ACM Workshop on Wireless Security, 2003.

Analysis of Factors Inhibiting e-Tailing in NCR Region

Sandeep Puri, Mayank Sahajwani, Aabhas Rastogi and Paras Arora

IMT, Ghaziabad

ABSTRACT

Internet retailing in India is experiencing immense growth, and is providing huge opportunities to marketers to facilitate their customers with online retailing experience, but still Indian customers are reluctant go for online shopping and they prefer to buy from physical stores. The purpose of this study is to analyze the factors inhibiting online retailing for India consumers. The study is based on primary data; for which sample size of 130 respondents was chosen and questionnaires were circulated. Variables obtained from literature review were classified into four main factors using Exploratory Factor Analysis. The study highlights four main factors that inhibit online retailing among Indian customers- Website Genuineness, Product Specifications, Product assessment and Website aesthetics & reviews. The study will assist marketers in formulating strategies to convince customers for online retailing and will also help them to differentiate themselves from competitors.

INTRODUCTION

Over the past decade potential of internet is evident as a radically different and highly effective communication channel: global reach, ease of access, enhanced interactivity, flexibility and speed, ability to communicate large amount of information, cost efficiency and ease of maintenance (Pyle, 1996; Vijayasarthy, 1998) are benefits that can be attributed to internet. However it was realized that internet had the maximum impact on retailing. Internet retailing is defined as 'retail format in which retailer and customer interact with each other through an interactive electronic network' (Levy and Weitz, 2001).

In India internet usage has shown a tremendous growth and is expected to grow at much higher pace, according to IAMAI 2011 report, as of September 2011, there are 112 Mn claimed Internet users: 88 million from urban cities and 24 Mn from rural villages, compared to last year there has been a growth of around 13%. The momentum is expected to hold up and by December 2011, it is expected that there will be 121 Mn claimed Internet users; therefore online shopping will soon be inevitable. Indian retail websites Snapdeal.com, Ebay.in,

Flipkart.com, infibeam.com, Shopping.rediff.com and many others will have to change their marketing strategies in order to maintain and increase their market share. US has witnessed an enormous growth in internet retailing, and in coming years India is also following the same trend, this is evident from the Boston Consulting Group reports, which indicated online retail in India could be a $84-billion industry by 2016 — more than 10 times its worth in 2010 — and will account for 4.5 per cent of total retail. India has become the third-largest Internet market, based on the total number of users, and 60 per cent of these come from smaller towns. More than a decade after MakeMyTrip was founded, 75 per cent of the Business to consumer online market is still dominated by the travel industry, according to a Dec 2011 Edelweiss report.

Extensive researches have been conducted (Constantinides, 2004; Mukherjee and Nath, 2007; Chen and Dhillon, 2003; Law and Bai, 2008; Scmidt et al., 2007; Tapscott and Williams, 2006; Donthu and Garcia, 1999; Teo and Liu, 2007) to know the factors that affect customers' online buying behavior. However, relatively less research has been conducted for analyzing factors inhibiting Indian consumers' online buying behavior.

LITERATURE REVIEW

Early studies by Doddy and Davidson (1967) presented a powerful vision of how the future of retailing lies in hands of consumers directly using computer terminals to order their goods directly from central warehouse. Advancement in technology and the scenario of Web 2.0 era in which social marketing plays a powerful role, it has become necessary for retailers to know more and more about their customers and determine their online buying behaviour. Extensive study has been conducted to determine the factors and their relevance to online buying behaviour.

Different researchers have identified and analysed various factors such as convenience, web store environment, web shopping enjoyment, customer service , trust as factors which affect online buying (Prasad and Aryasri, 2009; Constantinied2004) and analysed their impact and the way they influence consumers' internet shopping behaviour. Trust has been defined as a willingness to rely on an exchange partner in whom one has confidence, reliability, integrity (Morgan and Hunt, 1994; Moorman et al., 1992). When consumers trustsan online firm before a potential transaction, they feel secure, feel that their privacy will remain intact, and believe that the firm has good reputation (Barnes et al., 2007). Researchers have pointed that lack of online trust is the main barrier to consumer participation in e-commerce, thus trust becomes as an important element to consider.

Constantinides (2004) ascribed different elements of trust; First- transaction security and customer data safety; this element is most closely related to perceived risk and trust. The Second element of trust is clear ordering, payment and refunding procedures, all these leads to perception of ease. This element defines usability for consumers and enhances their willingness to purchase online as perceived risk is reduced to a greater extent and trust is instilled for online retailer. Third element of trust is customer data abuse, fourth is guarantees and returns policies and last is uncertainty reducing elements which comprise of frequently asked questions (FAQs) and conflict resolution policies. An influential web experience also leads to reduced perceived risk and leads to increased level of online purchase intentions (Schlosser et al., 2006).O'Cass and Fenech (2003) analyzed that perception of ease in terms of usefulness is greatly dependent on web experiences (perceived security, satisfaction during the visit, shopping compatibility, or internet self-efficacy). Website quality is a matter of delivering both hedonic and utilitarian elements (Bauer et al., 2006; Collier and Bienstock, 2006;Yoo and Donthu, 2001)E-tailer faces three challenges while developing a design: the site must provide a hedonic experience, providing retailing functionality, and must be easy to use(Charles F. Hofacker, 2008). Nah and Davis (2002) defined web usability as the ability to find one's way around the web , to locate desired information , to know what to do next and to do it with minimal effort, these all elements in one or the other way affect consumers' online experience of retailers' site. Consumers of internet retailers' main concern is related to the product quality they are going to receive, inferior product quality, and delayed deliveries impact not only the brand image but also increases perceived product risk for all the future transactions, that is bad past experience makes consumer more sceptical about online shopping.

Online consumers are negatively influenced by various determinants of online shopping, which not only increase their level of perceived risk but also reduce their re-purchase intentions. Extensive study has already been done on factors influencing internet retailing, whereas less research has been conducted on analysing inhibiting factors in respect to Indian consumers. Indian Consumers are greatly influenced by various elements of online shopping;hence in order to identify the factors inhibiting online shopping following methodology was applied.

RESEARCH METHODOLOGY

In order to identify the factors inhibiting Internet Retailing, an online survey was conducted. Online questionnaire was prepared by using facility to make online forms available on Google documents and the questionnaire was mailed to 150 respondents in Delhi NCR. The questionnaire was developed with the help of the literature, consultation with academicians and teenagers. Both male and female respondents of all age groups were taken for sampling. The type of sampling used is purposive sampling and the respondents were asked to fulfil the criteria of having past experience of online shopping. Overall; the questionnaire yielded 150 responses out of which around twenty responses were not relevant for the study due to irregularities in filling the questionnaire. Questionnaire comprised of open ended, closed ended, rating questions. On the basis of 21 variables obtained through literature review, rating questions were formulated. Respondents were asked to rate 21 statements relating to internet shopping. Responses to all these statements in questionnaire were measured on five-point Likert scale ranging from 1= Strongly agree to 5= Strongly disagree. Demographic information such as age, gender, income, education was also obtained.Data collected from the rating questions were processed in statistical package of SPSS-19, and Exploratory Factor Analysis (EFA) was conducted to determine the inhibiting factors for internet retailing. 21 variables obtained were deduced into four major factors.

The following table shows the demographics of the respondents, which have been segregated based on Education,Age,Gender and Income Levels.

Table 1. Respondents' Profile

Demographic Variables		Percentage
Education	Higher Secondary	22%
	Graduate	35%
	Post- Graduate	43%
Age (in Years)	below 18	22%
	18-25	31%
	25-35	47%
Gender	Male	68%
	Female	32%
Income (Rs.)	Less than 25000	35%
	25001-40000	24%
	40001-60000	30%
	Above 60000	11%

EMPIRICAL RESULTS

Data obtained from the sample through questionnaire was processes and analysed, it revealed that out of 130 responses 69% of population preferred to buy from physical retailer over the internet retailer (as shown in Figure 1). As shown in Figure 2; Respondents were also asked about their purpose of visiting the internet retailing website, of 130 responses 98 replied with their purpose as 'checking prices', followed by 92 who visited website to 'purchase the products' online, and the least preferred purpose of visiting internet retailing website was 'to read and write reviews'.

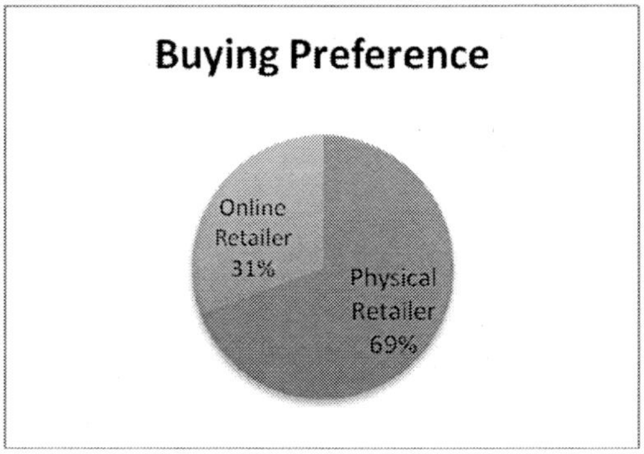

Fig. 1

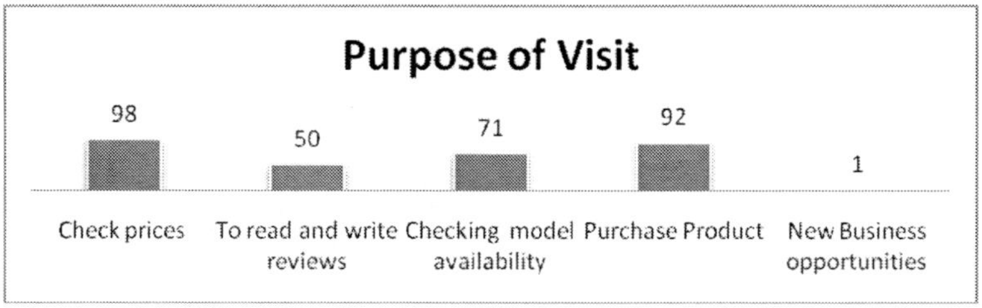

Fig. 2

EXPLORATORY FACTOR ANALYSIS

An exploratory factor analysis was carried out to determine the factors inhibiting online shopping behaviour of Indian consumers. Principal Component analysis was employed for extracting factors and orthogonal rotation with Varimax was applied. Latent root criterion was used for extraction of factors. The factors have been given appropriate names on the basis of variables represented in each case. The names of the factors, the statements, the labels and factor loading have been summarised in Table 2. Four major factors were obtained that inhibit internet retailing.21 variables were subjected to EFA and a final four factor model was estimated, factor loadings of variables ranged from .271 to as high as .883.The four factor solution accounted for 48.272% of the total variance, and exhibited a KMO measure of sampling adequacy of .712 .it is a pretty good extraction because we were able to economize on the number of choice factors (from 21 to 4 underlying factors). The percentages of variance explained by factors one to four are 12.908, 11.982, 11.841, and 11.541 respectively. The first factor, Website Genuineness accounted for the largest proportion, that is, 12.908% of the total explained variance. This factor was defined by seven scale items was primarily related to genunity of websites. The second factor, Product Specifications, explained 11.982% of the variance and was constructed on five scale items, which were primarily associated with the product and its specifications. The third factor, Product assessment, explained 11.841% of the variance and was constructed by three scale item which were associated with physically testing the product. Finally, the fourth factor, Intricate website explained 11.541% of the variance and encompassed five items. Varimax rotated factor analysis results for internet shopping inhibiting factors are shown in Table 3 which indicates communalities of each of 21 items. It also indicates that 48.272% of the variance of variable 1 is being captured by 4 extracted factors together. The proportion of the variance in any one of the original variable which is being captured by the extracted factors is known as communality (Nargundkar, 2002).

Table 2. KMO and Bartlett's Test

Kaiser-Meyer-Olkin Measure of Sampling Adequacy.		.712
Bartlett's Test of Sphericity	Approx. Chi-Square	742.453
	df	210
	Sig.	.000

Table 3

Variables	*Factor 1*	*Factor 2*	*Factor 3*	*Factor 4*	*Communalities*
Many_Adds	.738				.563
Corrupt_images	.718				.560
Money_Back_Gaurantee	.638				.481
Hidden_Costs	.602				.631
Confidential_Data	.487				.323
Website_Inauthetication	.468				.366
Bargaining	.337				.228
Inadequate_Details		.719			.537
Right_Categorization		.716			.536
Damaged_Product		.572			.468
Full_View		.539			.509
Registering		.526			.288
Physical_Testing			.833		.792
Touch_Feel			.856		.759
Low_Grade_Product			.593		.392
Less_Reviews				.785	.675
Unanswered_Facts				.757	.586
Uninteresting_Website				.658	.489
Low_Ranking				.586	.389
Unfavourable_Comments				.477	.313
Financing_Options				.271	.251
% of Variance	12.908	11.982	11.841	11.541	
Cumulative %	12.908	24.890	36.731	48.272	

DISCUSSIONS AND MANAGERIAL IMPLICATIONS

Prior researches relating to online shopping behaviour have been conducted which are likely to vary and these researches didn't focus their attention for Indian consumers, findings for this study primarily focuses on Indian consumers and the factors that play key role in making them reluctant towards online shopping. Our findings reveal Webiste genuineness, Product Specifications, Product Assessment and Intricate Website as four important factors that inhibit Indian consumers for e-tailing.

First Dimension, Website Genuineness

This factor comprises of variables that are more or less related to genuinity of websites and its features. If a website displays many ads and pop-ups it makes shopping experience disruptive.Corrupt or blank images do not create positive impression on customers. Indian consumers always have fear of losing their confidential data to third party, lack of money back guarantee in case the desired product is not delivered however money-back guarantees reduce the inhibition level exerted on consumers (Shimp and Bearden, 1982). There are many internet retailing websites whose addresses cannot be authenticated; these websites affect consumers trust and increases perceived risk.

Second Dimension, Product Specifications

Every consumers desires of viewing the product from all sides prior to its purchase, getting complete details about the product, and while searching for products wants it to be placed under right category, but if all these are not fulfilled on a website his/her shopping experience becomes difficult. Information asymmetry is more on online shopping as compared to offline shopping. Most websites want their customers to register before purchasing products, and many times registering becomes tedious and eventually makes consumers reluctant towards online shopping. Indian consumers are sceptical of receiving damaged product which affects their trust towards internet retailing. Thus companies like Flipkart.com, lenskart.com, Infibeam.com and many other Indian sites should consider this factor and design their websites accordingly.

Third Dimension, Product Assessment

To touch & feel the product is habit of Indian consumers but this proves to be a major limitation for online shopping behaviour, they desire of physically testing the product and are highly sceptical of receiving low grade products, inconsistency between expectation and perceived performance in service experience of consumers, was termed as cross-channel quality inconsistency (CCQI) (Payne and Frow, 2005; Van Birgelen et al., 2006), this inconsistency affects customer relationship, influences feeling of users (Cadotte et al., 1987) and their satisfaction level (Davis and Heineke, 1998; Oliver, 1980; Prenshaw et al., 2006) which thereby has impact on loyalty and re-purchase intentions (Ha and Janda, 2008).

Fourth Dimension, Website Aesthetics & Reviews

Aesthetics of websites greatly influence the purchase intentions; it also influences the credibility of retailer (Fogg et al., 2002).Providing an efficient web experience is one phase of online retailing which encompasses client interaction and this phase is followed by second phase which is fulfillment phase (Bauer et al., 2006; Posselt and Gerstner, 2005) in which products are delivered to consumers, thus to attract consumers it becomes necessary for companies to handle initial phase with much care. This dimension also includes the feedbacks obtained from the consumers, consumers prior to their purchase are influenced by online consumer reviews (OCRs), which contains information and recommendations of the product from the customer's perspective (Park et al., 2007). OCRs are considered to be part of consumer endorsements and these endorsements improve the overall attitude towards the product and thereby increasing expected price (Fireworker and Friedman, 1977).

CONCLUSION

Trends in online shopping are changing rapidly and marketers are not always certain how the consumers will behave with changing trends. An understanding of inhibiting factors of internet retailing can be of great importance for marketers. This study indicates that website genuineness is most important factor affecting internet retailing among Indian consumers followed by product specifications as second major factor. The insight gained from this study could help companies providing internet retailing experience to focus more on providing desired quality products, making their websites more attractive and user friendly. With increase in internet retailing in India many companies have come up with innovative ideas like Cash on delivery, money back guarantees, 360 degree view of the product, tracking the shipment of product, and efficient customer services, all these changes have created a positive word of mouth for online shopping experience, but internet retailing provides a large scope for further developments so that Indian e-tailing business could be at par with that of US. Moreover the results of this paper will act as benchmark for managers of companies which are trying to go online and can help them develop an effective marketing strategy to gain a competitive advantage by focusing on factors that affect Indian consumers' online buying behaviour. It adds significantly to the meagre body of knowledge in this area in Indian context.

REFERENCES

[1] Ashworth, C., Schmidt, R., Pioch, E. and Hallsworth, A. (2006), "An approach to sustainable 'fashion' e-retail: a five stage evolutionary strategy for clicks and mortar and pure play enterprises", Journal of Retailing and Consumer Services, Vol. 13 No. 4, pp. 289-99.

[2] Ackerman et al., 1999: Ackerman, M.S., Cranor, L.F. and Reagle, J. (1999), "Privacy in e-commerce: examining user scenarios and privacy preferences", Proceedings of the First ACM Conference on Electronic Commerce, Denver, CO, USA.

[3] Bauer et al., 2006; Bauer, H.H., Falk, T. and Hammerschmidt, M. (2006), "eTransQual: a transaction process-based approach for capturing service quality in online shopping", Journal of Business Research, Vol. 59, pp. 866-75.

[4] Cheung, C.M.K., Zhu, L., Kwong, T., Chan, G.W.W. and Limayem, M. (2003), "Online consumer behavior: a review and agenda for future research", Proceedings of the 16th Bled eCommerce Conference, Bled, 9-11 June.

[5] Constantinides, E. (2004), "Influencing the online consumer'sbehavior: the web experience", Internet Research, Vol. 14 No. 2, pp. 111-26.

[6] Chen, S.C. and Dhillon, G. (2003), "Interpreting dimensions of consumer trust in e-commerce", Information and Technology Management, Vol. 4 Nos 2/3, pp. 303-18.

[7] Doddy, A.F. and Davidson, W.R. (1967), "Next revolution in retailing", Harvard Business School, Vol. 45, May-June, pp. 4-16

[8] Eroglu, S.A., Machleit, K.A. and Davis, L.M. (2003), "Empirical testing of a model of online store atmospherics and shopper responses", Psychology & Marketing, Vol. 20 No. 2, pp. 139-50.

[9] Kuan, H.H., Bock, G.W. and Vathanophas, V. (2008), "Comparing the effects of web site quality on customer initial purchase and continued purchase at e-commerce web sites", Behaviour and Information Technology, Vol. 27 No. 1, pp. 3-16.

[10] Law, R. and Ngai, C. (2005), "Usability of travel web sites: a case study of the perceptions of Hong Kong travelers", Journal of Hospitality and Leisure Marketing, Vol. 13 No. 2, pp. 19-31.

[11] Mukherjee and Nath, 2007 Mukherjee, A. and Nath, P. (2007), "Role of electronic trust in online retailing", European Journal of Marketing, Vol. 41 Nos 9/10, pp. 1173-202.

[12] Moorman, C., Zaltman, G. and Deshpande´, R. (1992), "Relationships between providers and users of market research: the dynamics of trust within and between organizations", Journal of Marketing Research, Vol. 29, pp. 314-28.

[13] Nah, F.F.-H.and Davis, S. (2002), "HCI Internet research issues in e-commerce", Journal of Electronic Commerce Research, Special Issue: Human Factors in Web-based Interaction, Vol. 3 No. 3, available at: www.csulb.edu/web/journals/ jecr/issues/20023/paper1.pdf

[14] Oliver, R.L. (1980), "A cognitive model of the antecedents and consequences of satisfaction decisions", Journal of Marketing Research, Vol. 17 No. 4, pp. 460-9.

[15] Payne, A. and Frow, P. (2004), "The role of multichannel integration in customer relationship management", Industrial Marketing Management, Vol. 33 No. 6, pp. 527-38.

[16] Posselt, T. and Gerstner, E. (2005), "Pre-sale vs. post-sale e-satisfaction: impact on repurchase intention and overall satisfaction", Journal of Interactive Marketing, Vol. 19, pp. 35-45

[17] Park, J. and Stoel, L. (2005), "Effect of brand familiarity, experience and information on online apparel purchase", International Journal of Retail & Distribution Management, Vol. 33 No. 2, pp. 148-60.

[18] Rosenbloom, B. (2002),"The ten deadly myths of e-commerce", Business Horizons, Vol. 45, pp. 1-6.

[19] Shimp and Bearden, 1982: Shimp, T. A., & Bearden, W. O. (1982). Warranty and other extrinsic cue effects on consumers' risk perceptions. Journal of Consumer Research, 9(June), 938–946.

Authenticity Check of Professional Degrees through Cloud Computing in India

Prashanta K. Bhuyan, Susmi Routray[1] and Suvalaxmi Singh[2]

Department of Computer Science & Engineering, HRCTGI, Ghaziabad
[1]IMT Ghaziabad
[2]TCS Noida

ABSTRACT

In the last two decades there has been a surge of deemed and Private Universities in India which adds up to the total count of Universities. The increase in the number of universities makes the task of verifying the authenticity of the degrees of the job applicant difficult for the employers. Information technology can make the task easier for the employers. Authenticity of professional degrees in varied areas such as Engineering, Medical Science, Computer Applications and Managementcan be verified through an Online System with user friendly environment. This paper describes a cost effective approach using cloud computing to verify the authenticity of degrees. The employers will get benefited to recruit the professionals for their organizations in a simplest approach as compared to present scenario. The system implementation will help in curbing corruption in the field of Education which is the backbone of the country's overall growth and development.

INTRODUCTION

Cloud Computing

Cloud computing is a model for enabling ubiquitous, convenient, on-demand network access to a shared pool of configurable computing resources [1](e.g., networks, servers, storage, applications, and services) that can be rapidly provisioned and released with minimal management effort or service provider interaction.

Cloud Computing is rapidly changing the landscape for Service Consumers, Service Providers, and the Businesses that relies on them. It represents a major shift in information technology architecture, altering the way services are sourced and delivered. The key element of Cloud Computing is that there is no need to know the underlying infrastructure as this underlying infrastructure becomes the 'Cloud', where the services delivered are paid according to the mount a user. In short, Cloud Computing is an alternative delivery and acquisition model in that anything and everything is offered as a service (X-as-a-Service).

X-as-a- Service [2]

The three main tenets of Cloud computing are instance availability of services, pay per use model and massive scalability. Cloud architecture is build and hence is highly flexible and modular and can integrate with other systems.

There are three layers of cloud computing:

Infrastructure as a Service (IaaS)

Infrastructure as a service virtualizes the hardware/network and storage aspects of the datacenter. A Storage Area Network must also be in place in order to fully realize the benefits of cloud E-Governance initiatives. Cloud architectures present a common infrastructure for all applications to work which is easy to use and deploy.

Platform as a Service (PaaS)

Cloud offers standard platforms in terms of providing different kinds of systems, middleware and integration systems. Some of the standard platforms they provide are:

- OS provisioning
- Queuing Service
- Database Services

- Middleware Services
- Workflow Services

Government departments requiring resources can request and get resources instantly as compared to traditional methods where they have to wait till they purchase, deploy, etc. Applications requiring middleware services can be provided instantly.

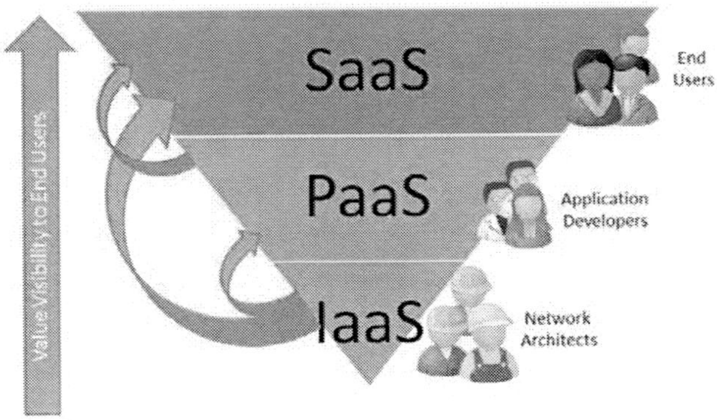

Cloud Computing Service Model [3]

Software as a Service (SaaS)

Cloud offers applications as a service. Imagine a case of new district deciding to move to E-Governance solution for some application for their citizens. The district need not purchase applications, hardware and software. They can make a request for a particular service from the cloud provider. Applications instances can then be created for their use. Numerous applications [4]. can be provided as standard services, where departments can request and manage. Some of the applications can be:

- Complaint Resolution System
- Employee Management Systems
- Attendance Resolutions Systems
- E-police, E-court
- Municipal Maintenance
- Water Boards, Billing, Payment Systems
- District Management Solutions
- Service Desk

Cloud fits in right into the requirements and can offer excellent service in this regard. Instead of each department hosting hardware, software and applications, they can get all the applications for a district instantly to be provisioned and operational [18]. Hence cloud accelerates the implementation of Governance services. This one feature can reduce the cost of E-Governance to a great extent.

Four Deployment Models [4]

(i) **Public Cloud**: In simple terms, public cloud services are characterized as being available to clients from a third party service provider via the Internet. The term "public" does not always mean free, even though it can be free or fairly inexpensive to use. A public cloud does not mean that a user's data is publically visible; public cloud vendors typically provide an access control mechanism for their users. Public clouds provide an elastic, cost effective means to deploy solutions.

(ii) **Private Cloud**: A private cloud offers many of the benefits of a public cloud computing environment, such as being elastic and service based. The difference between a private cloud and a public cloud is that in a private cloud-based service, data and processes are managed within the organization without the restrictions of network bandwidth, security exposures and legal requirements that using public cloud services might entail. In addition, private cloud services offer the provider and the user greater control of the cloud infrastructure, improving security and resiliency because user access and the networks used are restricted and designated.

(iii) **Community Cloud**: A community cloud is controlled and used by a group of organizations that have shared interests, such as specific security requirements or a common mission. The members of the community share access to the data and applications in the cloud.

(iv) **Hybrid Cloud**: A hybrid cloud is a combination of a public and private cloud that interoperates. In this model users typically outsource nonbusiness critical information and processing to the public cloud, while keeping business-critical services and data in their control.

Present Educational Scenarios

In India there are many universities those are awarding professional degrees, they are:

- Autonomous Body
- Deemed University
- Foreign University
- Central University
- State University
- Private University

Autonomous Body

Many Institutions in India are granted the permission to autonomously award the professional degrees in the field of ***Engineering, Medical Science, Computer Applications and Management***, in official documents they are called "autonomous bodies". They usually fall under the administrative control of the Department of Higher Education[5]. The institutions are as:

- Indian Institutes of Technology (IITs) [6]
- School of Planning and Architecture (SPAs)
- National Institutes of Technology (NITs) [7]
- Indian Institutes of Management (IIMs) [8]
- Indian Institutes of Science Education and Research (IISERs)
- All India Institute of Medical Sciences (AIIMS)

Central University

A **Central University** or a **Union University** in India is established by Act of Parliament and are under the purview of the Department of Higher Education in the Union Human Resource Development Ministry.[9. In general, universities in India are recognized by the University Grants Commission (UGC), which draws its power from the *University Grants Commission Act, 1956*.[10. In addition, 15 Professional Councils are established, controlling different aspects of accreditation and coordination.[11. Central universities, in addition, are covered by the *Central Universities Act, 2009*, which regulates their purpose, powers governance etc., and established 12 new universities.[12. The list of central universities published by the UGC includes 42 central universities.[13.However, as Central University of Jammu has not started operating as of June 2011,[14. there are, in effect, 41.

State University

In India, to develop each states's academic **state universities**are funded by the State government of the States of India.State take care every activities of the university.

Deemed University

Deemed university is a status of autonomy granted to high performing institutes and departments of various universities in India. This status of "Deemed-to-be-University", is granted by Department of Higher Education, Union Human Resource Development Ministry, on the advice of the University Grants Commission (UGC) of India, under Section 3 of the University Grants Commission (UGC) Act, 1956.[15][16]

Universities having deemed university status are known and recognized for good quality education.[17]

Private Universities

The higher education system in India includes both private and public universities. Public universities are supported by the Government of India and the state governments, while private universities are mostly supported by various bodies and societies. Universities in India are recognized by the University Grants Commission (UGC), which draws its power from the *University Grants Commission Act, 1956*.[18. In addition, 15 Professional Councils are established, controlling different aspects of accreditation and coordination.[19 Private universities in India are regulated under the UGC (Establishment and Maintenance of Standards in Private Universities) Regulations, 2003.[20. Per the UGC act and these regulations, private universities are established by an act of a local legislative assembly and listed by the UGC in the Gazette upon receiving the act. As confirmed by ruling of the Supreme Court of India, recognition by the UGC is required for the university to operate.[21. Also per the 2003 regulations, the UGC sends committees to inspect the private universities and publishes their inspection report.

Foreign University

In future government of India planning to allow many foreign universities to establish in India and to award professional degrees to enhance the educational system of India.

All above universities are awarding the professional degrees and they do not have any centralized system to get the status in central level.

ONLINE SYSTEM THROUGH CLOUD COMPUTING

All universities must connect through a centralized system. The protocols and policies must be centralized. The system must be as:

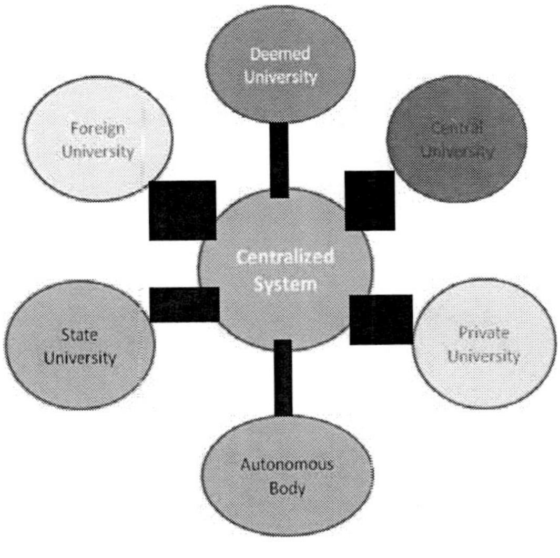

To implement centralized system for educational field to award professional degrees.India must be divided into two parts:

- North Zone
- South Zone

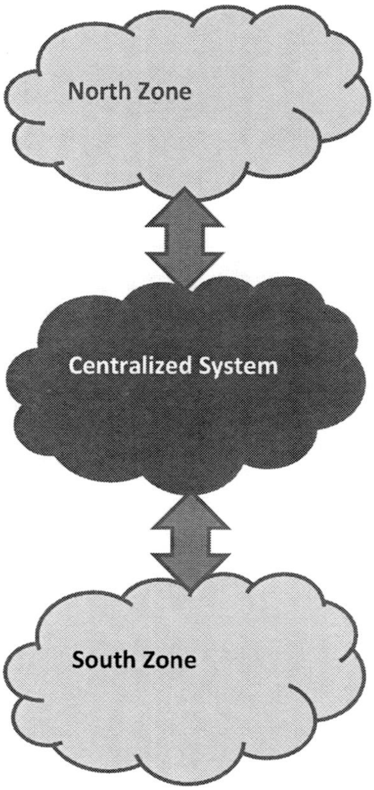

North Zone

North Zone will be the as per the physical location of North part of the country. All universities related to the northern part they must connected to North Zone. These universities will directly interacted with the North Zone System.

South Zone

South Zone will be the as per the physical location of South part of the country. All universities related to the southern part they must connected to SouthZone. These universities will directly interacted with the South Zone System.

Both North Zone and South Zone System will connected to a centralized System of the Country.

To implement this whole system in a centralized way a huge infrastructure is required and the implementation is complicated in nature. Through Cloud Computing technology the implementation can be easy and cost effective.

The implementation of centralized system at high level may be done by putting different main servers and back up servers in both North Zone and South Zone and at central place there must be also main and back up servers. Main servers will work at regular basis and for any failure of the service of main servers, to get the data recovered the back up servers must be used.

The workflow to the system must be made to authenticate the profile of professionals at very low level, i.e. Institutions level to high level, i.e. University level. Profile uploading and to get the unique ID the overburden must be with the professionals and approval to the data must be made at different level.

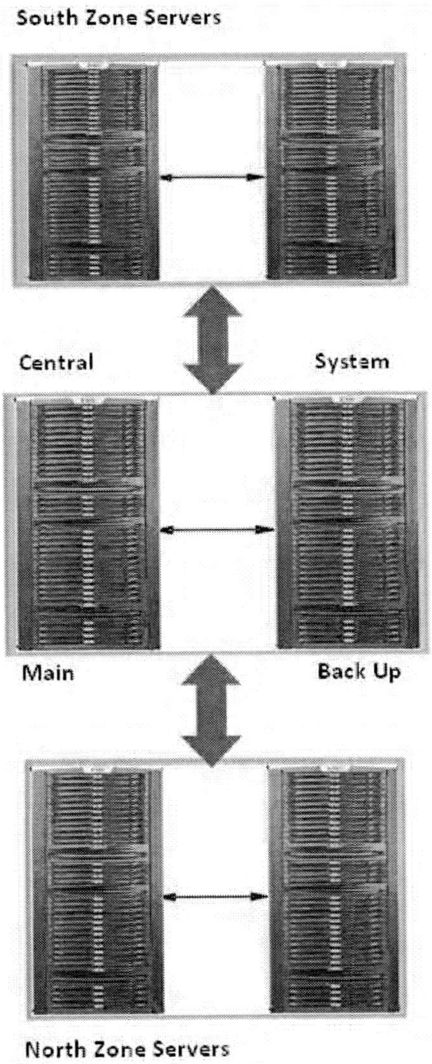
South Zone Servers
Central
System
Main
Back Up
North Zone Servers

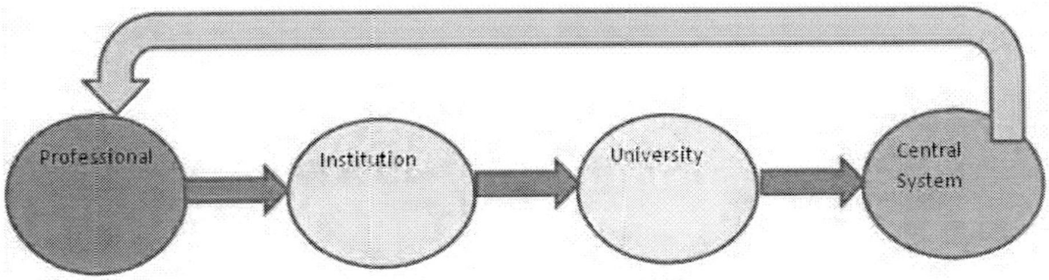
Professional
Institution
University
Central System

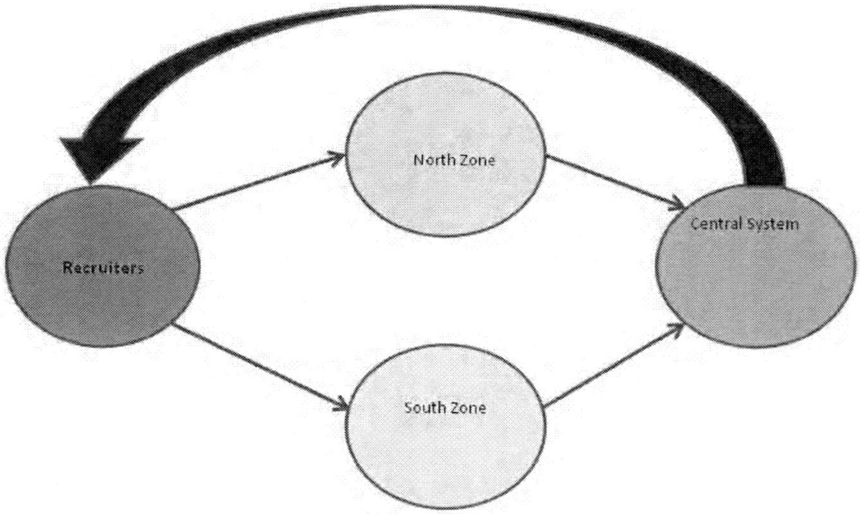

To implement the entire project application huge infrastructure, human resources and maintenance are required in terms of financials. Government of India may implement the centralized system by means of any Indian MNC those are providing the CloudServices. Initial cost can be invested by the Company itself and at long term the company will get the cost from professionals as well as from the recruiters.

Advantages of Centralized ONLINE System through Cloud Computing

- More user friendly application
- Cost effective approach
- Easy and Robust implementation
- Pay as per the service used
- Faster and healthy environment
- Access from any where any time
- Authenticity of Data
- Easy recruitment process for entire country

CONCLUSION

The online centralized system for authenticity of professional degrees is a foremost requirement to the country. The professionals overhead in terms of carrying and keeping their certificates from place to place can be minimized. The recruiters will not face any problem related to the professionals authenticity of the degrees as now the company spending a huge money to check the degrees and an overhead to the company and delay in entire recruitment process. The government of India must take this initiative to implement the application to help the professionals as well as the recruiters and to make the country a corruption free country in the field of Educational System for better development of the country.

REFERENCES

[1] Goldstein, P (2009), The Tower, the Cloud, and the IT leader and workforce, in Katz,R (ed) (2009), The Tower and the Cloud: Higher Education in the Age of Cloud Computing, Educause.

[2] General Services Administration, Federal Cloud Computing Services, Cloud FAQ, https://apps.gov/cloud/advantage/information/page.do

[3] Cloud computing for e-Governance: http://www.iiit.ac.in/~vasu Computing and Information Technology, 16:4, 2008, 235–246.

[4] Government Cloud Computing: http://Cloudcomputing.dataline.com

[5] "Autonomous Bodies – Higher Education". *education.nic.in*. Union Human Resource Development Ministry. Archived from the original on 17 December 2010. Retrieved 30 June 2011.

[6] "The Institutes of Technology Act, 1961" (PDF). Indian Institute of Technology, Bombay. 24 May 2005. Retrieved 14 May 2006.

[7] "National Institutes of Technology Act, 2007" (PDF). Press Information Bureau. Retrieved 3 September 2011.

[8] "Technical Education – Centrally funded Institutions – Management Education". *education.nic.in*. Union Human Resource Development Ministry. Retrieved 30 June 2011.

[9] "Central Universities}". *mhrd.gov.in*. Union Human Resource Development Ministry. Retrieved 13 March 2012.

[10] "University Grants Commission Act, 1956" (PDF). Union Human Resource Development Ministry.Retrieved 3 September 2011.

[11] "Professional Councils-Inside H E – University Grants Commission". *ugc.ac.in*. University Grants Commission. Retrieved 11 August 2011.

[12] "Central Universities Act, 2009" (PDF). Central University of Bihar.Retrieved 24 February 2012.

[13] "Central Universities". *ugc.ac.in*. University Grants Commission. Retrieved 22 June 2011.

[14] "Watts, Archit (10 June 2011). "CentralUniversity of Jammu Local to be appointed VC soon, says minister"

[15] "Indian Institute of Space Science and Technology (IISST) Thiruvanathapuram Declared as Deemed to be University". Union Human Resource Development Ministry, Press Information Bureau. July 14, 2008.

[16] "IIST gets deemed university status". The Hindu. Jul 15, 2008.

[17] "Deemed University - University Grants Commission". *ugc.ac.in*. 23 June 2008. Retrieved 16 June 2011. "23rd June, 2008"

[18] "University Grants Commission Act, 1956" (PDF). Union Human Resource Development Ministry.Retrieved 3 September 2011.

[19] "Professional Councils-Inside H E – University Grants Commission". *ugc.ac.in*. University Grants Commission. Retrieved 11 August 2011.

[20] "UGC (Establishment and Maintenance of Standards in Private Universities) Regulations, 2003" (PDF). University Grants Commission.Retrieved 22 February 2012.

[21] "Supreme Court Judgment on Private Universities in Chhattisgarh". *ugc.ac.in*. University Grants Commission. Retrieved 22 February 2012.

Big Data Analytics: Need of Present Era

Sapna Sinha and Vishal Bhatnagar[1]

IT Department, ASET, Amity University, Noida
[1]CSE Department., AIACT & R, Delhi

ABSTRACT

Data Deluge is almost drowning today's world. Every one is busy in exploiting potential of big data. With the advent of big data, data scientists are trying to harness new software technologies, hardware and cloud computing. Organizations are visualizing this huge mountain of data as a game changer to get insight to provide better customer satisfaction and making huge profit. The goal of this paper is to contribute to clear understanding of the use and technological requirements for Big Data Analytics and the various challenges associated with it implementation.

INTRODUCTION

With the use of technology in every walks of life, huge amount of data is being generated every seconds. We are surrounded by electronic gadgets like: mobile phones, sensors, CCTV cameras, those who are contributing in data deluge. For instance 150 Exabyte's of data was generated by mankind in 2005, 1200 Exabyte's in 2010 and as per IBM this figure will rise to 35000 Exabyte's in 2020. Also organizations across the globe have identified that best business decisions are base on fact instead of gut feel and these facts can be extracted using big data analytics. Group of researchers from both industry and academia are trying to find out the ways and methods to make use of this data effectively. For this they have started developing tools like Hadoop, MapReduce, etc. for extracting value out of this huge data.

Companies like Greenplum, EMC, IBM, Google and Yahoo are also doing research in this upcoming field. New methods of data analytics are coming into the picture, which focuses on inference. Inference is the process of deriving conclusion based on existing knowledge of researchers. To gain an insight of how organizations are leveraging business analytics IBM conducted survey and found that almost all top performing companies are using big data analytics. Organizations are deriving business benefits from analyzing ever larger and more complex data sets that increasingly requires real time or near real time capabilities. This proves that organization can leverage advanced analytics to create competitive advantage.

Social networking sites are handling massive load, 20 billion events per day, this shows the glimpse of the size of data available on the net. This data can be used to extract meaningful patterns which can highlight different issues related to day to day life. Facebook and Twitter the popular social networking site has started using big data analytics for risk analysis, sentiment analysis, requests per day, average latency, signups, SMS, duplicate detection, counts; like, comments, shares tweets and identifying the features get re-tweeted, etc. Companies like Walmart and Kohl's are using big data analytics for market basket analysis, customer categorization, item positioning, etc. hence proving its importance in retail sector too. Similarly Google is using big data analytics for improving their search algorithms by knowing their customers.

Nate Silver, statistician used a data driven approach to predict 49 of the 50 states results in the recent US election, he has also developed model to predict baseball players future performance. This show how data driven approaches are used and will be used in near future.

This paper discusses issues related to big data, and will highlight the need of big data analytics in near future. The whole paper is organized into X sections, section II discusses the areas in which research is required in big data analytics, section III is the introduction of big data, section IV focuses on the need of big data in the present era. Section V describes disparity between traditional and big data analytics and data warehouses for big data analytics. Section VI discusses different components of Big Data processing along with its layers of abstractions. Section VII discusses about the challenges with big data implementation, section VIII contains description how big data analytics is used in different walks of life. Section IX tells about implications of big data research and the final, section X is a conclusion.

RELATED RESEARCH AND MOTIVATION

The motivation behind the preparation of this research paper is based on the hype big data analytics is getting in the present scenario. Predictive power of big data analytics has generated the interest of the many researchers. Viability of existing storage, database technologies and analytics are needed to be re-evaluated to check if it can cater the need of big data analytics, therefore new tools and technologies are needed. The demand of new hardware and algorithms to handle big data has opened doors of new area of research. National Institute of Standards and Technology (NIST) has categorized research in the field of big data into four areas, specific to security and implementation of big data [14]. According to NIST research is required in the area of computer science of big data which includes designing of new frameworks, use of framework for specific classes of problem, metrics, techniques to enhance security of big data, development of tools to enhance processing capacity. Parallelism, real time analytics are the key issues in the field of big data analytics. So new tools and techniques can be designed and developed to exploit parallelism.

According to IBM the area of research in the field of big data includes designing of processing technologies, storage units, workloads, framework, model, metrics, network design, benchmark, workload optimization system, fault tolerance issues, debugging of data intensive applications, evaluation of tools, operating systems, etc. [2]. Lots of tools and methods have been already developed and yet to be developed to handle this big data.

BIG DATA: AN INTRODUCTION

What is big data? Loukides (2010) stated that big data is "When the size of the data itself becomes part of the problem" and "traditional techniques for working with data run out of steam".[15]

Gartner (2011) discussed other dimensions of data too, besides its size. The other dimensions focused are 3V's : Volume, Velocity and Variety. He has also included fourth characteristics of the big data as complexity.[15]

IDC (2012) has defined Big Data technologies as new generation of technologies and architectures, designed to extract value at low cost by trapping this high velocity data and analysis. Also big data are the data sets that grow very large and very fast which are difficult to handle by using traditional tools and techniques.[17]

The term given to this huge data is "Big Data", this term was first coined by Roger Magolus from O'Really in 2005. The term refers to data which has huge volume, variety, velocity and veracity of data processing [1]. Complexity, the fifth characteristics added by the Gartner. Volume refers to scale and size of the data usually in Terabytes or Zeta bytes. Variety of data refers to the format of data, it can be structured, semi structured and unstructured and velocity refers to the frequency at which data arrives for processing. Veracity is the quality of information [2].

The scale, distribution, diversity and timeliness of Big Data, needs the use of new technical architecture for better insight to unlock value of this data. These data can't be analyzed efficiently using only traditional databases or methods, hence it needs new data analysis algorithms and technologies to store, manage and realize the business benefits.

Big Data comes in multiple forms, from highly structured financial data to structured text files, to multimedia files and genetic mappings. Cloud computing and cheap storage technology let big data to be stored on multiple storage units. Volume is the consistent characteristics due to this the preferred approach of processing big data is in parallel computing environments and Massively Parallel Processing (MPP) is used. Traditional database technologies has limitations that does not scale up, therefore distributed in-memory databases are used. Complex event processing wants data to be processed as it comes with extremely low latency is required.

In the information technology age data analytics is used in many industries helping organizations in decision making. Data analytics is different from data mining in respect of scope, purpose and focus of analysis whereas data analytics focuses on inference, the process of deriving a conclusion based solely on what is already known by the researcher. Big data analytics is the use of advanced analytic techniques and explores he details of business operations and customer interactions.

NEED OF THE BIG DATA

All business uses information in different processes, from marketing to decision making. Information available on internet has stimulated the interest. Web data, use of social media, software's, sensors, mobile phones are generating Trillion bytes of data every seconds, which is visualized by business houses as a money bank. Data communicated, browsed, buying, sharing, searching creates enormous trails of data which can be aggregated, stored and analyzed is playing economic role too. These data can be analyzed to draw best decisions, cost cutting and increasing sales. Organizations have started exploiting this abundance data and using it to get competitive edge. Tweets, posts and blogs available on the social media are exploited for sentiment analysis and to check how idea spreads, Log data is exploited to unhide unusual patterns or to identify the known patterns to drive meaning out of it. Section 8 discusses the various areas in which big data is used and how it can benefiting us. [16]. Commodity hardware and cloud computing has completely transformed the world. they proved beneficial for the implementation of big data analytics. It has proved as important tool to combat global issues like security and epidemics too.

Data Analytics and Data mining are used by organizations to keep updated with monitoring and analyzing unstructured data which was earlier rejected during cleaning process of data in Enterprise Data Warehouse (EDW). Predictive nature of big data helps business to analyze the trends through portals, social networking sites and web blogs; and help enterprise to their product lines. Customer churn, price analysis, pricing, economics and demographic data can easily be categorized.

DIVERGENCE BETWEEN TRADITIONAL AND BIG DATA ANALYTICS

Growing size of data generated has changed the need of infrastructure and algorithm used to handle big data analytics. In traditional analytics data loaded inside a data warehouse is well understood, structured, cleansed and in line with the business metadata, traditional analytics are build on the top of Relational Data Model means relationship between subjects are already created and it is a batch oriented and transformation jobs is needed to be done before the analysis. Parallelism is achieved through costly hardware like MPP(Massively Parallel Processing) systems[6]. Traditional analytical systems are not able to handle unstructured data available on internet.

Big data targets unstructured, not clean and erroneous data, due to unstructured nature of data it is difficult to establish relationship between information. It aims at near real time analysis of the data using the support of the software meant for it. Parallelism is achieved by the use of appliances available in market, commodity hardware and new generation of analytical software like hadoop or other analytical database[6]. Distributed databases have made possible to store Big data in multiple databases on multiple storage units.

In Big Data analytics data is collected from multiple sources and distributed at multiple physical location. In-memory analytics is used, loaded fast, queries are executed on the nodes, to provide high scalability. Figure 1 shows difference between traditional data warehouse and big data analytics. [7].

Kapil Bakshi, 2012 discussed techniques to address unstructured data analysis. According to him all techniques share common characteristics of scalability, in-memory processing, elasticity, fast loading, real time analytics and high availability.[8].

SQL is used for query in traditional data ware house but due to unstructured nature of big data it can not be used. For big data NoSQL (Not Only SQL) is used, it separates data management and storage. It provides high performance.

Scalable data storage and allows data management task to be defined at application layer. NoSQL databases are also called schema free databases. Hbase databases are the example of NoSQL implementation. HBase is distributed column oriented and build on the top of HDFS (Hadoop Distributed File System).

Yahoo! Cloud Serving Benchmark (YCSB) is key benchmark of NoSQL database. It provides online read and write access to data. YCSB contains workload generating clients, it can be read-intensive or write-intensive workloads. Workloads defines operations size and query distribution.[9].[12].

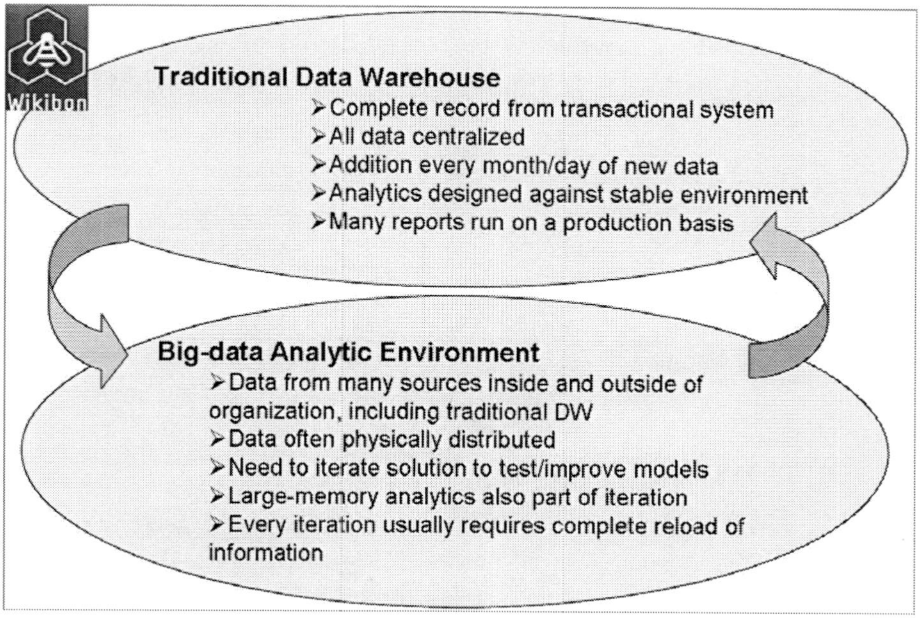

Fig. 1. Difference Between Traditional Data Warehouse and Big Data Analytics

Source: Wikibon 2011

Software and tools, which can help in collecting data by large group like web. Business Intelligence tools used to create report, analyze and present results are not restricted to periodic basis display, instead real time management dashboards are the need. For example, technologies like Cassandra and HBase handles big data on distributed system. MapReduce combines data presentation or functionality from two or more sources to create new services and Hadoop, is a open source software framework for processing huge datasets stored on distributed systems.

COMPONENT OF BIG DATA PROCESSING

Big data projects have different layers of abstractions, like Analytic applications layer at the top, followed by Fast-loading analytic database, modeling, management & security, higher level languages, job & task trackers, location-aware file systems, processing & original data.[7].

Table 1 shows different layer of abstractions of big data project from top to bottom, along with tools used at each layer. [7].

MAD(Magnetic, Agile and Deep) approaches are the future of analytics. Magnetic means unlike traditional data ware houses, data bases for big data analytics should attract data from all the data sources. Agile means the modern warehouses should allow analyst to absorb, digest, produce and adapt data near real time. Deep means the data bases for big data analytics should provide deep data repository and sophisticated real time algorithm. [13].

Table 1. Layer of Abstractions of Big Data Project

No. of Layer	*Name of the Abstraction Layer*	*Tools Used*
1	Analytic Application Layer	ClickFox, Merced, Etc
2	Fast-loading Analytic Database	Greenplum Netezza
3	Modeling	ETL, Modeling Tools, e.g. CR-X
4	Management & Security	Kerberos, Cascading
5	Higher Level Languages	PIG, Hive(DW)
6	Job & Task Trackers	Map Reduce Engine
7	Location-aware File Systems	HDFS, HBase, Cassandra
8	Processing & original data	processors and data storage devices

CHALLENGES WITH BIG DATA

A characteristic of Heterogeneity, scale, timeliness, complexity, and security problems with big data has generated challenges in all phases of big data project. Data acquisition from diverse sources itself is the major challenge, as data from tweets, posts and blogs are unstructured text, where as images and videos are structured but cannot used for semantic content and search. In Data Integration, usually data are generated digitally, it very difficult to influence the creation for automatically linkage with previously created data. Due to lack of scalability algorithms and complexity of data, Data Analysis is the major challenge and finally presentation of results and its interpretation by lay man is crucial. These problems led to many technology advances. [3]

Big data can be classified into five types [4],

1. Web and social media – data generated from click stream and interaction data from social media like Facebook, Twitter, LinkedIn and Blogs.
2. Machine-to-Machine(M2M)- data readings from electronic devices like sensors, meters, etc.
3. Big transaction data – data generated through healthcare claims, telecommunications call detail records and utility billing.
4. Biometrics data- data of fingerprints, genetics, handwriting, retinal scans etc.
5. Human generated data - data generated by humans such as notes, audio recording, emails, paper documents surveys and electronic medical records.

Big Data has different framework depending on industry and its functions. Most of the big data is unstructured in nature, transforming such data into structured form is itself a big challenge.

Data policies specific to organization is also issue of concern, as it decides privacy and security of information. Ownership of data is also important issue when incorrect data is processed and needs clarifications. Organizational mindset and lack of available talents are also deciding factor in implementation of big data analytics. Industries having less completion, is slow in adopting big data analytics and taking benefit out of it.

APPLICATION AREAS OF BIG DATA ANALYTICS

Big data analytics can be used in all the sectors, following section discusses about how analytics is unlocking the power of data in various sectors are[4].[5] :

1. **Healthcare** – Data about patients, claims, clinical trials, electronic medical records, medical image, utilization of care, patient behavior and preferences are collected. Analytics are used for patient monitoring, predictive modeling based on electronic medical records.
2. **Power and Utilities** – Data are collected from smart meters, bills, load etc. Analytics are used for load forecasting, demand estimation etc.
3. **Stock Exchange & Regulatory bodies** – Data about daily trade is collected and analyzed. Analytics is used to identify investors and relationship between them, fraud detection and identifying patterns of investments by investors.
4. **Retail** – Data about customer spending pattern, purchase, preferences are collected. Analytics is used for analysis of merchandising, assortment & inventory management, Loyalty program, real time prediction of sales, etc.

5. **Banking & Finance Sectors** – Customers/client data collected from the transaction, loan, credit history etc. Analytics are used for risk management, credit collections, claims investigation, fraud detection, campaign management, etc.
6. **Government & PSU's** – Census data is collected and analyzed. Analytics is used by policy makers for drafting citizen welfare policies in areas of healthcare, security, and customs.
7. **Rail Roads** – Travel data and statistics are collected. Analytics are used for preventive maintenance.
8. **Customer Services** – Analytics are used for call monitoring.
9. **Information Technology** – Analytics is used for log analytics.
10. **Marketing** – Analytics are used for Sentiment Analysis and customer categorization.
11. **Information Security** – Network logs are examined, Analytics are used for network analysis, intrusion detection, etc.
12. **Telecommunications** – Call details, number of calls made, usage data are collected. Analytics are used address issue like customer churn, cross-sell/up-sell, price plan optimization and network optimization to areas of identifying potential users, drafting tariff plan, etc.

RESEARCH IMPLICATIONS AND DISCUSSION

To exploit the data deluge, McKinsey Global Institute projected in 2011, the need of 140,000 to 190,000 worker with Deep analytical skills, in United States, alone. One can easily visualize the requirement of data scientists throughout the world. New techniques like artificial intelligence, natural language processing, pattern recognition and machine learning are yet to be use in the field of big data analytics.[16. Use of big data analytics and its accurate prediction in sports and politics has widened the arena, it is expected that in the times to come more and more models will come into the existence, specific to different domains.

CONCLUSION

The paper was organized to provide comprehensive overview of big data analytics. It introduces different aspects of big data analytics, like - challenges associated with big data analytics and its use. The paper clearly differentiates between traditional and big data analytics. Components of big data processing are also discussed. Overall we found that lots of industry people are coming forward for the research in the field of big data analytics. EMC, Greenplum, Alpine Data Labs, Oracle, Google, yahoo and IBM are the pioneer one. The paper does not include internal structure of the tools used for big data analytics. More sectors, tools and technologies are yet to be discovered.

REFERENCES

[1] T. Morgan. IBM Global Technology Outlook 2012. In Technology Innovation Exchange, IBM Warwick, 2012 .

[2] Jian Li, IBM Research. Understanding Systems and Architectures for Big Data, IBM Research Technical Report. July 10, 2012.

[3] Challenges with Big Data, available at cra.org/eee/docs/init/bigdatawhitepaper.pdf

[4] A Framework that Focuses on the "Data" in the Big Data Governance, available at : http:/ /ibmdatamag,com/2012/06/a-framework -that-focuses-on-the-data-in-big-data-governance/

[5] How Analytics is unlocking the power of data in India, available at http:// sasindia.wordpress.com/2012/05/11/how -analytics -is-unlocking-the-power-of-data-in-india/

[6] Traditional vs Big Data Analytics, available at http://soa.sys-con.com/node/1968472

[7] Flover David, 2012, Enterprise Big-data, available at http://wikibon.org/wiki/v/ Enterprise_Big-data

[8] Bakshi k., 2012, Considerations for Big Data: Architecture and Approach, available at : http://ieeexplore.ieee.org/stamp/stamp.jsp?arnumber=06187357

[9] B.F. Cooper, Adam Silberstein, Erwin Tam, Raghu Ramakrishnan, and Russell Sears. Benchmarking Cloud Serving Systems with YCSB. In ACM Symposium on Cloud Computing, 2010.

[10] IBM InforSphere Big Insights. Available at http://www-01.ibm.com/software/data/ infosphere/biginsights/

[11] J. Cohen, B. Dolan, M. Dunlap, J. M. Hellerstein, and C. Welton. MAD Skills: New Analysis Practices for Big Data. Under Submission, March 2009.

[12] Big Data in the Enterprise: Network Design Considerations, Cisco White Paper, available at http://www.cisco.com/en/US/prod/collateral/switches/ps9441/ps9670/white_paper_c11-690561.pdf

[13] Devlin B., "From, Business Intelligence to Enterprise IT Architecture, "B-eye-Network, (2010), available at http://www.b-eye-network.com/view/13926

[14] Michael Cooper & Peter Mell, Tackling Big Data, available at http://csrc.nist.gov/groups/ SMA/forum/documents/june2012presentations/fcsm_june2012_cooper_mell.pdf

[15] Big Data and the Web: Algorithms for Data Intensive Scalable Computing available at: *http://melmeric.files.wordpress.com/2012/03/big-data-and-the-web.pdf*

[16] Steve Lohr, 2012, The Age of Big Data, available at: *http://www.nytimes.com/2012/02/12/ sunday-review/big-datas-impact-in-the-world.html?pagewanted=all&_r=0*

[17] Alys Woodward, 2012, Big Data Analytics: The Mature, the New, and the incredible.

Building Institutional Intelligence in Higher Educational Institutions using Knowledge Management and Data Mining Techniques

Mamta Bhusry and Jayanthi Ranjan[1]

Singhania University, Rajasthan
[1]*Institute of Management Technology, Ghaziabad*

ABSTRACT

Academic, research and administrative activities in higher educational institutions (HEIs) result in generation of significant amount of institutional knowledge. Today, HEIs face the challenge of deployment of the institutional knowledge towards better performance outcomes. To derive greater value from the knowledge generated, institutions need to better assess, analyze and utilize the institutional knowledge in order to extract existing relationships, associations, patterns and trends in knowledge and position these towards process improvement, performance enhancement and decision making. In order to meet these requirements, the paper outlines the importance of converting institutional knowledge into institutional intelligence using knowledge management and data mining methods and proposes a holistic and reliable approach towards effective capture and analysis of the institutional knowledge and its transformation into institutional intelligence.

The approach uses a three phase process: (1) Identification and assessment of multiple variables called the performance indicators that influence the performance in HEIs. (2) A transformation model to convert the institutional knowledge into institutional intelligence. (3) Modelling the transformation process using knowledge management and data mining techniques for functional domains in HEIs. The structuring of knowledge management and data mining applications for the transformation of institutional knowledge into institutional intelligence using the proposed model will lead to an overall quality management system in HEIs.

INTRODUCTION

Higher educational institutions (HEIs) are a nested system consisting of a number of subsystems of functional domains, each determined by a set of performance indicators that impact the performance. Significant amount of knowledge is created in HEIs as a result of the activities performed in the functional domains. Deployment of the institutional knowledge towards better performance and decision making outcomes will yield effective results which is deficient in the current scenario. In order to generate the desired outcomes, the institutions need to better assess, analyze and utilize the institutional knowledge for extracting existing relationships, associations, patterns and trends in the knowledge (Bhusry, 2012). The discovered patterns and relationships enable the stakeholders to derive greater value from the institutional knowledge than simple query and analysis approach (Chen, Han and Yu, 1996). According to Delavari, Beikzadeh and Amnuaisuk (2005), making the most use of the institutional knowledge, a strategic resource, will lead to the main objective of HEIs which is improving the quality of processes and performance.

Higher educational institutions are complex systems that encompass the measurement and management of academic, administrative and research issues. The need for data integration, institutional metrics and higher education analytics is apparent and unarguable (Wells, 2007). McMaster (2000) referred to organizational intelligence as the capacity of an organization as a whole to gather information, to innovate, to generate knowledge and to act effectively based on the knowledge it had generated. In the context of this paper, the authors describe institutional intelligence as the collaboration of patterns, associations, rules and relationships that exist in the institutional data and can be retrieved by applying the principles of knowledge management and data mining. The capabilities of institutional intelligence contribute greatly towards strategic planning and decision making and are critical to institutional success (Wells, 2007).

Conversion of institutional knowledge to institutional intelligence and its usage requires the identification of knowledge parameters in HEIs and their capture and storage followed by a transformation process that converts the knowledge chunks, explicit as well as implicit, into explicit and objective constructs and finally the dissemination of the institutional knowledge to the points of use. In order to achieve this, the authors propose a holistic approach towards management of the institutional knowledge and its transformation into institutional intelligence using a three phase process-identification of the performance indicators that impact the performance in HEI functional domains, a tiered architecture for conversion of institutional knowledge into institutional intelligence and modeling the architecture using data mining methods.

Application of knowledge management and data mining methods to analyze and process the institutional knowledge and its conversion to institutional intelligence will have manifold benefits for the stakeholders. A range of benefits including student performance (Ma et al., 2000 and Shyamala and Rajagopalan, 2006), domain expertise (Delmater and Handcock, 2001), enhanced efficiency and resource utilization (Luan, 2002), quality assurance (Waiyamai, 2003), student affairs (Barros and Verdejo, 2000), student counseling (Talavera and Gaudioso, 2004)and admission requirements and effective alumni interaction will not only contribute towards an educational institution in delivering better quality education experience, but also aid the institution in effectiveness of administrative services and research activities (Ranjan and Ranjan, 2010).

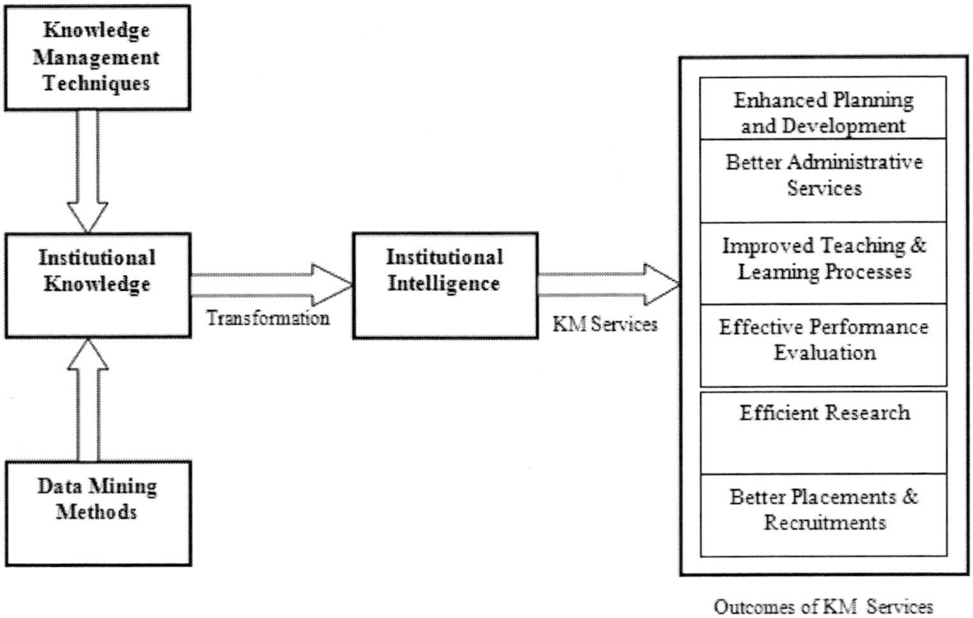

Fig. 1. Transformation of Institutional Knowledge to Institutional Intelligence

KNOWLEDGE MANAGEMENT AND DATA MINING APPLICATIONS – BACKGROUND AND RESEARCH

Knowledge management and data mining have been interesting areas of research in the educational domain. Kidwell, et al.(2000, pp. 28-33) discussed how an institution wide approach to KM can lead to exponential improvements in knowledge sharing in educational institutions and the subsequent surge benefits. Ranjan and Khalil (2007, pp. 15-25) argued that in order to build and develop a robust and thriving knowledge environment the institutions need to look beyond technology and develop the overall culture of accessing, collaborating and managing knowledge. Huveida, Shams, and Hooshmand(2008, pp. 695-702) demonstrated the relevance of problem solving and decision making theory in assessing the purpose of organizational KM activities and suggested new ways to conceptualize KM practices. Nagad and Amin (2006, pp. 60-65) concluded that effective KM may require significant change in culture and value, organizational structures and reward systems. Rowley (2000, pp. 325-333)in the study on KM in higher education said that KM challenges lie in the creation of a knowledge environment and the recognition of knowledge as intellectual capital and emphasized that effective KM in higher education requires significant change in the culture and values, organizational structures and reward systems.

Researchers have explored various applications of data mining in context of education. Luan (2001) introduced a decision support tool using data mining in the context of knowledge management. Shyamala and Rajagopalan (2006) developed a model for prediction of student performance by finding similar patterns from data gathered. Ranjan and Malik (2007) proposed a framework for effective student counseling process using data mining techniques. Ranjan and Ranjan (2010) explored the application of data mining techniques in higher education from the Indian perspective. Sahay and Mehta (2010) developed a software system to assist higher education in assessing and predicting key issues related to student success using data mining algorithms. Ehlers et al. (2009), reported on a decision support system for research management for higher education using clustering technique of data mining to bridge the inherent ambiguity across different academic disciplines. Delavari (2004) proposed a model for improving the efficiency and effectiveness of higher educational processes using the capabilities of data mining technologies.

Though there are many established research activities available on KM intervention in higher education, few studies have focused on data mining enabled knowledge management intervention. This is the motivation for this paper.

RESEARCH DESIGN

The research adopted a three phase approach, the first phase consisting of an interview and questionnaire method for the identification, verification and validation of the functional domains and performance indicators, the second phase consisting of a tiered architecture using knowledge management and data mining techniques to capture, store, transform and disseminate the knowledge and the third phase constituting the modeling the architecture.

Identification of the Functional Domains and Performance Indicators

A large percentage of knowledge created in the HEIs is fuzzy and difficult to quantify. For any institution, it is a challenging task to effectively capture, analyze and understand all the factors, perceptions, results, views and attributes that determine the performance of the institution. These are both qualitative and quantitative in nature and if improperly understood or expressed in abstract, can lead to vague and incorrect inferences.

Interviews with faculty members and other functionaries in engineering colleges and business schools, observation of procedures and processes as well as study of work already done (Ashish and Arun, 2006, Ranjan and Khalil, 2007) were used to identify the functional domains and performance indicators that impact them. Content analysis technique was applied to obtain a list of performance indicators in each functional domain.

The list of performance indicators identified in the functional domains was distributed to only senior faculty members with experience more than 7 years, heads of departments and deans for rating on a five point likert scale (1 for not important and 5 for most important). 152

faculty members participated and only those performance indicators with standard deviation (SD) of 1.0 or less and average rating of 3.5 out of 5 and above were considered in the study and the rest were eliminated. The criteria (SD < 1.0 and mean >= 3.5/5) offer a suitable definition of threshold for stability (Yeoh and Koronios, 2009) and hence considered appropriate.

The study facilitated to identify eight major functional domains namely Institutinal Planning and Development, Institutional Research, Placement Services, Institutional Teaching and Learning, Faculty Performance, Student Performance, Institutional Administrative Services and Student Affairs in HEIs and a set of performance indicators in each domain.

Constructing the Institutional Intelligence Model from Institutional Knowledge: A Knowledge Management and Data Mining Approach

This section presents the proposed architecture based on the capture and storage of institutional knowledge, its transformation to institutional intelligence and dissemination of institutional intelligence to various points of use.

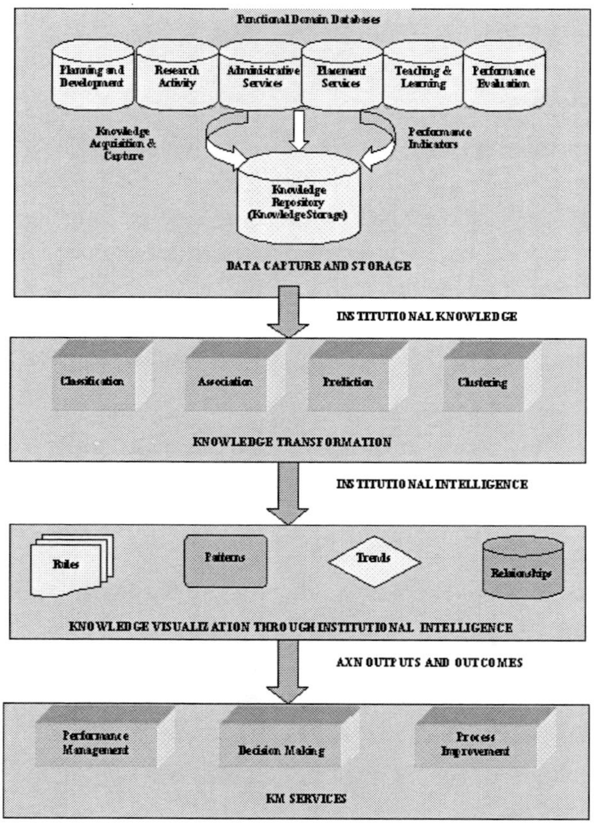

Fig. 2. A Tiered Architecture for Transformation of Institutional Knowledge to Institutional Intelligence

The institutional knowledge is generated in the form of performance indicators as a result of interaction between processes, people and environment within the HEI functional domains. The knowledge is captured and stored in a central knowledge base called the knowledge repository. The knowledge repository is a structured collection of the institutional knowledge that ensures the availability of related knowledge quickly and efficiently at the same place. Data mining techniques such as clustering, classification, prediction and association are applied to the stored knowledge to create institutional intelligence in the form of patterns, trends, rules and relationships.

The main objective of the proposed architecture is to identify how each performance indicator can be improved through data mining techniques leading to the overall improvement in the functional domain. The data mining functions are applied to the performance indicators in order to achieve useful outcomes in the form of institutional intelligence and the stakeholders can draw benefits by deployment of the institutional intelligence to their decisions and actions. The outcomes of the data mining process and the benefits to the stakeholders are illustrated in table 1. Only three functional domains have been considered in this paper due to lack of space.

Modelling the Proposed Architecture using Data Mining Techniques

The CRISP methodology (Chapman et al., 2000) is followed for the creation of the data mining model. The methodology consists of understanding the objectives, data collection, data cleaning and transformation, data mining modeling and interpretation and evaluation of results. Based on the first phase of the CRISP methodology, the objective of the modeling is to convert institutional knowledge to institutional intelligence.

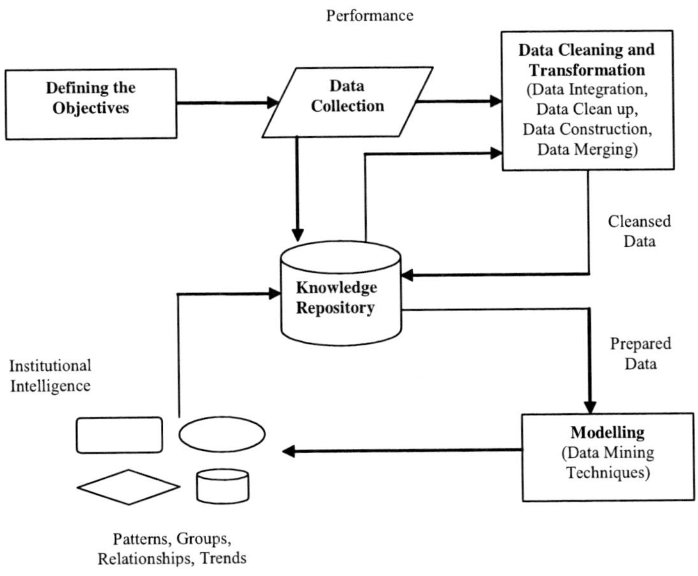

Fig. 3. Phases of the CRISP Methodology for Modelling the Architecture

The goal of the data collection phase is to extract the data relevant to the data mining analysis. The data is captured and stored in a knowledge repository. The data collected will consist of ambiguities, inconsistencies, missing links, duplicity and redundancy. The data cleaning and transformation phase consists of cleansing the data by removing noise and irrelevant information from the data set to construct the final data that can be used for modeling (Sahay and Mehta, 2010). Various data preparation operations such as data integration, cleanup, construction and merging are applied on the data. These represent a critical success factor for the knowledge repository and the data mining techniques (Berson and Smith, 2004). The data integration phase allows the information to be merged for each faculty. Data cleaning involves fixing the inconsistent values such as different ways of coding the values that have the same meaning. Data construction consists of deducing some derived attributes. The capability to merge data from multiple data sources and elimination of replicated data reduces the amount of data processing overheads.

The next phase is the data mining phase. The purpose is to analyze the data using appropriate algorithm to discover meaningful patterns, rules, relationships and associations in the data (Sahay and Mehta, 2010). For modeling the architecture, data mining techniques as shown in table 1 are used.

Classification is a data mining function used to classify the data group into pre-defined classes based on certain criteria. Classification assigns items in a collection to target categories or classes with the goal to accurately predict the target class for each case in the data (Oracle® Data Mining Concepts, 2008). Clustering is used to segment a dataset into subsets or clusters based on a set of attributes. It results into a division of data into groups of similar objects where each cluster consists of objects that are similar between themselves and dissimilar to other objects (Wanner, 2004). Prediction focuses on predicting certain events or behavior based on historical information. Association consists in finding affinities among a collection of data objects. Association rules help to detect relationships or associations between specific values of categorical variables in large data sets (StatSoft, Inc., 2011).

The final phase of interpretation and evaluation of results involves using the results for useful decisions. For the proposed architecture, the results are used in the form of KM services of decision making, institutional performance management and process improvement.

CONCLUSION AND FUTURE WORK

The higher educational institutions today desire high levels of institutional intelligence in order to achieve their educational goals and objectives. Till very recently technology was not amenable to the intelligence levels required. Recent years have experienced information technology as a tool to capture, store, transform and distribute knowledge. However the utilization of the institutional knowledge into actionable intelligence has not been exploited by HEIs to enhance and deliver their services better. HEIs need to capture the institutional knowledge and convert it into institutional intelligence to be used for decision making, planning and implementing the institutional processes.

In order to establish the priority for constructing institutional intelligence from institutional knowledge, the authors have discussed a holistic approach for the capture of institutional knowledge in the form of performance indicators in functional domains and its transformation into institutional intelligence using knowledge management and data mining techniques.

REFERENCES

[1] Ashish, Arun, 2006, "IT Based KM in Indian Higher Education System: Addressing Quality Concerns and Setting the Priorities Right", Journal of Knowledge Management Practice, vol. 7, No. 3.

[2] Barros, B. and Verdejo, M. F. (2000), "Analyzing Student Interaction Processes In Order To Improve Collaboration: The Degree Approach", International Journal of Artificial Intelligence in Education, Vol.-11, pp. 221-241.

[3] Berson, A., Smith, S,J., 2004, "Data Warehousing, Data Mining and OLAP", Tata McGraw-Hill Publishing Co. Ltd., India.

[4] Bhusry, 2012, "Institutional Knowledge to Institutional Intelligence : A Data Mining Enabled Knowledge Management Approach", International Journal of Computational Engineering Research, Vol. 2, Issue 5.

[5] Chapman, P., Clinton, J., Kerber, R., Khabaza, T., Reinartz, T., Shearer, C. and Wirth, R., 2000, CRISP-DM 1.0: Step-by-Step Data Mining Guide. hal-00588765.

[6] Chen, M.S., Han, J., Yu, P.S., 1996, "Data Mining: An Overview from a Database Perspecive", IEEE Transaction on Knowledge and Data Engineering.

[7] Delavari, N. and Beikzadeh,M.R., 2004, "A new analysis model for data mining processes in higher educational systems", MMU International Symposium on Information and Communications Technologies 2004 inConjunction with the 5th National Conference on Telecommunication Technology 2004. Putrajaya, Malaysia.

[8] Delavari, N., et al., 2005, "Application of Enhanced Analysis Model for Data Mining Processes in Higher Educational System", ITHET 6th Annual International Conference.

[9] Delmater R., and Handcock M., 2001, "Data Mining Explained: A Manager's Guide to Customer- Centric Business Intelligence", Digital Press, Boston.

[10] Ehlers, K., Jpubert, M., Kinghorn, J., Zyl, A., 2009, "A Decision Support System for Institutional Research Management in Higher Education", International Conference on Computational Science and Engineering.

[11] Huveida, R., Shams, G., Hooshmand, A., 2008, "Knowledge Management Practices in Higher Education Institutions : A Different Approach", IEEE 978-1-4244-2917-2, pp. 695-702.

[12] Kidwell, J., Linde, V., Johnson, S., 2000, "Applying corporate Knowledge Management Practices in Higher Education", Educause Quarterly, November 2000.

[13] Luan, J., 2001, "Data Mining applications in Higher Education", A chapter in the upcoming "New Directions for Institutional Research", 1st edition, Josse Bass, San Francisco.

[14] Luan, J., 2002, "Data Mining and Its Applications in Higher Education", Knowledge Management: Building a Competitive Advantage fir Higher Education. New Directions for Institutional Research, No. 113. San Francisco, CA: Jossey Bass.

[15] Ma, Y., Liu, B., Wong, C.K., Yu, P.S., Lee, S. M., 2000, "Targeting the right students using data mining", Proceedings of the sixth ACM SIGKDD international conference on Knowledge discovery and data mining, Boston, pp 457-464.

[16] McMaster, M., 2000, "The Intelligence Advantage: Organizing for Complexity", The Press of Sichuan People, 2000.

[17] Nagad, W., Amin, G., 2006, "Higher Education in Sudan and Knowledge Management Applications", IEEE 0-7803-9521-2/06, pp. 60-65.

[18] Oracle® Data Mining Concepts, 2008, 11g Release 1 (11.1), B28129-04.

[19] Ranjan, J., Malik, K., 2007, "Effective Educational Process : A Data Mining Approach", VINE, Vol. 37, Issue 4, pp. 502-515.

[20] Ranjan, J., Khalil, S., 2007, "Application of Knowledge Management in Management Education : A Conceptual Framework", Journal of Theoretical and Applied Information Technology, pp. 15-25.

[21] Ranjan, J., Ranjan, R., 2010, "Application of Data mining Techniques in Higher Education in India", Journal of Knowledge Management Practice, Vol. 11, Special Issue 1, January 2010.

[22] Rowley, J., 2000, "Is Higher Education Ready for Knowledge Management", The International Journal of Educational Management, vol 14, No. 7, pp. 325-333.

[23] Sahay, A., Mehta, K., 2010, "Assisting Higher Education in Assessing, Predicting, and Managing Issues Related to Student Success: A Web-based Software using Data Mining and Quality Function Deployment", Academic and Business Research Institute Conference, Las Vegas, 2010.

[24] Shyamala, K., Rajagopalan, S.P., 2006, "Data Mining Model for a Better Higher Educational System", Information Technology Journal, Vol. 5, No. 3, pp. 560-564.

[25] StatSoft, Inc. 2011, Electronic Statistics Textbook. Tulsa, OK: StatSoft. available at *http://www.statsoft.com/textbook/*

[26] Talavera, L. and Gaudioso, E., 2004, "Mining Student Data to Characterize Similar Behavior Groups In Unstructured Collaboration Spaces", presented at Workshop on Artificial Intelligence in Computer Supported Collaborative Learning at European Conference on Artificial Intelligence, Valencia, Spain, pp. 17-23.

[27] Waiyamai, K., 2003, "Improving Quality of Graduate Students by Data Mining", Kasetsart University, Bangkok, Thailand.

[28] Wanner, L., 2004, "Introduction to Clustering Techniques, IULA.

[29] Wells. D., 2007, "Applying Business Intelligence Principles to Higher Education", The Data Warehousing Institute's (TDWI) Spring 2007 World Conference.

[30] Yeoh, W., Koronios, A., 2009, "Critical Success Factors for Business Intelligence Systems", Journal of Computer Information Systems, Spring 2010, pp 23-32.

APPENDIX

Table 1

Input Knowledge (Performance Parameters in Functional Domains)	*Outcome of Data Mining Process / Institutional Intelligence*	*Benefits to the Stakeholders*	*Data Mining Function*
	Placement Services		
Data on salary packages and job profiles offered by Companies	• Clusters of companies based on job profiles offered • Patterns of human resource (HR) requirement by companies • Prediction of patterns in placement • Patterns of salary packages	• Prediction of salary packages • Prediction of industry requirements • Organizing campus placements • Preparing students for interviews • Supplementing curriculum to meet the current industry trends	• Clustering • Classification • Prediction
Data on previous placements (companies, positions, pay packages, number of placements)	• Patterns of placements	• Prediction of placements	• Classification • Prediction
Feedback from companies about alumni employed with them	• Performance patterns of alumni • Patterns of deficiencies exhibited	• Motivating students to perform in jobs • Preparing students better for interviews • Guiding students on industry requirements	• Prediction • Classification
Nature of interview sessions	• Performance patterns in interviews	• Preparing students better for interviews	• Prediction
	Faculty Performance		
Courses taught by faculty	• Clusters of expertise of faculty	Assignment of courses to faculty	• Clustering
Results in courses taught by faculty	• Patterns of results based on pre defined parameters	• Evaluation of faculty • Assignment of courses to faculty • Design of strategies for faculty improvement • Awards and recognition to faculty	• Classification • Clustering
Research activity	• Patterns of research areas of faculty • Clusters of related research areas • Clusters of related research literature • Clusters of available guidance	• Identification of research areas • Prediction of research trends • Research guidance • Availability of research literature • Awards and recognition to faculty	• Classification • Prediction
Student feedback	• Patterns in student feedback based on pre-defined parameters • Patterns in competencies / skills most sought for • Patterns in missing / deficient skills and competencies	• Faculty recognition • Faculty counselling • Designing strategies for faculty improvement • Career development plans • Self improvement	• Classification • Clustering

Peer rating	• Patterns of peer rating based on pre defined parameters • Patterns in skills most sought for • Patterns in missing / deficient skills	• Self improvement • Team work • Counselling	• Clustering • Classification
Seminars, workshops and conferences organized by the faculty	• Clusters of faculty contribution in organizing seminars, workshops and conferences • Patterns of organizing skills of faculty	• Rewards and recognition • Skills development • New initiatives	• Classification • Clustering
Seminars, workshops and conferences attended by the faculty	• Patterns of interest areas of faculty • Clusters of knowledge gained in related areas	• Assigning faculty for attending conference, seminars and workshops • Knowledge sharing	• Classification • Clustering • Association
Initiatives for self improvement and career development	• Patterns of self improvement and career development initiatives • Patterns of success rates of self improvement and career development initiatives career development initiatives	• Support for self improvement • Career development plans	• Classification
Institutional Planning and Development			
Institutional goals, objectives, vision, mission, targets and quality policy	• Association of goals, objectives, and targets achieved with those stated	• Creating meaningful objectives • Analyzing reasons for failures	• Association
Plans and policies outlined by important functionaries of the institute	• Relationship between developmental progress and plans and policies • Clusters of plans and policies in related areas	• Strategic Planning	• Association • Clustering
Reports by review committees and accreditation bodies on the compliance of the institute to norms	• Characteristic patterns of non-compliance and conformity to standards • Patterns of factors contributing to non-compliance	• Formulation of corrective and preventive measures • Strategic planning for future development • Prediction of new developmental avenues • Analysis of factors responsible for non compliance	• Clustering • Prediction
Reports on competitor data	• Patterns of competitor performance	• Strategic planning to overcome competition	• Prediction
Results of assessment of procedures and processes	• Clusters of processes and procedures for functional domains • Clusters of redundant procedures	• Elimination of redundant and duplicate procedures and processes • Enhancement of procedures and processes	• Clustering

Business Intelligence Application in Financial Sector – Credit Scoring of Retail Loans using a Hybrid Modeling Approach

S. Chandrasekhar

FORE School of Management, New Delhi

ABSTRACT

Retail Loans now-a-days form a major proportion of Loan Portfolio. Broadly they can be classified as (i) Loans for Small and medium Sector and (ii) Loans for Individuals. The objective of Credit Scoring is that we use enough of precaution before the sanction of the loan so that the loans do not go bad after disbursement. This will increase to the bottom line of the financial institution and also reduce the Credit Risk.

Techniques used to perform Credit Scoring Varies for the above two classes of loans. In this paper, we concentrate on the application of Credit Scoring for individual or so called personal loans like – Auto loan, buying goods like Televisions, Refrigerators etc. Large numbers of loans are being disbursed in these areas. Though the size of the loan may be small, when compared to Small/Medium Scale Industry, if one does not control the defaults, the consequences will be disastrous.

From the characteristics of borrower, product characteristics a Credit Score is computed for each applicant. If the Score exceeds a given threshold loan is sanctioned. If it is below the threshold, loan is sanctioned. In practice a buffer zone is created near the threshold so that those Credit Scores that fall in buffer zone, detailed investigation will be done before a decision is taken.

In this Research Paper, a combination of Decision Tree and Logistic Regression is used to determine the weights that are to be assigned to different characteristics of the borrower. Decision Tree is used at first level of analysis to narrow down the importance of Variables and overall weights that needs to be assigned. It is also used for optimum groupings of numeric and non-numeric Variables. At second level, Logistic Regression is used to compute odd ratios a variant of probability,which in turn is used to assign weights foran attribute and to individual levels in an attribute.

This has been tested on real life data and found to work better compared to methods using a single stage models. An accuracy of around 80% in decision is obtained which is good for any modeling study as there is no model which gives 100% accuracy.

INTRODUCTION

Credit Scoring forms an important process in any lending system [1][2]. In the absence of any Scoring the Financial Institution may end up taking a huge risk as most of loans may go bad. This severely affects the bottom line and image of the Institution [1].

Two broad classes of Scoring Model exists (i) Subjective Scoring [3] and (ii) Statistical Scoring [3].

Subjective Scoring is based on intuitive judgement. Subjective Scoring works but there is scope for improvement one limitation is prediction of risk is person dependent and focuses on few characteristics and may be mistakenly focusing on wrong characteristics.

Statistical Scoring uses hardcore data of borrower characteristics, product characteristics and uses mathematical models to predict the risk. The relation is expressed in the form of an equation which finally gets converted to a score. Subjectivity will be reduced and variable(s) that are important to scoring are identified based on strong mathematical foundation.

Different Models have been used in Credit Scoring like Regression, Decision Tree, Discriminate Analysis and Logistic Regression [4]. Most of the times, a single model is used to compute the Credit Score. This method works well when the underlying decision rule is simple and when the rule becomes complex, the accuracy of the model diminishes very fast.

Methodology and Results

A sample data of about Three Hundred and Seventy Nine Records were taken from a Bank Database. The following Variables were used for the Analysis.

Table 1. Variables and their attributes

Sex	:	Male/Female
Age	:	Customer Age – Continuous
Time-at-Address	:	How Long The Customer Is Living At This Address
Residence Status	:	Owner, Rented
Telephone	:	Yes/No
Time-Bank		How Long Is Customer With The Bank ; Numeric
Home Expenses	:	Numeric
Decision	:	Sanctioned/Rejected
Occupation	:	Creative, Driver, Guard, Labourer, Manager, Office-Staff, Production, Professional, Sales, Semi-Production
Job Status	:	Government, Private, Self-Employed
Time-Employed	:	Length Of Employment - Numeric
Liab. - Reference	:	True/False
Acc. - Reference	:	Given/Other Instructions
Balance	:	Numeric

Since the Independent Variables are a Combination of Numeric and Non-numeric Variable(s), and Dependent Variable Non-numeric, Decision Tree using Chi-square Interaction Detection (CHAID)Method is used to analyse the data. We cannot use regression. Out of 379 Cases, 53% (201) Cases are rejected and 47% (178) have been accepted. Table 2 and Fig. 1 gives the details of results of running a Decision Tree.

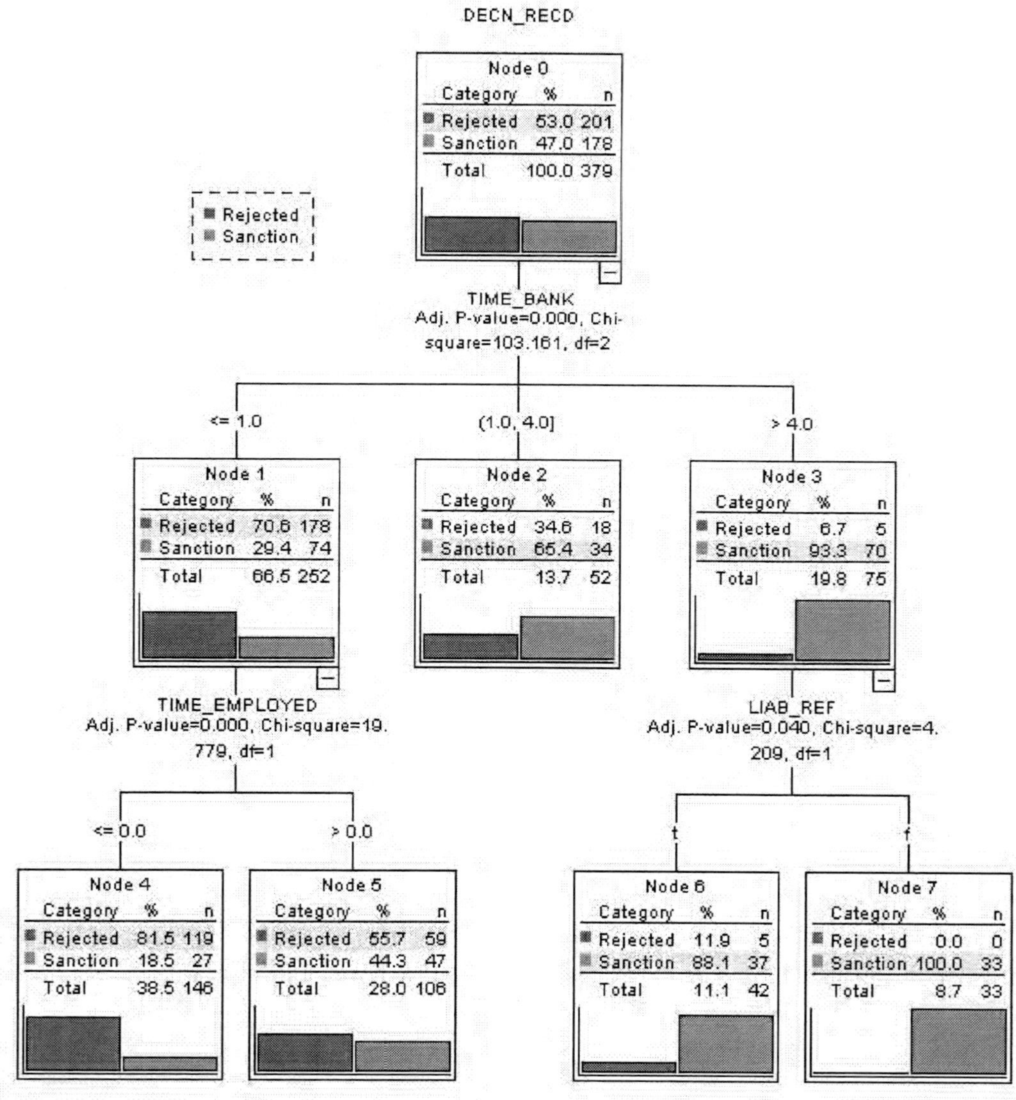

Fig. 1. Graphical Representation of Decision Tree

Table 2. Summary of Decision Tree

Model Summary		
Specifications	Growing Method	Chaid
	Dependent Variable	Decn_Recd (Decision)
	Independent Variables	Sex, Age, Time_At_Address, Res_Status, Telephone, Occupation, Job_Status, Time_Employed, Time_Bank, Liab_Ref, Acc_Ref, Home_Expn, Balance
Results	Independent Variables Included	Time_Bank, Time_Employed
	Number of Nodes	8
	Number of Terminal Nodes	5
	Depth	2

Classification Accuracy of the Tree is given in Table 3.

Table 3. Classification Accuracy

Classification			
Observed	*Predicted*		
	Rejected	*Sanction*	*Percent Correct*
Rejected	178	23	88.6%
Sanction	74	104	58.4%
Overall Percentage	66.5%	33.5%	74.4%
Growing Method: CHAID Dependent Variable: DECN_RECD			

If you look at Table 2, the model has identified Time-Bank, Time-Employed, as important Variables for Prediction and it has rejected all other Variables. The overall classification accuracy is about 74%. All Non-numeric Variables like Occupation, Job Status, Residential Status etc. are ignored.

One reason for rejecting all other Non-numeric Variables may be due to sample size of the data set and heavy influence of Numeric Variables. In practice, Non-numeric Variables also play an important role in Credit Scoring. To validate this assumption, in the next step, Two Decision Trees have been built – One taking only Numeric IndependentVariables: Time-At-Address, Time-Bank, Home-Expenses, and Balance. The classification accuracy is 77%. This is shown in Table 3.

Then for Second Tree using only Non-numeric Independent Variables like Occupation, Job Status, Residence Status, etc., are considered. The Classification accuracy was 66% which is not low. The Dependent Variable is Decision.

Hence one can include both Numeric and Non-numeric Variable but with a slightly higher weightage for Numeric compared to Non-numeric Variables. The weights will be inversely proportional to error, i.e. if the error is high weight will be less and vice-versa.

So, the overall weightage assigned to Numeric Variables are: (77/ (77+66)) × 100 = 54%; it is (66/ (77+66)) × 100 = 46% for non-numeric Variable(s).

The next step is to assign Individual Weights to different levels within Numeric and Non-numeric Variables keeping overall weights to 54% and 46%.

Logistic Regression is used for assigning Individual Weights.

Logistic Regression gives a functional relation between Dependent and Independent Variables. The only difference between Logistic Regression and Usual Regression is the Dependent Variable is categorical and has only two states of nature like Loan Application Accepted/Rejected, Person defaulting a loan/not defaulting, etc.

The functional form can be expressed as:

$$L_n\left\{\text{Probability}\left(\frac{\text{Loan rejected}}{\text{Loan sanctioned}}\right)\right\} = \alpha_0+\alpha_1{*}\text{Time-at-Address}+\alpha_2{*}\text{Time-employed}+\ldots\ldots$$

α_0, α_1 , α_2,......................are called the Logit Coefficients and will be estimated using sample data using maximum likelihood estimation.

Out of all the Independent Variables taken for model building, I have explained below methodology of assigning Individual Weights for different attribute level values. One example for Numeric Variable and another for Non-numeric Variable. This methodology is repeated for all other Numeric and Non-numeric Independent Variables.

When all the Numeric Variables are taken as Independent Variable(s), and DECISION as Dependent Variable, Logistic Regression is run. Based on the significance the following Variables are retained:

TIME-BANK (1.53)	TIME-EMPLOYED (1.20)	BALANCE (1.0)

The numbers in the bracket indicate the odd ratio and all are significant at 5%. Alternatively what it means is these Coefficients are correct 95% of time. Only 5% of time they may be wrong. COX_NELL R Square of about 0.4 Validates the Hypothesis, that Logistic Regression fits the data. If value of COX_NELL RSquare isbelow 0.05 one can conclude Logistic Regression does not fit the data.

Out of Total Weight of 54% assigned to all Numeric Variables, the break-up of Weights for THREE significant Numeric Variables are worked out as follows using the Logit Coefficients:

$$\text{TIME-BANK} = (1.53/(1.53 + 1.20 + 1.0)) \times 54 = 22$$
$$\text{TIME-EMPLOYED} = (1.20/(1.53 + 1.20 + 1.0)) \times 54 = 17$$
$$\text{BALANCE} = (1.0/1.53 + 1.20 + 1.0)) \times 54 = 15$$

At the next level let us take one Variable used in scoring i.e. TIME-BANK. The total weight for this is 22 and this Variable takes on values in the range: 0-67. The total weight of 22 needs to be broken into different bins and the binning should be automatic instead of person dependent.

For this, the methodology used is as follows:

The histogram was displayed and using Visual binning techniques the Variable TIME-BANK was binned into 5 bins. This may not be optimum. The next step was to use the Decision Tree to automatically determine the number of bins. The DependentVariable is DECISION and Independent Variable is TIME-BANK grouped into 5 bins. The output of the Decision Tree is given in Fig. 2.

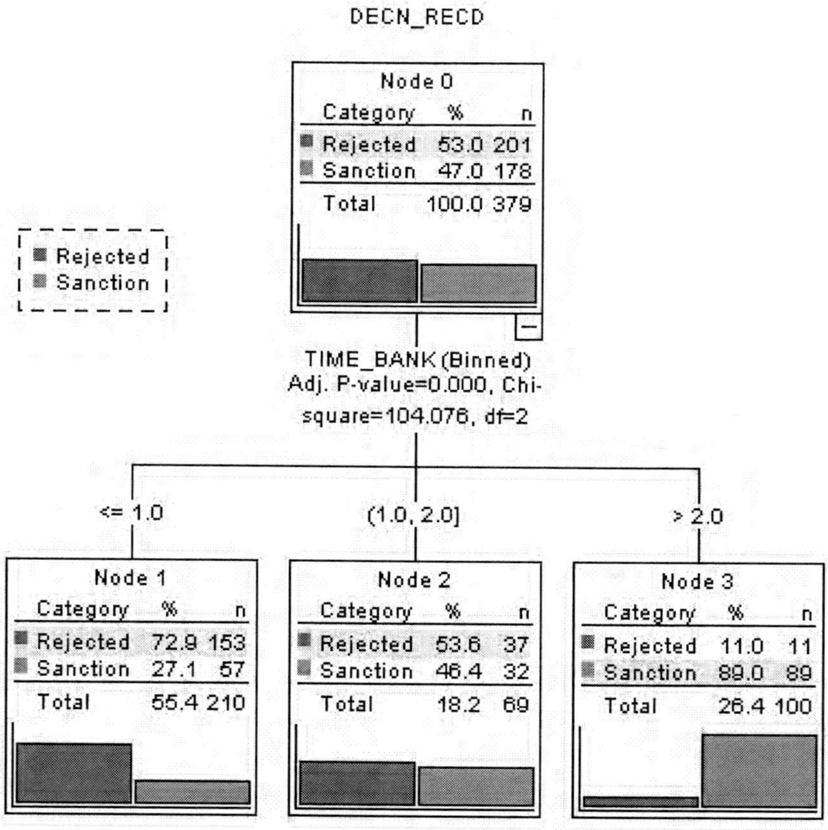

Fig. 2. Automatic Binning using Decision Tree

Looking at the Tree output shown above it is clear that only THREE bins are optimum compared to manual FIVE bins. The following bins are given in Table 4.

Table 4. Bins Identified Using Decision Tree

Time-Employed	≤ 1.0	Bin 1
1.0 < Time-Employed	≤ 3.0	Bin 2
Time-Employed	> 3.0	Bin 3

Again Logistic Regression is used to determine Individual Weights for each bin.

The Logit Coefficients for Bin 1, Bin 2 and Bin 3 are 0.4, 3.0 and 19.0 respectively.

The weights assigned to different bins are in Table 5.

Table 5. Weights Assigned to Different Bins of TIME-EMPLOYED

$$\text{TIME-EMPLOYED} \leq 1.0;\ \text{wt} = \frac{0.4}{0.4+3.0+19.0} \times 22 = 0.4$$

$$1.0 < \text{TIME-EMPLOYED} \leq 3.0;\ \text{wt} = \frac{3.0}{0.4+3.0+19.0} \times 22 = 3.0$$

$$\text{TIME-EMPLOYED} > 3.0;\ \text{wt} = \frac{19.0}{0.4+3.0+19.0} \times 22 = 18.6$$

$$\text{TOTAL WT. FOR TIME-EMPLOYED} \quad 22.00$$

Similar process is repeated for other Two Variables, i.e. TIME-WITH-BANK and BALANCE.

When the decision tree model was applied to Non-numeric Variables like JOB-STATUS, OCCUPATION, RESIDENTIAL STATUS, ACC.-REF. and TELEPHONE only TWO Variables were significant. They were: OCCUPATION, JOB STATUS.

Total of 46% weight for Non-numeric Variables is split into two parts using the odd ratios. Result:OCCUPATION: 40 and JOB STATUS: 6. Using Decision Tree and Logistic Regression the Weights for different attribute values under Occupation are given in Table 6.

Table 6. Weights Assigned to Different Attributes

Professional	12.5	Creative	2.80	Government	2.4
Semi-professional	9.5	Sales	1.92	Self-employed	2.5
Office Staff	5.2	Driver	1.00	Private	1
Production	2.9	Labourer	1.27		
		Guard	0.86		
		TOTAL	40	TOTAL	6.0

When once the Weights for all Independent Variables of significance have been computed using Decision Tree – Logistic Regression iteratively the data will be ready for scoring.

The Credit Score for each Record will be sum of Weight of the Bin to which each attribute level falls. Data will be sorted in Descending Order of Credit Score.

A part of Scored Data is given in Table 7.

Table 7. Sample Scored Data

DECN_RECD	BAL_BINED_TWO_LVL	TIMES_EMPL_BIN3	TIME_BNK_BIN3	TIMES_EMPLOYED_SCORE	TIME_BANK_SCORE	JOB_STAT_SCORE	OCCUPATION_SCORE	BALANCE_SCORE	Total_credit_Score
Rejected	2	1	1	0.9	0.4	1	9.5	0.5	12.3
Rejected	2	1	1	0.9	0.4	1	1	0.5	3.8
Rejected	2	2	1	4.4	0.4	2.4	1.92	0.5	9.62
Sanction	2	1	2	0.9	3	1	9.5	0.5	14.9
Sanction	2	1	3	0.9	18.6	1	9.5	0.5	30.5
Sanction	1	1	3	0.9	18.6	1	12.5	13.5	46.5
Rejected	2	1	1	0.9	0.4	1	2.9	0.5	5.7
Sanction	2	2	3	4.4	18.6	1	12.5	0.5	37
Rejected	2	1	2	0.9	3	1	5.2	0.5	10.6
Rejected	2	2	2	4.4	3	1	2.8	0.5	11.7
Rejected	2	1	1	0.9	0.4	2.4	2.8	0.5	7
Sanction	1	3	3	11.8	18.6	1	2.8	13.5	47.7
Rejected	2	1	1	0.9	0.4	1	2.8	0.5	5.6
Rejected	2	1	2	0.9	3	1	1.92	0.5	7.32
Sanction	2	1	3	0.9	18.6	1	2.8	0.5	23.8
Sanction	2	3	1	11.8	0.4	2.4	2.9	0.5	18
Rejected	2	3	1	11.8	0.4	1	1.95	0.5	15.65
Sanction	2	3	3	11.8	18.6	2.4	2.9	0.5	36.2
Rejected	2	1	1	0.9	0.4	2.4	1	0.5	5.2

Now one can try different cut off's and see how the accuracy changes. As an example let us put a cut off score of 14 i.e. for these whose Credit Score is greater than or equal to 14, Loan will be sanctioned and for those less than 14, the loan will be rejected. The total number rejected with this threshold is 165 out of Total Number of 201 rejected cases. The accuracy of rejection is 82%. Similarly, there are 124 accept cases for threshold 14.

CONCLUSION

The paper illustrates Hybrid model for Credit Scoring Using Decision Tree and Logistic Regression in a recursive manner. SPSS Software has been used for Model building and Data analysis. It also optimizes the Bins for both numeric and non-numeric Variables using Decision Tree. Many times subjective Weights are used based on experience of loan manager. This paper explores how financial institution specific data can be used to derive the Weights automatically. One can compare and fine tune the subjective scores based on actual data. Further work involves integration of an optimization technique like Linear/Goal programming to fine tune the Weights.

REFERENCES

[1] Lyn Thomas Et.al......, *Credit Scoring and its applications*, SIAM Publication, June 2002.

[2] E.M. Lewis, San Rafael, *An Introduction to Credit Scoring,* Athena Press, 1992.

[3] Naeem Siddique, *Developing and Implementing Intelligent Credit Scoring*, John Wiley and SAS Series, 2005.

[4] R.A. Eisenbeis, *"Recent developments in the application of Credit Scoring Techniques to the evaluation of commercial loans"* (1996), *IMA J. Math. Appl. Business& Industry.* Vol. 7, PP 271-290, 1996.

Eliminating the Need for Multiple Layer-2 Network for Better Traffic Management

Prabhjot Kaur

Data Meghe College of Engineering, Navi Mumbai

ABSTRACT

MPLS is a mechanism in high-performance telecommunications network http://en.wikipedia.org/wiki/Telecommunications_network *that directs data from one network node to the next based on short path labels rather than long network addresses, avoiding complex lookups in a routing table. The labels identify virtual links (paths) between distant nodes rather than endpoints. MPLS can encapsulate packets of various network protocols and supports a range of access technologies, including T1/E1, ATM, Frame Relay, and DSL. It makes easy to commit network resources in such a way as to balance the load in the face of a given demand and to commit to differential levels of support to meet various user traffic requirements. The ability to dynamically define routes, plan resource commitments on the basis of known demand, and optimize network utilization is referred to as* traffic engineering. *It operates at a "layer 2.5" protocol, designed to provide a unified data-carrying service for both circuit-based clients and packet-switching clients which provide a datagram service model. It can be used to carry many different kinds of traffic, including IP packets, as well as native ATM, SONET, and Ethernet frames.This paper provides an overview of Multiprotocol Label Switching – Transport Profile (MPLS-TP), with information on the benefits of a combined MPLS-TP and IP/MPLS-based solution, and how Pseudowire-based MPLS can be adopted for transport network services.*

INTRODUCTION

Multiprotocol Label Switching(MPLS) is a promising effort toprovide the kind of traffic management and connectionoriented *Quality of Service* (QoS) support found in *Asynchronous Transfer Mode* (ATM) networks, to speed up the IPpacket-forwarding process, and to retain the flexibility of an IP-basednetworking approach.

The roots of MPLS go back to numerous efforts in the mid-1990s to combine IP and ATM technologies. The first such effort to reach the marketplace was IP switching, developed by Ipsilon. To compete with this offering, numerous other companies announced their own products, notably Cisco Systems (Tag Switching), IBM (aggregate route based IP switching), and Cascade (IP Navigator). The goal of all these products was to improve the throughput and delay performance of IP, and all took the same basic approach: Use a standard routing protocol such as *Open Shortest Path First* (OSPF) to define paths between endpoints;assign packets to these paths as they enter the network; and useATM switches to move packets along the paths. When these products came out, ATM switches were much faster than IP routers, and the intent was to improve performance by pushing as much of the traffic as possible down to the ATM level and using ATM switching hardware. In response to these proprietary initiatives, the *Internet EngineeringTask Force* (IETF) set up the MPLS working group in 1997 to develop acommon, standardized approach. The working group issued its first setof Proposed Standards in 2001. Meanwhile, however, the market didnot stand still. The late 1990s saw the introduction of many routers thatare as fast as ATM switches, eliminating the need to provide both ATMand IP technology in the same network.

Traffic management is an important mechanism for Internet network providersseeking to optimize network performance and traffic delivery.MPLS makes it easy to commit network resources in such a way as tobalance the load in the face of a given demand and to commit to differentiallevels of support to meet various user traffic requirements.

The multiprotocol label switching transportprofile (MPLS-TP) is a networking scheme for packet transport networks (PTNs) that specifies a connection-oriented, packet-switched architecture.MPLS-TP needs to be efficient when supporting packetswitchedtraffic with multiple classes and characteristics.

TRAFFIC ENGINEERING

MPLS makes it easy to commit network resources in such a way as to balance the load in the face of a given demand and to commit to differential levels of support to meet various user traffic requirements. Theability to dynamically define routes, plan resource commitments on the basis of known demand, and optimize network utilization is referred to as *traffic engineering*.With the basic IP mechanism, there is a primitive form of automated traffic engineering. Specifically, routing protocols such as OSPF enable routers to dynamically change the route to a given destination on a

Packet-by-packet basis to try to balance load. But such dynamic routing reacts in a very simple manner to congestion and does not provide a way to support QoS. All traffic between two endpoints follows the same route, which may be changed when congestion occurs. MPLS, on the other hand, is aware of not just individual packets, but flows of packets in which each flow has certain QoS requirements and a predictable traffic demand. With MPLS, it is possible to set up routes on the basis of these individual flows, with two different flows between the same endpoints perhaps following different routers. Further, when congestion threatens, MPLS paths can be rerouted intelligently. That is, instead of simply changing the route on a packet-by-packet basis, with MPLS, the routes are changed on a flow-by-flow basis, taking advantage of the known traffic demands of each flow. Effective use of traffic engineering can substantially increase usable network capacity.

WHAT IS MPLS-TP?

MPLS-TP is a set of MPLS protocols that are being defined in IETF. It is a simplified version of MPLS for transport networks with some of the MPLS functions turned off, such as Penultimate Hop Popping (PHP), Label-Switched Paths (LSPs) merge, and Equal Cost Multi Path (ECMP). MPLS-TP does not require MPLS control plane capabilities and enables the management plane to set up LSPs manually. Its OAM may operate without any IP layer functionalities.

The essential features of MPLS-TP defined by IETF and ITU-T are:

- MPLS forwarding plane with restrictions
- PWE3 Pseudo wire architecture
- Control Plane: static or dynamic Generalized MPLS (G-MPLS)
- Enhanced OAM functionality
- OAM monitors and drives protection switching
- Use of Generic Associated Channel (G-ACh) to support fault, configuration, accounting, performance, and security (FCAPS) functions

The below figure shows the MPLS-TP Network Model.

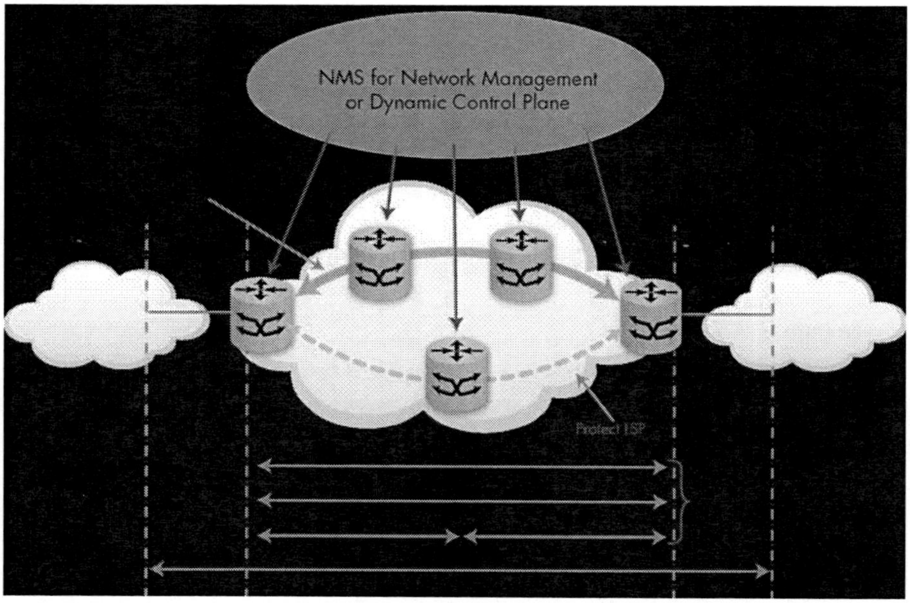

GOAL OF MPLS-TP

The goal of MPLS-TP is to provide connection-oriented transport for packet and TDM services over optical networks leveraging the widely deployed MPLS technology. Key to this effort is the definition and implementation of OAM and resiliency features to ensure the capabilities needed for carrier-grade transport networks – scalable operations, high availability, performance monitoring and multi-domain support.

MPLS-TP key characteristics are:

- It is strictly connection oriented.
- It is client-agnostic (can carry L3, L2, L1 services).
- It is physical layer agnostic (can run over IEEE Ethernet PHYs, SONET/SDH [G.783] and OTN [G.709],[G.872] using GFP [G.7041], WDM, etc.)
- It provides strong operations, administration and maintenance (OAM) functions similar to those available in traditional optical transport networks (e.g., SONET/SDH, OTN); these OAM functions are an integral part of the MPLSTP data plane and are independent from the control plane.
- It provides several protection schemes at the data plane similar to those available in traditional optical transport networks.
- It allows network provisioning via a centralized NMS and/or a distributed control plane
- The GMPLS control plane is also applicable to the MPLS-TP client or server layers and allows to use a common approach for management and control of multi-layer transport networks Current transport networks (e.g. SONET/SDH) are typically operated from a network operation centre (NOC) using a centralized network management system (NMS) that communicates with the network elements (NEs) in the field via the telecommunications management network (TMN, see ITU-T Recommendation M.3010 [M.3010]). The NMS provides well-known FCAPS management functions which are: fault, configuration, accounting, performance, and security management as defined in ITU-T Recommendation M.3400 [M.3400]. Together with survivability functions such as protection and restoration, availability figures of >99,999% have been achieved thanks to the highly sophisticated OAM functions that are existing, e.g. in SONET/SDH transport networks. This well proven network management paradigm has been taken as basis for the development of the new MPLS-TP packet transport network technology.

Moreover, MPLS-TP provides dynamic provisioning of MPLS-TP transport paths via a control plane. The control plane is mainly used to provide restoration functions for improved network survivability in the presence of failures and it facilitates end-to-end path provisioning across network or operator domains. The operator has the choice to enable the control plane or to operate the network in a traditional way without control plane by means of an NMS. It shall be noted that the control plane does not make the NMS obsolete – the NMS needs to configure the control plane and also needs to interact with the control plane for connection management purposes.

HOW DOES MPLS-TP WORKS?

- MPLS-TP uses Generalized MPLS (GMPLS) to provide deterministic and connection oriented behaviour using LSPs (Label Switched Paths), making it a dependable transport protocol.
- MPLS-TP also uses Targeted LDP (T-LDP) to set up pseudo wires (PWs) over GMPLS LSPs, to provide VPWS (Virtual Private Wire Service) and VPLS (Virtual Private LAN Service).
- MPLS-TP mandates running protocols such as BFD (Bidirectional Forwarding Detection) over GMPLS LSPs and PWs, to provide OAM functionality.
- MPLS-TP does not assume IP connectivity between devices, and explicitly rules out related features of normal MPLS, such as PHP (Penultimate Hop Popping, ECMP (Equal Cost Multipath), and LSP Merge.
- MPLS-TP specifies how very fast protection and restoration will be achieved using switchover to backup paths.
- MPLS-TP allows LSPs and PWs to be signalled using a control plane (using RSVP-based GMPLS signalling and Targeted LDP signalling), or to be statically configured.
- A typical MPLS-TP service is depicted below, showing three PWs that have been stitched together. In this example, the access networks LSPs are statically configured, and the backbone uses signalling. However, all combinations are possible - the backbone could use statically configured LSPs, and the access networks could use signalling.

For fault detection and localization, each device in the diagram would run BFD over each PW and each underlying LSP. This works as follows.

- Both ends of each LSP send BFD packets over the LSP, typically with very short intervals (10ms being common).
- If either end sees an interval between received BFD packets above a certain threshold, it will raise an alarm for the specific service, and report the problem in the content of the BFD packets it transmits.
- If either end sees such a problem reported in received BFD packets, it will also raise an alarm for that LSP.

To distinguish BFD packets from other labelled data flowing over the LSP, the BFD packets are pre-pended with a special well-known MPLS label, the "GAL" (GAch Label), which sits at the bottom of the MPLS label stack, and a GAch (Generic Associated Channel) header. The terminating device will use the GAL label to determine that the packet is not part of the normal data stream, and the GAch header to determine what sort of OAM traffic it is.

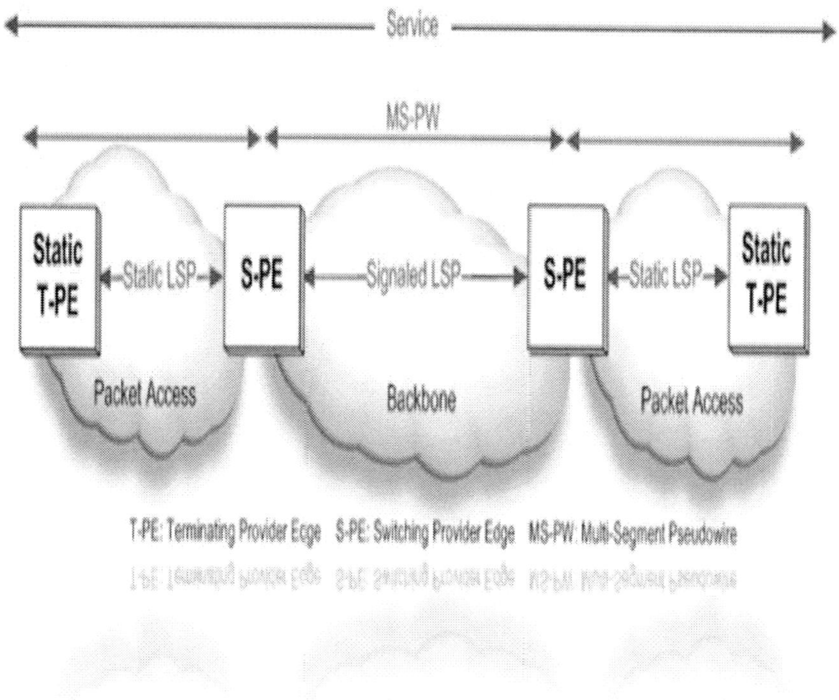

When BFD is used over the PW rather than over the underlying LSP, it does not use the GAL label. Instead, all data traversing the PW contains an initial header (the "GAch header", or "Control Word") which the terminating device can use to detect whether a packet is normal data or a BFD packet.

CONCLUSIONS

MPLS-TP is intended to enable next-generation converged packet networks tying together service routing and transport platforms. Major advantages are consistent operations and OAM functions across the different network layers and the seamless interworking with IP/MPLS networks. MPLS-TP is highly scalable due to its multiplexing capability that can be used to create a network with multiple hierarchical layers. MPLS-TP supports a huge variety of services that are encapsulated into pseudo wires and it can be carried over the existing and evolving transport network infrastructure

REFERENCES

[1] MPLS Working Group, *http://datatracker.ietf.org/wg/mpls/*

[2] E. Rosen, A. Viswanathan, and R. Callon, "MultiprotocolLabel Switching Architecture," IETF RFC 3031, Jan. 2001.

[3] D. Thaler and B. Aboba," What Makes for a Successful Protocol?," IETF RFC 5218, July 2008.

[4] RFC 5654: Requirements of an MPLS Transport Profile.

[5] RFC 5921: A Framework for MPLS in Transport Networks.

[6] RFC 5659: An architecture for Multi-Segment Pseudo wire Emulation Edge-to-Edge.

[7] Bryant *et al.*, "Pseudo Wire Emulation Edge-to-Edge (PWE3) Architecture," IETF RFC 3985, Mar. 2005.

[8] Martini *et al.*, "Pseudowire Setup and Maintenance Using the Label Distribution Protocol (LDP)," IETF RFC 4447, Apr. 2006.

[9] P. Trimintzioset *al.*, "A Management and Control Architecture for Providing IP Differentiated Services in MPLSBased Networks," *IEEE Commun. Mag.*, May 2001 F. Le Faucheur and W. Lai, Maximum Allocation Bandwidth.

ICT Enabled Technologies

Neeraj Awasthy and Sukriti Tayal

IMT, Ghaziabad

ABSTRACT

India has become a test bed for innovations in information andCommunication technologies (ICT) serving the rural user.India has more than 70% of its population living in rural areas with agriculture as their main livelihood. There exists a hope that ICT can surmount at least some of rural India's social, political, and administrative challenges and create a viable technology for the provision of health, education and other social services.

The gradual shift of the rural user base from the traditional ICT tools (radio, television and print media) to the new ICT tools (internet, PC's and mobiles) is well evident and is attributed to the increased tele-density and growth of the cellular mobile sector in addition to the telecom network. The overall tele-density in India as of March, 2012 is 77.57% out of which rural areas contribute close to 38%. The rural subscriber base is 330 million out of the 930 million country-wide. These new tools provide benefits such as increased accessibility to the user, enhanced knowledge flow and connectivity, timely and cost-effective format for the user.

Initiatives have been taken by the government and some private firms towards building a better knowledge management base and hence the infrastructure. They want to establish a support structure for the sustainable livelihood opportunities.

1. *By medium of Telecommunication networks and Internet accessibility*
   - *kiosks/ knowledge centres/common service centres*
   - *e-portals*
2. *By medium of Mobiles*
   - *messages*
   - *Audio and video conferencing*
3. *By medium of community radios*

The objective of study of these modes of e-governance is to build upon a model of the most appropriate means of implementing the technology after looking at the various factors which influence the dissemination of information in rural areas.

INTRODUCTION

ICTs generally refer to an expanding assembly of technologies that are used to handleinformation and aid communication. These include hardware, software, media for collection, storage, processing, transmission and presentation of information in any format (i.e. voice,data, text and image), computers, the Internet, CD-ROMs, email, telephone, radio, television,video, digital cameras, etc. While radio, television and print media were primarily used toperform these tasks earlier, with the advent of the new ICTs, these have now been considered as traditional ICTs. However, many of these traditional ICTs are effective than web-basedsolution, as they can resolve issues such as language, literacy or access to the Internet (UNDAW, 2002).

> *The new information and communications technologies are among the driving forces forGlobalisation. They are bringing people together, and bringing decision makersunprecedented new tools for development. At the same time, however, the gap betweeninformation 'haves' and 'have-nots' is widening, and there is a real danger that the world'spoor will be excluded from the emerging knowledge-based global economy.* *(Kofi Anan, 2002).*

Not surprisingly, the digital divide mirrors divides in other resources that have amore insidious effect, such as the disparities in access to education, health care,capital, shelter, employment, clean water and food. These other divides canarguably be viewed as being a result of an imbalance in access to information—in short, the digital divide—than its cause. Information is critical to the social andeconomic activities that comprise the development process. Thus, ICTs, as ameans of sharing information, are a link in the chain of the development processitself (ILO, 2001).

In India, the rural population accounts for about 72% of the total population and the percentage of totalpopulation below the poverty line is 22%1. For BOP families, the cost of accessing a service at the taluk level varies from ₹ 200 to 300.

The role of ICT is catalytic in the complex task of poverty reduction by leveraging the effects on earning opportunities, on educational and health services, on good governance and on promoting democracies. This suggests the centrality of a holistic approach in evaluating the impact of ICT's. The goal of using ICT with rural people is not only about overcoming the digital divide, but rather enforcing and furthering the process of social inclusion. It has been proposed (UNDP 2001 b) that strong linkages need to be established between direct ICT interventions and national- level programmes that deploy ICT as an enabler in development.[1]

The information and communication technologies includes traditional tools like newspaper, wireless local loops, village kiosks, rural radio broadcasting. Modern ICT's includes –

1. Global system of mobile communication (GSM) and digital radio
2. Computers, personal data assistants (PDA's) , e-mail, speech recognition technologies, global positioning system (GPS) and internet

Since opportunities abound around the globe, it is very important for Government to provide connectivity to its citizens to make them "Information rich". ICT can strengthen the role of each governance pillar in rural development and poverty reduction. It can facilitate speedy, transparent, accountable, efficient and effective interaction between the public, citizens, business and other agencies. [1]

Typical ICT Infrastructure Required for e-Governance

The rural ICT solutions are normally offered through internet portals hosted on a delivery web server to provide access to the citizens through inexpensive internet medium. The information flow between the delivery server and the other departments is accomplished through Intranet/ LAN connectivity with servers of these departments (if exist). Often, due to non-computerization of back-end systems, the transactions are manually exchanged and response data is keyed in manually through the nodes on the delivery server.

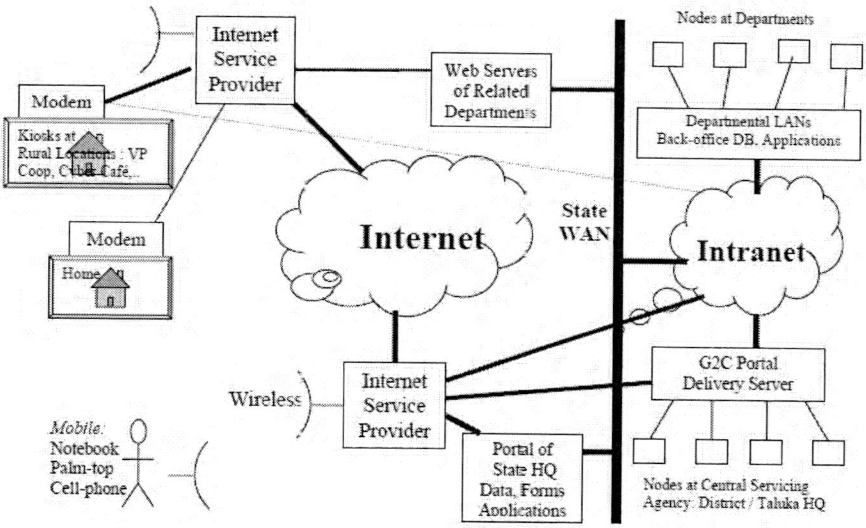

Fig. 1. Typical ICT Infrastructure for Rural Applications

The various benefits of rural development by ICT's would be:

1. Societal Upliftment
2. Employment
3. Health Services
4. Privacy and Security
5. Improved economic performance
6. Increased Citizen participation
7. Education
8. Innovation and Research
9. Poverty Alleviation

TRADITIONAL TOOLS

Radio

India's post-independence experiments with ICT in agricultural development started withradio. The government established a network of All India Radio (AIR) stations across the country to broadcast programmes in regional languages.

Television

Doordarshan, the government television has been playing an important role in communicating rural and agricultural news and information to rural communities. Doordarshan currently reaches 92 per cent of the Indian population through a network ofl, 414 terrestrial transmitters. It telecasts programmes on agriculture, rural development,women, children, family welfare, adult education, youth, civic sense and public awareness, science & technology and also telecasts special programmes during natural calamities such asflood, earth quake, epidemics, etc.

Newspapers

Newspapers (especially local language dailies) are one of the important sources ofinformation for farmers. According to the New Delhi-based Indian Newspaper Society, India has more than 62,000 newspapers, with a staggering 90% of them in local languages. Most of the regional language dailies devote at least one page every week for news and articles on different aspects of agriculture.

MODERN TOOLS

Mobile Telecommunication

The rural areas in the country have experienced rapid growth in telecom services and the tele-density (defined as the number of persons per hundred owning a telephone connection) has risen from 21.16 per cent in December 2009 to 60.99 per cent in September 2010. The total number of rural connections at the end of September 2010 was 236.21 million compared to 47 million at the start of the Eleventh Plan. As on September 2010, 5.69 lakhs of village public telephones (98 per cent) have been provided. The latest figures released bythe Telecom Regulatory Authority of India show that tele-density in rural India was 28.42 in September 2010, compared to 137.25 for urban areas As on September 2010, the Internet subscriber base stood at 17.90 million, out of which the number of Broadband subscribers was 10.31 million and the share of Broadband subscription in total Internetsubscription was 57.6 per cent. [4]

The first three indicators A1, A2 and A3, viz., fixed telephones per 100 inhabitants,Mobile telephones per 100 inhabitants'; and computers per 100 inhabitants, are regularly maintained month wise by the department of telecommunication under the ministry ofinformation and communication technology.

M-commerce, defined as the buying and selling of goods and services using wirelesshandheld devices such as mobile telephones or personal data assistants (PDAs),is growing at a rapid pace.This rapid growth stems from the cost advantageof mobile infrastructure over fixed-line installation and from the fact that mobilenetwork consumers can simply buy a handset and a prepaid card and start using itas soon as the first base stations are in place. [6]

Challenges for Telecommunication

1. Very capital-heavy to connect the last mile in reaching a village, maintenance is also expensive
2. Low returns make it economically non-feasible, considering the extremely low traffic expectation.

Internet Enabled Computer Centres (Kiosks/Telecentres)

Rural kiosks could provide the first computing experience for as much as 700 million people in India. Kiosks help impoverished villagers improve their standard of living by expanding livelihood options and empowering them with information, tools, goods, and services (such as education and healthcare). Telecentres is a physical place providing public access to communication and information services.Under the National e Governance Plan (NeGP) the Government is making a concerted effort to create 100,000 Citizen Service Centres (CSC) in rural areas where citizens will be able to access eservices. There are approximately 0.6 million inhabited villages in India of which nearly 91% are connected to the fixed line telecom network. Inadequate power supply and lastmile connectivity problems have prevented a fast rollout of the CSCs only 40,000 CSCs have been created so far. [3]

Fig. 2. The Dimensions Covered by the ICT Usage

Commercial Initiatives Run by Large Enterprise

1. ITC's e-Choupal supplies market information through village kiosks to entice farmers to sell directly to ITC.
2. ITC's Digitalmandi offers the farmers all the information they need to enhance farm productivity by using better technology, improve farm produce price realization and cut transaction costs. Farmers can access latest local and global information on weather, scientific farming practices as well as market prices at the village itself through this Bilingual web portal.
3. Hindustan Lever Limited's e-Shakti online store for rural markets.

Community-Oriented Entrepreneurial Projects

1. Drishtee aids government computerize bureaucracies. Applications range from filling out forms, applying for licenses and birth certificates, filing petitions and grievances, printing land records.
2. N-Logue offers communication services that leverage their unique connectivity solution. These wireless connectivity solutions also provide some villages with their only phone. Public AccessInternet Kiosks' have been established in 30 villages under the SARI project in association with n-logue.
3. Tarahaat utilizes fine graphics and animations to convey general introductory information about their services. The site also uses voice effectively for dissemination of information.

Government-Led Initiatives

1. Akshaya project in Kerala seeks to make 100% of the state's households computer literate.
2. Bhoomi, in Karnataka makes citizen land records accessible online. It has computerized 20 million records ofland ownership of 6.7 million farmers in the state.
3. Gyandoot hasbeen making government more accessible to villagers. It reduces the time and money peoplespend trying to communicate with public officials and provide immediate,transparent access to local government data and documentation.[9]

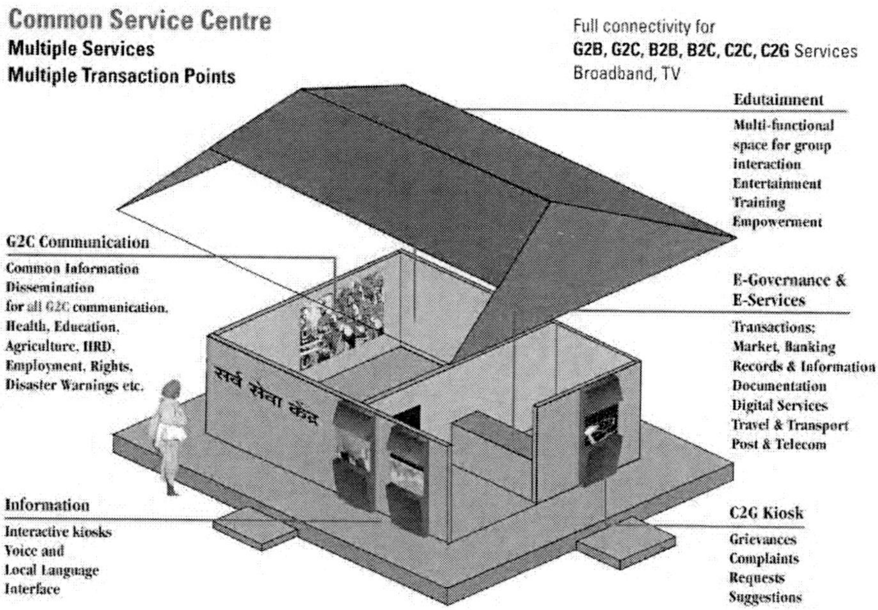

Fig. 3. The Fundamental Aspect of a Common Service Centre

Operational Challenges with the Internet Enabled Computer Centers

- Start-up costs are high
- Infrastructural obstacles are severe.
- Kiosks are critically dependent on good kiosk operators.
- Kiosks are sensitive to location and population density.

Technology Needs of these kiosks

- Power management
- Connectivity: Poor connectivity is handled through VSAT satellite dishes or specially developed wireless access solutions (e.g., n-Logue's corDECT). Mobile wireless, Wi-Fi, and WiMAX technologies are likely to become more important as time goes on.

Alternatives to PC-Based Kiosks

Mobile phones seem the most likely candidate to serve as a viable alternative to PC-based kiosks. Leap-frogging landline infrastructure, mobile phones are becoming common among the poor. Providing connectivity at reasonable costs and increasingly greater processing power, they could easily supplant PCs as the gateway to information and electronic services. [5]

E-Portals

1. Agmarknet (*http://www.agmarknet.nic.in/): -* This home page links you to the various Ministries of Government catering to different needs of rural India.
2. Agriwatch (http://www.agriwatch.com/): This website provides the SMS facility for alerts on prices of particular commodities.[11]

Community Radio

A community radio (CR) station can be roughly defined as a short range radio station that caters to the information needs of communities living in surrounding areas. CR stations often involve local community members in program production, centred around topics including discussions on civic amenities in the area, health and hygiene, advice on common economic activities such as agriculture, and even local folk songs and cultural events. [10]

MOST EFFECTIVE TOOL

The phones contribute to reduce poverty and improve rural livelihoods through a number of ways. First, by expanding and strengthening social networks; increase people's ability to deal with emergencies and to work together thereby reducing costs and increasing productivity.

Secondly, mobile phones enable rural people to cut down travel costs; minimize physical risks; maximize the outcomes of necessary journeys; increase temporal accessibility; amplify efficiency of activities; and send and receive money. Thirdly, mobile phones help rural traders and farmers to secure better markets and prices; save time and money; and promptly communicate business-related information. However, mobile phones have not made important contributions to improve incomes of rural households. [2]

RECOMMENDATION

Recommendations keeping in mind the challenges for implementation of ICT in rural India

1. Illiteracy – you cannot use much of textual information
2. Middlemen – Physical distances makes it difficult to provide proper info
3. Language – Multiplicity and highly specific local languages
4. Easy loans – Reluctance of banks to provide soft loans to farmers.
5. Affordability – Any new technology must be economical.

REFERENCES

[1] Department of information technology, government of India (2008). Impact assessment of e-governanceprojects. retrieved April 11, 2009 from *http://www.mit.gov.in/download/impactassessmentreportdraft.pdf* - Google Search [WWW Document], 2012.

[2] I. hammond (2008, June). Mobiles telecoms in rural areas. i4d (information for development)magazine, VI (6). available: http://*www.i4donline.net* - Google Search [WWW Document], 2012.

[3] S. Gandhi, s. Mittal and g. Tripathi (2009, January). The impact of mobiles on agriculturalproductivity. TheVodafone public policy paper series, number 9. Available: *http://www.vodafone.com/publicpolicyseries* - Google Search [WWW Document], 2012.

[4] UNDP. (2006). human development report 2006 (263). RetrievedMay 5, 2009, from *http://hdr.undp.org/hdr2006/pdfs/report/hdr06-complete.pdf* - Google Search [WWW Document], 2012.

[5] Exploring Conditions for Delivery of Successful M-Government Services to the Bottom of the Pyramid (BOP) in India by Subhash Bhatnagar/ : SSRN [WWW Document], 2012a. URL *http://papers.ssrn.com/sol3/papers.cfm?abstract_id=1618169*

[6] Mobile Government: An Emerging Direction in E-government: Ibrahim Kushchu: 9781591408840: Amazon.com: Books [WWW Document], 2012. . URL *http://www.amazon.com/Mobile-Government-Emerging-Direction-government/dp/1591408849*

[7] The opportunity for mobile operators. Available: *http://www.vnl.in/solutions/theopportunity/* - Google Search [WWW Document], 2012.

[8] Department of Telecommunication (Govt. of India), Annual Report 2004

[9] India 2006; a Reference Annual, New Delhi: Publication Division, Ministry of Information and Broadcasting

[10] Bridges (2001). Spanning the Digital Divide, Bridges.org Report *http://www.bridges.org/spanningchpt4.html*

[11] CRISP (2009), Reaching Rural Women- Designing programmes that meet their needsthrough a consultative design process. *www.reachingruralwomen.org.*

Integrating Layered Approach With CRF to Build More Efficient Intrusion Detection System

Vaishali T. Deshmukh and Shubhangi Vaikole[1]

Shreeram Polytechnic, Airoli, Navi Mumbai
[1]Datta Meghe College of Engg., Airoli, Navi Mumbai

ABSTRACT

Today the use of the network becomes a crucial part of our routine life. Most of us keep and access sensitive data online. So the security of network system becomes important. Intruder is one of the most publicized threats to security. Network Intrusion Detection Systems (NIDS) have become a standard component in network security infrastructures. An intrusion detection system must reliably detect malicious activities in a network and must perform efficiently to cope with the large amount of network traffic. In this paper, we address Conditional Random Fields and Layered Approach for intrusion detection. The CRFs can be effective in improving the attack detection accuracy by reducing the number of false alarms, while the Layered Approach can be implemented to improve the overall system efficiency. Hence, by integrating both we build a single system that is accurate in attacks detection and efficient in operation.

INTRODUCTION

Today, intrusion detection is one of the high priority and challenging tasks for network administrators and security professionals. Every day the attacker comes up with newer and more advanced penetration methods to defeat the installed security systems [16] and [17]. Thus, it becomes important to protect the networks from known vulnerabilities and at the same time take steps to detect new and unseen, but possible system abuses by developing more reliable and efficient intrusion detection systems. Its prime purpose is to detect as many attacks as possible with minimum number of false alarms, i.e. the system must be accurate in detecting attacks.

However, an accurate system is always slow in decision making. We desire a system that detects most of the attacks, gives very few false alarms, copes with large amount of data, and is fast enough to make real-time decisions.

In this paper we have addressed a system where the study is limited to one system application (Network Based College Administration System).The attacks are categorised into four groups (DOS, Probe, U2R, R2L). All the possible attack will be shown with this application and detected at that particular layer of attack. Each layer is modelled separately with a set of features. The sequence labelling and the classification can be done with CRF. Customization of a system can be done according to the requirements.

VARIOUS INTRUSION DETECTION SYSTEMS (IDS)

Intrusion detection (ID) system is a type of security management system for computers and networks. An ID system gathers and analyzes information from various areas within a computer or a network to identify possible security breaches, which include both intrusions and misuse functions, does following

- Monitors and analyzes user and system activities
- Analyzes system configurations and vulnerabilities
- Assess system and file integrity
- Recognizes patterns of typical attacks
- Analyses abnormal activity patterns
- Tracks user policy violations

Intrusion detection started in around 1980s and can also be classified as:

- Network intrusion detection system (NIDS)
- Host-based intrusion detection system (HIDS)
- Protocol-based IDS(PIDS)
- Application protocol-based intrusion detection system (APIDS).

As we are dealing with only the network packets we are using NIDS. A network intrusion detection system is a system that also tries to detect malicious activity such as denial of service attacks [3], port scans or even attempts to crack into computers by monitoring network traffic [11]. The NIDS does this by reading all the incoming packets and try to find out suspicious patterns. If, for example, a large number of TCP connection requests to a very large number of different ports are observed, one could assume that there is someone conducting a port scan of some or all of the computer(s) in the network.NIDS is not limited to inspecting incoming network traffic only. Often valuable information about an ongoing intrusion can be learned from outgoing or local traffic as well.

RELATED WORK

Intrusion detection and network security has been introduced around since late 1980s. Since then, many methods and frameworks have been proposed and many systems have been built to detect intrusions.

Association Rule Mining

These are based on building classifiers by discovering relevant patterns of program and user behaviour. Association rules are used to learn the record patterns that describe user behaviour. These methods can deal with symbolic data, and the features can be defined in the form of packet and connection details. However, mining of features is limited to entry level of the packet and requires the number of records to be large and sparsely populated. Otherwise, they tend to produce a large number of rules that increase the complexity of the system.

Data Clustering Methods k-Means and the Fuzzy c-Means

Clustering technique is based on calculating numeric distance between the observations, and hence, the observations must be numeric [18]. Observations with symbolic features cannot be easily used for the clustering methods. It considers the features independently and is unable to capture the relationship between different features of a single record, which further degrades attack detection accuracy.

Naive Baye's Classifiers

These make strict independence assumption between the attributes in an observation resulting in lower attack detection accuracy when the features are correlated, which is often the case for intrusion detection. Bayesian network can also be used for intrusion detection. However, they tend to be attack specific and build a decision network based on special characteristics of individual attacks. Thus, the size of a Bayesian network increases rapidly as the number of features and the type of attacks modelled by a Bayesian network increases [9]. To detect anomalous traces of system calls in privileged processes, hidden Markov models (HMMs) have been applied in and however, modelling the system calls alone may not always provide accurate classification as in such cases various connection level features are ignored. Further, HMMs are generative systems and fail to modelling-range dependencies between the observations.

Decision Trees

This method selects the finest features for each decision node during the construction of the tree based on some well defined criteria [8]. One such criterion is to use the information gain ratio. Decision trees generally have very high speed of operation and high attack detection accuracy.

Neural Networks

According to Debar[19] though the neural networks can work effectively with noisy data, they require large amount of data for training and it is often hard to select the best possible architecture for a neural network.

Support Vector Machines

Support vector machines have also been used for detecting intrusions. Support vector machines map real valued input feature vector to a higher dimensional feature space through nonlinear mapping[6].This can also provide real-time detection capability, deal with large dimensionality of data, and can be used for binary-class as well as multiclass classification.

Other approaches for detecting intrusion include the use of autonomous and probabilistic agents for intrusion detection. These methods are generally aimed at developing a distributed intrusion detection system. To overcome the weakness of a single intrusion detection system, a number of frameworks have been proposed, which describe the collaborative use of network-based and host based systems, systems that employ both signature based and behaviour-based techniques. The data analyzed by the intrusion detection system for classification often has a number of features that are highly correlated and complex relationships exist between them. When classifying network connections as either normal or as attack, a system may consider features such as "logged in" and "number of file creations" [2]. When these features are analyzed individually, they do not provide any information that can assist in detecting attacks. However, when these features are analyzed together, they can provide meaningful information, which can be helpful for the classification task [15].

CONDITIONAL RANDOM FIELDS FOR INTRUSION DETECTION

Conditional models are probabilistic systems that are used to model the conditional distribution over a set of random variables.

The CRFs have proven to be very successful in such tasks, as they do not make any unwarranted assumptions about the data. Hence, we explore the suitability of CRFs for intrusion detection system may consider features such as "logged in" and "number of file creations."When these features are analyzed individually, they do not provide any information that can aid in detecting attacks.

However, when these features are analyzed together, they can provide meaningful information, which can be helpful for the classification task.

Let X be the random variable over data sequence to be labelled and Y the corresponding label sequence. In addition, let *G = (V,E)* be a graph such that $Y = (Y_v)_{v \in (V)}$, so that Y is indexed by the vertices of G. Then, *(X,Y)* is a CRF, when conditioned on X, the random variables Yv obey the Markov property with respect to the graph

$$p(Y_v|X, Y_w, w \neq v) = p(Y_v|X.Y_w, w \sim v)$$

where $w \sim v$ means that *w* and *v* are neighbours in *G*, i.e., a CRF is a random field globally conditioned on X. For a simple sequence (or chain) modelling, as in our case, the joint distribution over the label sequence Y given X has the following form:

$$p_\theta(y|x) \propto \exp\left(\sum_{e\in E,k} \lambda_k f_k(e, y|_e, x) + \sum_{v\in V,k} \mu_k g_k(v, y|_v, x)\right),$$

where x is the data sequence, y is a label sequence, and $y|s$ is the set of components of y associated with the vertices or edges in sub graph S. In addition, the features fk and gk are assumed to be given and fixed. For example, a Boolean edge feature fk might be true if the observation Xi is "protocol = tcp," tag $Yi\text{-}1$ is "normal," and tag Yi is "normal." Similarly, a Boolean vertex feature gk might be true if the observation Xi is "service = ftp" and tag Yi is "attack."

We showed that the sequence labelling methods such as the CRFs can be very effective in detecting attacks.

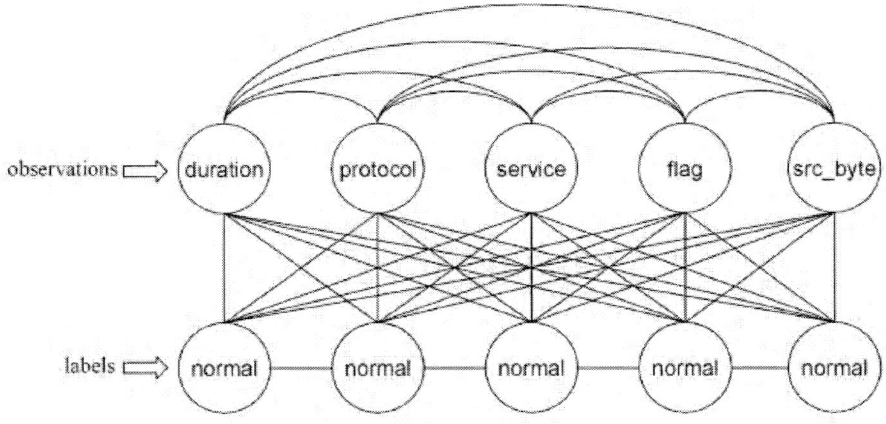

Fig. 1. Graphical representation of a CRF

In the proposed system each record represents a separate connection, and hence, we consider every record as a separate sequence. We aim to model the relationships among features of individual connections using a CRF, as shown in Fig.1. In this figure, features such as duration, protocol, service, flag, and src_bytes take some possible value for every connection. During training, feature weights are learnt, and during testing, features are evaluated for the given observation, which is then labelled accordingly.

LAYERED APPROACH FOR INTRUSION DETECTION

The LIDS draws its motivation from what we call as the Airport Security model, where a number of security checks are performed one after the other in a sequence. Similar to this model, the LIDS represents a sequential Layered Approach and is based on ensuring availability, confidentiality, and integrity of data and (or) services over a network. Fig. 2 gives a generic representation of the framework.

The goal of using a layered model is to reduce computation and the overall time required to detect anomalous events. The time required to detect an intrusive event is significant and can be reduced by eliminating the communication overhead among different layers. This can be achieved by making the layers autonomous and self-sufficient to block an attack without the need of a central decision-maker. Every layer in the LIDS framework is trained separately and then deployed sequentially. We define four layers that correspond to the four attack groups mentioned in the data set. They are Probe layer, DoS layer, R2L layer, and U2R layer. Each layer is then separately trained with a small set of relevant features. Feature selection is significant for Layered Approach and discussed in the next section. In order to make the layers independent, some features may be present in more than one layer. The layers essentially act as filters that block any anomalous connection, thereby eliminating the need of further processing at subsequent layers enabling quick response to intrusion. The effect of such a sequence of layers is that the anomalous events are identified and blocked as soon as they are detected.

Our second goal is to improve the speed of operation of the system. Hence, we implement the LIDS and select a small set of features for every layer rather than using all the 41 features. This results in significant performance improvement during both the training and the testing of the system. In many situations, there is a trade-off between efficiency and accuracy of the system and there can be various avenues to improve system performance. Methods such as naive Bayes assume independence among the observed data. This certainly increases system efficiency, but it may severely affect the accuracy. To balance this trade-off, we use the CRFs that are more accurate, though expensive, but we implement the Layered Approach to improve overall system performance. The performance of our proposed system, Layered CRFs, is comparable to that of the decision trees and the naive Bayes, and our system has higher attack detection accuracy.

INTREGRATING LAYERED APPROACH WITH CONDITIONAL RANDOM FIELDS

In our system, every layer is separately trained to detect a single type of attack category. The attack groups are different in their impact, and hence, it becomes necessary to treat them differently. Hence, we select features for each layer based upon the type of attacks that the layer is trained to detect.

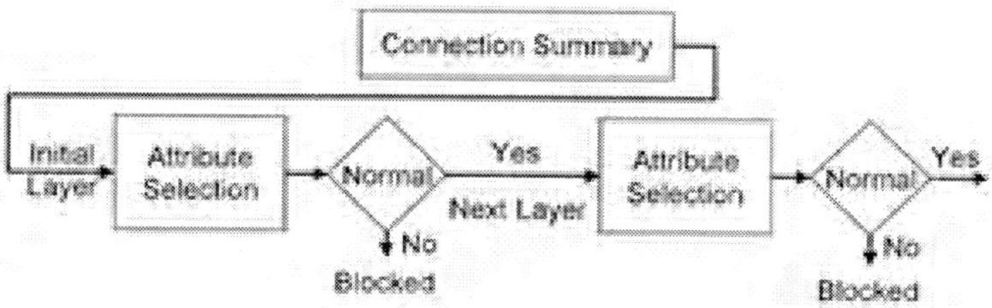

Fig. 2. Layered Representation

Probe Layer

The probe attacks are aimed at acquiring information about the target network from a source that is often external to the network. Hence, basic connection level features such as the "duration of connection" and "source bytes" are significant while features like "number of files creations" and "number of files accessed" are not expected to provide information for detecting probes.

DoS Layer

The DoS attacks are meant to force the target to stop the service(s) that is (are) provided by flooding it with illegitimate requests. Hence, for the Dos layer, traffic features such as the "percentage of connections having same destination host and same service" and packet level features such as the "source bytes" and "percentage of packets with errors" is significant. To detect DoS attacks, it may not be important to know whether a user is "logged in or not."

R2L Layer

The R2L attacks are one of the most difficult to detect as they involve the network level and the host level features. We therefore selected both the network level features such as the "duration of connection" and "service requested" and the host level features such as the "number of failed login attempts" among others for detecting R2L attacks.

U2R Layer

The U2R attacks involve the semantic details that are very difficult to capture at an early stage. Such attacks are often content based and target an application. Hence, for U2R attacks, we selected features such as "number of file creations" and "number of shell prompts invoked," while we ignored features such as "protocol" and "source bytes."

The algorithm for integrating CRFs with the Layered Approach.

Algorithm

Training

- **Step 1:** Select the number of layers, n, for the complete system.
- **Step 2:** Separately perform features selection for each layer.
- **Step 3:** Train a separate model with CRFs for each layer using the features selected from Step 2.
- **Step 4:** Plug in the trained models sequentially such that only the connections labelled as normal are passed to the next layer.

Testing

- **Step 5:** For each (next) test instance perform Steps 6 through 9.

- **Step 6:** Test the instance and label it either as attack or normal.
- **Step 7:** If the instance is labelled as attack, block it and identify it as an attack represented by the layer name at which it is detected and go to Step 5. Else pass the sequence to the next layer.
- **Step 8:** If the current layer is not the last layer in the system, test the instance and go to Step 7. Else go to Step 9.
- **Step 9:** Test the instance and label it either as normal or as an attack. If the instance is labelled as an attack, block it and identify it as an attack corresponding to the layer name.

IMPLEMENTATION

Most intrusions occur via network using the network protocols to attack their targets. Generally, there are four categories of attacks

They are:

1. DoS (denial-of-service), for example, ping-of death, syn flood, etc.
2. Probe, surveillance and probing, for example, port-scan, ping-sweep, etc.
3. R2L, unauthorized access from a remote machine, for example, guessing password.
4. U2R, unauthorized access to local super user privileges by a local unprivileged user, for example, various buffer overflow.

DOS and PROBE attacks involve many connections to some hosts in a very short period of time. While R2L and U2R attacks are related to data packets, and normally involve only a single connection.

In real scenario, we are not aware of the category of an attack. Rather, we are interested in identifying the attack category once the system detects an event as anomalous. In our work, we define features from the observations as well as from the observations and the previous labels and perform sequence labelling via the CRFs to label every feature in the observation. Layered Approach not only improves the attack detection, but it also helps identify the type of attack once detected because every layer is trained to detect only a particular category of attack. Hence, if an attack is detected at the U2R layer, it is very likely that the attack is of "U2R" type.

This enables to perform quick recovery and prevent similar attacks. Fig. 3 gives the real-time system representation. We integrate the four models (with feature selection) and develop the final system. In this experiment the data in the test set is relabelled either as normal or as attack and all the data from the test set is passed though the system starting from the first layer. If layer 1 detects any connection as an attack, it is blocked and labeled as "Probe." Only the events labeled as "Normal" are allowed to go to the next layer. The same process is repeated at the next layers where an attack is blocked and labelled as "DoS," "R2L," or "U2R" at layer 2, layer 3, and layer 4, respectively. Figure 4 shows how the DOS attack is detected in the particular DOS layer; once it is detected we blocked it immediately.

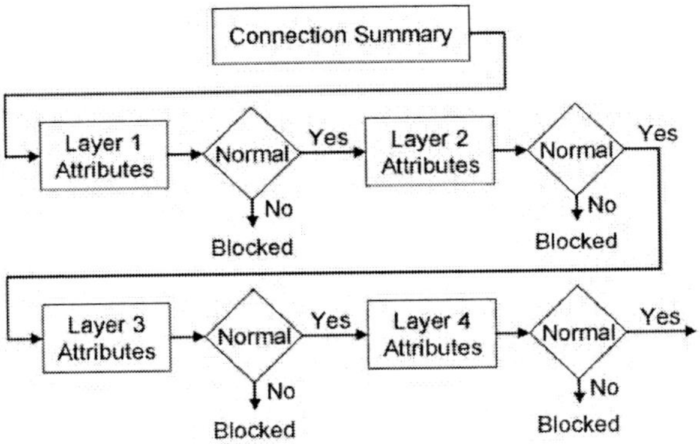

Fig. 3. Real-Time Representation of the System

CONCLUSIONS

In this system we addressed the dual problem of Accuracy and Efficiency for building robust and efficient intrusion detection systems. CRFs are very effective in improving the attack detection rate and decreasing the FAR. Having a low FAR is very important for any intrusion detection system. Further; feature selection and implementing the Layered Approach significantly reduce the time required to train and test the model.

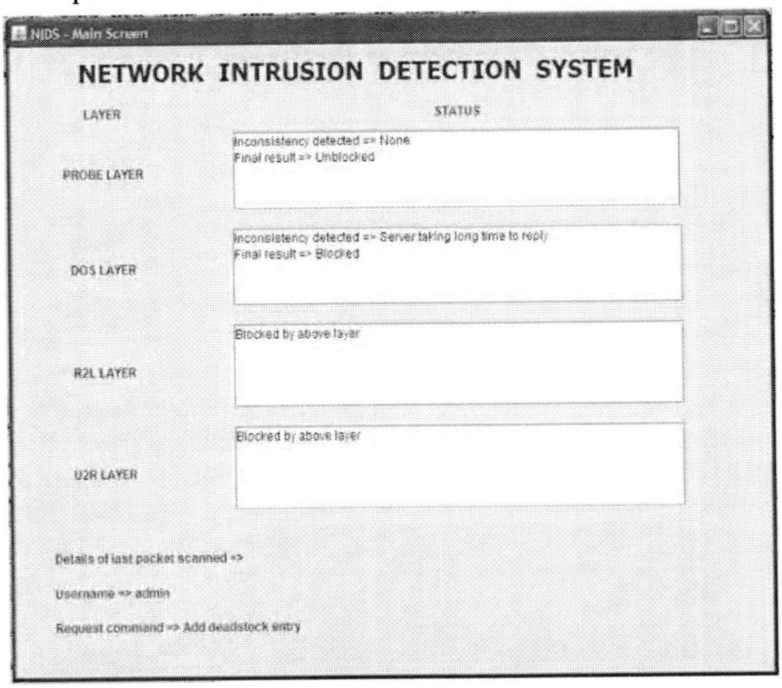

Fig. 4. Sample Result of DOS Attack

This method is much suitable for detecting R2L and U2R attacks.

Our system can help in identifying an attack once it is detected at a particular layer, which expedites the intrusion response mechanism, thus minimizing the impact of an attack. Our system has the advantage that the number of layers can be increased or decreased depending upon the environment in which the system is deployed, giving flexibility to the network administrator.

REFERENCES

[1] W. Lee, S. Stolfo, and K. Mok, "Mining Audit Data to Build Intrusion Detection Models," Proc. Fourth Int'l Conf. Knowledge Discovery and Data Mining (KDD '98), pp. 66-72, 1998.

[2] Boswell, Wendy (n.d.). *A Short History of the Internet.* http://websearch.about.com/od/whatistheinternet/a/historyinternet.htm.

[3] Chen, Qiang (2001). *Computer Intrusion Detection through Noise Cancellation.* Arizona: Arizona State University.

[4] Cisco (2007). *Understanding Delay in Packet Voice Networks.* http://www.cisco.com/warp/public/788/voip/delay-details.hml

[5] A. McCallum, "Efficiently Inducing Features of Conditional Random Fields," Proc. 19th Ann. Conf. Uncertainty in Artificial Intelligence (UAI '03), pp. 403-410, 2003.

[6] D.S. Kim and J.S. Park, "Network-Based Intrusion Detection with Support Vector Machines," Proc. Information Networking, Networking Technologies for Enhanced Internet Services Int'l Conf. (ICOIN '03), pp. 747-756, 2003.

[7] Inline (2005). *Snort Inline Part II.* Pete Savage. Retrieved on March 8, 2007 http://linuxgazette.net/118/savage.html.

[8] A. McCallum, D. Freitag, and F. Pereira, "Maximum Entropy Markov Models for Information Extraction and Segmentation," Proc. 17th Int'l Conf. Machine Learning (ICML '00), pp. 591-598,2000.

[9] N.B. Amor, S. Benferhat, and Z. Elouedi, "Naive Bayes vs. Decision Trees in Intrusion Detection Systems," Proc. ACM Symp. Applied Computing (SAC '04), pp. 420-424, 2004.

[10] NetOptics (n.d.). *White Paper: Deploying Network Taps with Intrusion Detection Systems.* Retrieved on April 4, 2007 http://www.netoptics.com/products/pdf/Taps-and-IDSs.pdf.

[11] Proctor, Paul E. (2001). *The Practical Intrusion Detection Handbook.* New Jersey: Prentice Hall.

[12] Puketza, Nicholas Joseph (2000). *Approaches to Computer Security: Filtering, Testing, and Detection.* California: University of California.

[13] Savage, Pete (2005). *Snort Inline Part I.* Retrieved on March 8, 2007 http://linuxgazette.net/117/savage.html.

[14] Snort (2007). *Snort Users Manual*. Retrieved March 8, 2007 from http://www.snort.org./docs/snort_htmanuals/htmanual_261.

[15] Zamboni, Diego (2001). *Using Internal Sensors for Computer Intrusion Detection*. Purdue: Purdue University LearningTechniques (ICML '01), pp. 282-289, 2001.

[16] K.K. Gupta, B. Nath, R. Kotagiri, and A. Kazi, "Attacking Confidentiality: An Agent Based Approach," Proc. IEEE Int'l Conf. Intelligence and Security Informatics (ISI '06), vol. 3975, pp. 285-296,2006.

[17] C. Ji and S. Ma, "Combinations of Weak Classifiers," IEEE Trans.Neural Networks, vol. 8, no. 1, pp. 32-42, 1997.

[18] H. Shah, J. Undercoffer, and A. Joshi, "Fuzzy Clustering for Intrusion Detection," Proc. 12th IEEE Int'l Conf. Fuzzy Systems (FUZZ-IEEE '03), vol. 2, pp. 1274-1278, 2003.

[19] H. Debar, M. Becke, and D. Siboni,"A Neural Network Component for an Intrusion Detection System," Proc. IEEE Symp..Research in Security and Privacy (RSP '92), pp. 240-250, 1992.

National Knowledge Management Framework

Vinay Kumar Ahlawat and Jayanthi Ranjan[1]

DMA-CIC, Rampur
[1]IMT, Ghaziabad

ABSTRACT

Further development of e-Government solutions is on demand to meet the needs of all citizens of the nation. The use of ICT is an excellent possibility to improve services to the citizens. This requires a framework of intensive knowledge transfer model which can play the role of catalyst towards the growth of a nation. This framework can be implemented in shape of a portal and participants (citizens) can be incorporated to the framework in different roles. The paper attempts to formulate the service delivery model of the framework with different nodal points (Citizen) in different roles.

INTRODUCTION

Today the use of new information and communication technologies is an excellent possibility to improve services hence Knowledge transfer for building better e-Government solutions is in demand. The core objective of the services offered by most web portals are of great variety, the web portals plays their incredible role in Knowledge producing for better future prospective. Knowledge portal are repositories to support its process effectively, empowering flexible knowledge acquiring and collecting providing knowledge refinement and maintenance with core object of thematic knowledge retrieval. It needs no prove that the Knowledge has become the most important producer of wealth in society as well as for any Nation. In today's economy corporate success comes from being able to acquire, codify and transfer knowledge more effectively and rapidly. The research on the importance of the knowledge community by Agarwal and Danny (2008) focuses on maximizing the knowledge and the potential of every people across different domains.Important aspect of knowledge management is extraction of the personal tacit knowledge that can be categorized into words and order for the best of its usage and attainment. Akin to this the portal on the experiences of people also assists to solve the problems practically.

Research in recent years proves that citizen participation is required to play the critical role in governance. Citizen participation research has been progressed significantly over the span of last two decades. Researchers and practitioners have emphasized citizen participation in public administration as a means of collaborating with citizens to promote democratic values such as transparency and accountability. In response to the demands of transparency in local governance, the study of Kim (2009) reflects that the local governments can enhance the level of transparency with their commitment to three core components of transparency, comprising openness, integrity and citizen empowerment.

This paper represents a framework that can be implemented in shape of a portal and participants (citizens) who can be incorporated to the framework in different roles. Proposed framework is the adoption of knowledge-based web portal approach in India. The step wise implementation of the work is as follows:

- Section 2: Presents the related and other published work in the field
- Section 3: Discusses the e-Government and citizen participation
- Section 4: Proposes the framework
- Section 5: Highlights the need for citizen participation in developingcountries like India
- Section 6: Summarises the expected benefits from the implementation of theframework
- Section 7: Discusses the future scope of work
- Section 8: The Findings and Conclusion.

LITERATURE REVIEW

The key to manage the knowledge must surely arise from understanding which is quite clear thatour learning has led us to research and reflect upon different aspects of knowledge. Rosenberg (2001) proposed four types of knowledge i.e. illustrated in Figure 1.

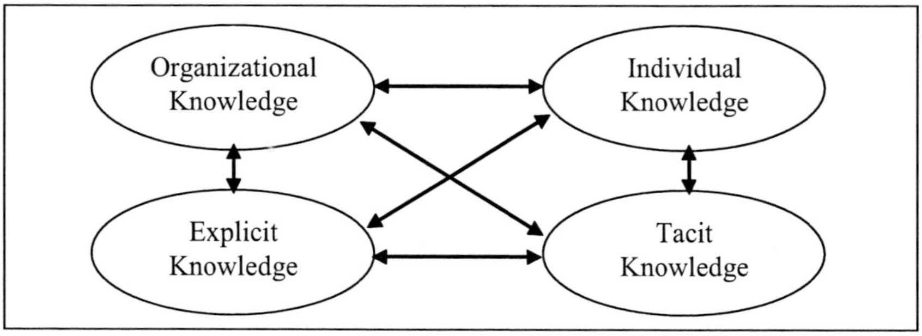

Fig. 1

Explicit: Gathered from internal and external sources easily able to codify into documents, processes and practices.

Tacit: Often embedded in the experiences and workpeople. It issomewhere difficult to record the document and teach but valuable and elusive.

Individual: Here the knowledge both tacit and explicit belongs and inherent in the individual.

Organizational: This focuses on the combined knowledge of individuals and retainsall the required information within an organization.

Davenport and Prusak (1998) in his research mirrors forth that knowledge takes place within a context of information and involves a mix of insights, framed experiences, values, judgments and ideals. True to say that Knowledge is dynamic within the social environment because it triggers ideas and actions. In the same context within a nation the knowledge of both individuals and the nation does not lie isolated rather it is exchanged and re-created through interactions between citizens. The study also signifies that while codify, store, retrieve and reuse of explicit knowledge, it lends itself to the use of ICT. In fact it is the capturing, storage and reusability of tacit knowledge that provides the leverage sought by Knowledge Management Systems.

The research by Nonaka and Takeuchi (1995) step wise describe the transfer of tacit knowledge in following four steps:

- **Tacit-to-tacit/socialization**: Where an individual acquires knowledge directly from others.
- **Tacit-to-explicit/externalization:**This step reflects how knowledge is converted into tangible form through dialogue.
- **Explicit-to-explicit/combination**: Here the knowledge is combined into an explicit form and documented or stored in database.
- **Explicit-to-tacit/internalization:** How the end-user internalizes the knowledge by learning or doing and incorporates this into their own body of knowledge.

The use of this knowledge base formed by citizens of nations can use implementing ICT. M. Janssen (2003) explored that Internet can be used for participative decision-making and in this way promote democracy. Government agencies can address citizen participation by actively searching for the views of the public and taking them into account in their decision making process. Governments in the developed countries have been using information and communication technologies (ICTs) including the internet to empower and facilitate their citizens.

Researchers in foresaid field like Robbins, Simonsen& Feldman (2008) Tolbert & McNeal (2003) Bertot, Jaeger & Grimes (2010) Phillips &Abey (2007) come to the findings that internet based interactive technology for facilitating citizen participation services not only serves the gauze citizen preferences in government decisions but also take the privilege to improve decision making and transparency.

In addition to this C. LestonBandeira (2007) with his qualitative and quantitative contribution explores that internet opens up possibilities for communicating with citizens through e-participation.

E-GOVERNMENT AND CITIZEN PARTICIPATION

The step third of the Paper focuses on the researcherJeong (2007) who defines E-Government and briefly summed up delivery models as digital interactions between a government and citizens (G2C) government and businesses/Commerce (G2B) government and employees (G2E) and also between government and governments/agencies (G2G). E-government allows for government transparency.

In Modern era where the effective rapid change in the context is witnessed the competence of government institutions/federal agencies are still being questioned which can be imperative for the government agencies to strive for improvement in performance. One goal of e-government will be aimed in reference to the citizen participation. It is noted that the participative democracy enables the active involvement of all citizens. Through the internet people from all over the country can interact with politicians or public servants and make their voices heard.The information society is one of the global trends that cause fundamental changes in the way of governing. Roland Traunmuller, GertiOrthofer and Helene Gieber (2006) describes the broader view on e-Government and governance wherethey explores e-participation on the rise and above all the role of citizens in the democratic process has clearly grown and evolved with the introduction of e-Government. As the society evolves towards information, the society with the government has to deal more and more with information and knowledge.

Citizen participation research has been progressed significantly over the last two decades. Researchers and practitioners have emphasized citizen participation in public administration as a means of collaborating with citizens to promote democratic values such as transparency and accountability that further argues that deliberative and collective action strategies of civic engagement are the most promising ways of involving the public and centering public management around the Nation. Scholars emphasize that the input in government performance evaluation and effort to provide more opportunities for citizen participation with best of their policy decision-making is truly an important strategy for putting trust in government.

Ranjan J. & Ahlawat V. (2010) remarkson the model of knowledge portal as *'an effective web tool based on citizen to citizen model which is named as AamAdmiSeva'* (a knowledge portal to serve the people, for the people, by the people). He proposes an effective web tool based on Citizen to Citizen interface for sharing various knowledge on different issues related to society and country. Main purpose to develop that model for this portal is to help common man through knowledge portal regarding the issues needs in their routine life, e.g. problems related to health, education, legal issues and so on. As the use of Internet is increasing day by day this proposed model can be revolutionary model in the development of nation.

NATIONAL KNOWLEDGE MANAGEMENT FRAMEWORK

This framework seeks to manage the knowledge resources of a nation through dynamic binding of citizens by capturing, storing, distributing and sharing the knowledge within the nation. A simple process-driven Knowledge Management Framework should seek to address the processes using technology as an enabler.

Our proposal for a National Knowledge Management Framework for any developing nation includes the following main elements (Figure 2):

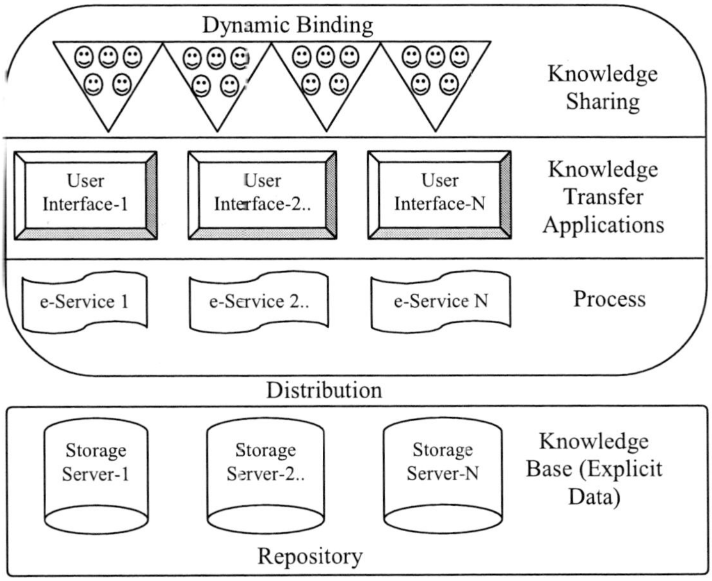

Fig. 2

Knowledge Sharing: Dynamic binding among citizens will act as participants. Citizens can be separated into three roles: service providers, service requesters and end users. The purpose of this layer is to provide citizens an approach to access User Interface and to share data and information that resides on distributed Knowledge Base via processes.

Knowledge Transfer Applications: All e-Services can be accessed through User Interfaces. These all called citizen's visible services where citizens can transfer knowledge via socialization (Tacit-to-tacit), externalization (Tacit-to-explicit), combination (Explicit-to-explicit) and internalization (Explicit-to-tacit).

Process: e-Services can be created with different languages and deployed on various platforms such as .Net and Java technology. E-Services can be categorized function wise. This layer of technology can enhance and support the above.

Knowledge Base: Repositories of explicit data and information.

The core objective of this model is to resolve the problem of common man with the help of common man. C2C model is web based so that more and more people can connect through web channel.Process follows with the input of problem and displayed on web portal through the suggestions of redresser citizen, who later gets the satisfactory output. The problems and their suggestions are placed on the web which would be easily visible to find out the suitable suggestions provided to them for the same. The benefit lies with this is that it can be kept as record or reference to those who have similar kind of problem in future.

THE PARTICIPATION OF CITIZEN IN DEVELOPING NATION

The next step in the study reflects the collective efforts and cooperative action that has been a part of human behavior right from the early days of civilization. Gradually such collective action led to formation of small habitations, communities, villages and thereafter to large cities and metropolises. They in turn created complex social groups and governmental organizations in fact in certain course of timethe government and the society no doubt became too big and formalized that resulted somewhat distant from the common man. Thus this created and evolved situation needs for mutual networking and interaction for the best of its solution of the raised issues. This practice requires the trust, mutual understanding, shared values and behavior that bind together the citizens of the nation and contribute in makingthe cooperative action possible. A sense of belonging and the concrete experience of social networking help in creating the relationships of trust and tolerance that evolveto bring great benefits to citizens.

The contribution of Rowe and Frewer (2005) is unturned. To prove the foresaid they categorize three different levels of citizen participation:

- **Citizen communication:** The information is conveyed from the government body to the public.
- **Citizen consultation:** The information flows from the public to the government.
- **Citizen participation:** The information is exchanged between the public and the government and some degree of dialogue takes place.

The research reflects the core values or goals of citizen participation programs and policies are to enhance transparency that includes the citizens' perception of openness, corruption, two-way communication with others. This adds further in reference to the fair and increased opportunities for them to participate in the decision making process.It is quite visible that several ways are there in which citizens' participation can improve government performance. First it can broaden government accountability for which the government must be responsive to citizens at large rather than to narrow sectarian interests. Secondly it should facilitate agreement where political preferences are particularly polarized. Thirdly it includes innovation and transparency in policymaking. Finally it enhances the efficiency of delivery of many services at the local level through involvement of residents.

THE EXPECTED BENEFITS

The paper shifts its study for finding the expected benefits on the mentioned subject. In reference to this the study can focus that the Governments should increase their effectiveness in delivering value through e-governmentinitiatives via their portals by treating various entities as true *citizens*. KM becomes animportant component in this effort by providing the mechanisms for creating, capturing,transforming and using knowledge. In addition e-government initiatives must facilitatecollaboration and knowledge flows between themselves and their users and also between auser and other users. In this section the study review three recent KM models for the Internet thatattempt to capture these mechanisms in portals and other Web sites.

This proposed framework is a crucial consideration in web portal for citizens of developing nation to ensure that knowledge flows efficiently between government and citizens and also among the different levels of citizens. In government affair each knowledge management intervention changes future citizen behavior such as loyalty, trust and honesty.

The unique feature of this framework is that that the information gathered is through citizen, the problems are dealt by the citizens. Thus we can exemplify that it is almost in control of citizens completely for their utility. It is noted that there are no set rules or limitations for this portal rather it can be modified as and when according to the need and requirement of the people.

THE FUTURE PROSPECTIVE

When making decisions on which knowledge management intervention to choose the government of developing nation needs to take into account the dynamic effect of each considered intervention on future consequence. To achieve this government needs to be treated as visionary in decision making which forms expectations on future citizen behavior that predicts consequences associated with each possible knowledge management intervention. It results with the calculated and satisfied implications of current services for qualitative achievements.

THE FINDINGS/CONCLUSION

The Paper contributes to the body of literature by develcping and evaluation framework known as *National Knowledge Management Framework* that includesKnowledge Management, Citizen Participation and Information and Communication Technology. This framework is implemented in the form of web portal and acts as an instrument of enhancing governmental effectiveness, improve and strengthen the capability of the administration to proactively partner with local community particularly in remote areas. Later it can bring better synergy between the government and the citizens which help in increasing the public interpersonal relationship and a positivity in thoughts for the administrative approaches.

REFERENCES

[1] Agarwal, N. K. and Poo, D. C. C. (2008), 'Capturing tacit knowledge across different domains: Knowledge Community (K-Comm)', International Journal of Business Information Systems 2008 - Vol. 3, No.6 pp. 668 - 685.

[2] Bertot, John C., Paul T. Jaeger, and Justin M. Grimes. 2010. "Using ICTs to create a culture of transparency: E-government and social media as openness and anti-corruption tools for societies." *Government Information Quarterly* 27: 264–271.

[3] C. Leston-Bandeira, "The Impact of the Internet on Parliaments: a Legislative Studies Framework," Parliamentary Affairs, vol. 60, pp. 665-674, 2007.

[4] Citrin, Jack and Christopher Muste. 1999. "Trust in government." In *Measures of Political Attitudes*, edited by John P. Robinson, Phillip R. Shaver & Lawrence S. Wrightsman, 462-532. New York: Academic Press.

[5] Cooper, Terry L., Thomas A. Bryer, and Jack W. Meek. 2006. "Citizen-Centered Collaborative Public Management." *Public Administration Review* 66(1): 76–88.

[6] Davenport, T. and Prusak, L. (1998) *Working Knowledge: How Organizations Manage What They Know,*Harward Business School Press.

[7] Fung, Archon. 2006. "Varieties of Participation in Complex Governance." *Public Administration Review* 66(1): 66-75.

[8] Irvin, Renee A. and John Stansbury. 2004. "Citizen Participation in Decision Making: Is it Worth the Effort?" *Public Administration Review* 64, no. 1: 55-65.

[9] Jeong Chun Hai @Ibrahim. (2007). Fundamental of Development Administration. Selangor: Scholar Press. ISBN 978-967-5-04508-0.

[10] Kim, Soonhee. 2009. *Management Strategy for Local Governments to Strengthen Transparency in Local Governance*. Seoul: United Nations Project Office on Governance.

[11] Kim, Soonhee. 2010. "Public Trust in Government in Japan and South Korea: Does the Rise of Critical Citizens Matter?" *Public Administration Review* 70(5): 801-810.

[12] King, Cheryl S., Kathryn M. Feltey, and Bridget O. Susel. 1998. "The Question of Participation: Toward Authentic Public Participation in Public Administration." *Public Administration Review* 58(4): 317-327.

[13] Kweit, Mary G. and Robert W. Kweit. 2007. "Participation, Perception of Participation, and Citizen Support." *American Politics Research* 35(3): 407-425.

[14] M. Janssen, "Guidelines for enhancing e-participation." in: Alexander Prosser, Robert Krimmer (eds.) e-Democracy: Technologie, Recht und Politik. Oesterreichische Computer Gesellschaft (in German), pp. 47-56, 2003.

[15] Nelson, Nici and Susan Wright. 1995. *Power and Participatory Development: Theory and Practice*. London: Intermediate Technology Publications.

[16] Nonaka, Ikujiro; Takeuchi, Hirotaka (1995), The knowledge creating company: how Japanese companies create the dynamics of innovation, New York: Oxford University Press, pp. 284, ISBN 978-0-19-509269-1.

[17] Phillips, Patricia, and Bernard Abey. 2007. "Using the web to increase transparency and accountability." *Government Finance Review*, 23(3): 32-38.

[18] Ranjan, J. and Ahlawat, V. (2010), *An effective web tool based on C2C (Citizen to Citizen) model, (A knowledge portal to serve the people, for the people, by the people)*, International

Joint Conference on Information and Communication Technology-2010, organized by Interscience Institute of Management & Technology, Bhubneshwar.

[19] Reddick, Christopher G. 2011. "Citizen Interaction and E-government: Evidence for the Managerial, Consultative, and Participatory Models." *Transforming Government: People, Process and Policy* 5(2): 167–184.

[20] Robbins, Mark D., Bill Simonsen, and Barry Feldman. 2008. "Citizens and Resource Allocation: Improving Decision Making with Interactive Web-Based Citizen Participation." *Public Administration Review* 68 (3): 564–575.

[21] Rosenberg, M.J. (2001). E-learning: Strategies for delivering knowledge in the digital age. New York: McGraw-Hill.

[22] Rowe, Gene, &Frewer, Lynn. J. (2005). A typology of public engagement mechanisms.

[23] *Science Technology and Human values*, 30(2), 251-290.

[24] Royo, Sonia, Ana Yetano, and BasilioAcerete. 2011. "Citizen Participation in German.

[25] and Spanish Local Governments: A Comparative Study." *International Journal of Public.*

[26] *Administration* 34, no. 3: 139-150.

[27] Scott, James K. 2006. "'E' the People: Do U.S. Municipal Government Web Sites Support Public Involvement?" *Public Administration Review* 66, no. 3: 341-353.

[28] Thomas, John Clayton. 1993. "Public Involvement and Governmental Effectiveness: A Decision-Making Model for Public Managers." *Administration & Society* 24, no. 4: 444-69.

[29] Tolbert, Caroline, and Ramona McNeal. 2003. "Unraveling the Effects of the Internet on Political Participation." *Political Research Quarterly* 56: 175-185.

[30] Weeks, Edward C. 2000. "The Practice of Deliberative Democracy: Results from Four Large-Scale Trials." *Public Administration Review* 60(4): 360-371.

[31] Yang, Kaifeng, and Kathe Callahan. 2005. "Assessing Citizen Involvement Efforts by Local Governments." *Public Performance & Management Review* 29(2): 191-216.

New Trends in Security Solution Architectures and Risk Assessment Strategies

Nirmalya Chakraborty, Jayanthi Ranjan[1] and Vandna Sharma[2]

UBS Investment Bank
[1]IMT, Ghaziabad
[2]Department of Management Studies, BIT, Meshra-Ranchi

ABSTRACT

Information Security is still predominating in all operations, technology and data in every organization. As enterprises are still targeted by cyber attacks through botnets, it is imperative to have an effective security in place that would shield against constant external and internal threats. Enterprises are also very conscious about insider threats and attacks that compromise data security and thus prevent exposure to exploitations. Insider controls have also been incorporated as a part of inherent enterprise security that fortifies its internal assets based on relevancy and sensitivity.

This research paper covers all the operations-data-technology-security composite elements as an integrated approach and highlights the modern trends in security architectures and procedures for IT Risk Management. The paper highlights the risks and threats that prevail in enterprise computing environment, and then depicts the various architectures that incorporate the controls and standards like ISO 27001 for protection. The risk assessment framework proposed in this paper would help any strategic 'head' to secure all corporate resources effectively and also comply with world security standards.

INTRODUCTION – GROUND 0

The security trends have taken an upturn surge that has made Information Security, paramount in all enterprises. Traditionally, infrastructure or perimeter security has been the essence of IT protection. New trends in security attacks have driven data-centric security; data being the most valuable asset of an organization. Applications that process, deliver, store and secure data thus require adequate controls for data protection. Application Security thus, has been the kernel of modern enterprise security.

Enterprises now have a staggering number of 'bad' programs and lines of codes already in production that enterprises are struggling to patch for their vulnerabilities [OWASP, 2010]. Attacks exploit these vulnerabilities seamlessly which are found in many such un-patched application software that expose critical enterprise assets. Enterprises are thus migrating towards secure platforms and aging out traditional and legacy systems.

Commercial web applications are generally most affected along with their browser platforms. Cross Site Scripting (XSS) and SQL Injections are the most frequent native vulnerabilities that are exploited to target enterprise resources [Cenzic Inc, 2010, OWASP, 2010]. Banking Trojans have expertise in the use of these exploits to sneak-in and dominate over financial targets and interrupt legitimate transactions. [McAfee Labs, 2010]

Botnets have also evolved drastically in comparison to other malicious threats. [GeorgiaTech Information Security Center, 2010] They are now an established infrastructure for the attackers as it provides a coordinated attacking launch-pad. Even VoIP networks host botnets [Gartner, 2010].

Spam storms are also a constant threat that enterprise mail exchange servers are always exposed to. It has been found that nine out of ten spam mails contains URLs mostly of genuine well-known sites used for social networking, blogging, file sharing and host other forms of user-generated content which are usually blocked inside enterprises [Symantec, 2010]. Process-intense Spam Management software manages and filters this traffic from the corporate networks.

There is still a steep rise in focused attacks on enterprises through reconnaissance of corporate sites as well as social networking sites like Facebook, Orkut, Linkedin, MySpace etc which have also become malware distribution centers [GeorgiaTech Information Security Center, 2010, McAfee Labs, 2010]. Employee awareness is still not adequate to stop exploitation and becoming victims.

Apart from IT controls Data protection Laws are also insignificant or light in many countries which make robust secure information architecture, the essence of a global business.

NEW TRENDS IN APPLICATION ARCHITECTURES

Every evolving organization is now built as a collection of software services, plug-ins, ActiveX controls and its security practices. Internal applications are either in-house developed or vendor applications are installed inside enterprise infrastructure. Some other applications link to vendor hosted solutions while others are internally hosted but face externally to clients/Internet.

Enterprises generally either operate on an active desktop or a virtual machine solution. Desktop solutions have its own risks while virtual solutions have the risk of cross-pollinating infections among different machines [Cybermedia, 2010]. Infrastructure (like servers, browser etc) are also locked down with rules and configurations along with tight physical security. Firewalls, proxies, application password expiration/rotation, CCTVs, SecurIDs, access control devices all work to enforce organizational security policies.

The Open Web Application Security Project (OWASP) is now dedicated to enabling organizations to develop, purchase, and maintain applications that can be trusted. Many application developers are following their frameworks to comply with the security standards.

In order to analyze enterprise security, each environment has to be scrutinized for threats and risks and to ascertain the minimum security requirements.

In-house Developed Applications

Applications that are developed by the internal or offshore development team dominate the enterprise IT domain. These applications are said to have been built using secure frameworks like OWASP (Open Web Application Security Project) etc. These applications seamlessly integrate with internal authentication systems like Kerberos and use session-based authentication on all sensitive objects. Some of these applications incorporate strict role-based security that manages entitlements, user migrations/terminations. Even the production IDs that are used for these applications are strictly monitored.

In-house applications are monitored by application owners who manages application distribution and life while and the security contacts manages the security model of the application and administers the security test and audits.

As per National Institute of Standards and Technology, the security requirements for in-house application should include: (i) access control; (ii) awareness and training; (iii) audit and accountability; (iv) certification, accreditation, and security assessments; (v) configuration management; (vi) contingency planning; (vii) identification and authentication; (viii) incident response; (ix) maintenance; (x) media protection; (xi) physical and environmental protection; (xii) planning; (xiii) personnel security; (xiv) risk assessment; (xv) systems and services acquisition; (xvi) system and communications protection; and (xvii) system and information integrity [Tom Olzak, 2006].

Special Sections of In-house Application Assessment

Assessment of In-house Applications is somewhat trusted applications but still requires certain aspects to be assessed and audited categorically. These are:

Whether all Sensitive Data in-feeds of the Application are Authenticated

Many applications gets data feeds from many other in-house or external applications. These feeds can be hourly, nightly or even every second. These feeds can have different levels of sensitivity. Independent access control for each feed must be strictly implemented in application design for the in-feeds. This will ensure and prevent un-authorized data extraction and exposure.

Many web syndication feeds are not meant to be displayed for the world to see. Every portal contains private and confidential data that is not made for every user, and especially not search. There are a few options for trying to keep things private in feed aggregator but the implementations require proper coding and privacy from all implementers. [Niall Kennedy, 2006]

How the Application Handles User Authentication and Manages User Credentials and Sessions

Authentication and session management should incorporate all aspects of user authentication and managing active sessions. Authentication is a critical aspect of the security process, but even solid authentication mechanisms can be undermined by flawed credential management functions, including password change, forgot my password, remember my password, account update, and other related functions. It should be ensured that credential management is reviewed and assessed adequately.

User authentication on the web typically involves the use of a userid and password. Stronger methods of authentication are commercially available such as software and hardware based cryptographic tokens or biometrics, but such mechanisms are cost prohibitive for most web applications. It must be ascertained that data sensitivity and type of exposure (internal/external) should determine the authentication method.

Web applications must establish sessions to keep track of the stream of requests from each user. HTTP does not provide this capability, so web applications must create and protect it themselves. [OWASP, 2010].

A bigger challenge is providing seamless access to applications and systems across corporate or network boundaries. It's no trouble for IT to define and manage user names and passwords on their own network, but it takes more work — or is nearly impossible — to extend access to internal systems to numerous external users or to manage local user access to a system outside of their control.[Keith Schultz, 2010]

How the Application Authenticates Between its Logical Components/Tiers

N-tier /distributed/Multitier applications are data applications that have separate processing in discrete tiers that are distributed between the client and the server. Each component must be authenticated adequately.

Multitier web application security may use SAML tokens and the back-end database, Kerberos token for authentication.

GRanularity, Audit, N-tier and Delegation (GRAND) Project from ISS (Information System and Services) in Newcastle University is investigating other approaches to address the areas of "Granularity and Delegation", "Audit and Accounting" and "N-tier authentication". They will develop technical tools, use cases and policy to support the deployment of advanced tools in access management.

How User Entitlements/Roles are Engineered into the Application

The essence of Role Based Access Control (RBAC) is for aggregating roles to privileges. Users are assigned roles and inherit predefined permissions by being members of roles. They are given entitlements — no more than what is required to perform their exact job function — based on the least privilege access principle.

Roles can be defined at an abstract level from a business perspective, or a context-specific level to an application/system from a technology perspective. At an abstract level, roles can be a simple label that defines the job function with a set of responsibilities and authority that goes with it.

Role engineering is the process of defining roles and related information, such as permissions, constraints, and role hierarchies, as they pertain to the user's functional use of systems, applications, and business processes.

To minimize deployment effort or to avoid any project scope creep, role definition is often not considered part of the initial project. Organizations frequently do not invest enough time to define roles in sufficient detail; rather, they tend to define high-level roles that do not reflect actual organizational job functions. Permissions mapped to high-level roles are usually generic in nature. The result of this random process is that additional efforts are required to manage job- and function-specific permissions manually, outside the Identity and Access Management Systems (IAM) system. This often results in IAM systems not delivering the expected business value, for example, adherence to compliance and reduced entitlement management costs. The process of defining roles should be based on a complete analysis of how an organization functions and should include input from a wide spectrum of users, including business line managers and human resources. [Srinivasan Vanamali, 2009]

Who Tracks and Manages the User Accounts and Roles

Migration of users needs to be tracked as well as escalation of user privileges made on-demand has to be monitored and logged appropriately. Accounts that are created, revoked or locked need to be audited under the supervision of the application owner/delegate. The enterprise delegated person and segregation of duties are to be reviewed and assessed.

How Platform/Library/Framework Dependencies Handles

Certain applications needs plug-ins like Office or Adobe plug-ins, or have platform dependencies like Java Runtime Environment or .NET frameworks or need some ActiveX controls or dll's which needs to be white-listed appropriately. These need to be assessed for any dangerous activities like opening of external ports or send internal network data offsite.

How Audit Logs are Captured and Maintained

Servers, Firewalls, IDS etc. create numerous logs which need to be reviewed and analyzed. It is imperative to assess how, where the logs are captured and how they are maintained.

Logs are wonderful for outages because, very often, all of the information necessary to determine what is causing (or caused) the outage can be found in the log files themselves.

During a crisis, staff often goes into reactive mode, sometimes relying on intuition, speculation, and atomic unrelated pieces of information to piece together what is going on or what happened. But logs are a record of what actually happened. Systems that allow staff to write and run reports in real-time based on outage information deliver the facts that response teams need to understand what's happening on the network.

Log management systems are excellent for aggregating and analyzing information from security devices for security awareness, but the information being gathered can be used for other purposes as well. For example, an organization "can analyze the customer experience for the top ten business relationships." Many trending and click track type Web application-reporting systems don't provide a granular view of the actual customer experience. Well-designed application logging would take the customer experience into account, and expands the utility of the log management well outside of the security box [Diana Kelley, 2010*]*.

The above sections help an assessor dig deep into application architecture and help articulate the risk and their countermeasures.

Vendor Applications Installed in Enterprise Infrastructure

Applications that are vendor developed and then installed inside enterprise infrastructure with legal and license agreements also hold a lot of enterprise IT space. These applications do not necessarily conform to internal security standards and as they are external vendor application, enterprises also do not much control on these applications.

These vendor applications can be rich applications like PeopleSoft, Documentum, Informatica, Radar or small tools like Tax calculators, Margin plotters, Office plug-ins etc. Due to the vastness of its functionalities they provide, business justification for its deployment may shadow any security implications.

These third party applications must be tested in Test/QA environment before a production (PROD) release. These tests would involve vulnerability scans and also penetration tests if the application has any external interfaces.

Many vendors like Fortify also provide On-Demand Vendor Security Management of other vendor applications that can be deployed securely in the enterprise infrastructure [Fortify, 2010].

Special Sections of Vendor Applications installed in Enterprise Infrastructure Security Assessment

Assessment of Vendor Applications installed in enterprise infrastructure are entrusted applications and thus requires certain aspects to be assessed and audited categorically. These are:

If Any Enterprise Sensitive Data is Sent Out of the Enterprise, where is the Data sent and Whether the Data is Authorized for Offsite Storage/Access by Infosec Guidelines/Assessment

Enterprise sensitive data that is sent / stored outside the enterprise need to be certified by an InfoSec team who will ascertain how sensitive the data is and whether offsite security controls are adequate for its data.

Whether the Application is Proxy Aware or Require any Firewall Rule Addition

If the in-house makes an external connection into the Internet, does it use a proxy aware capability is a point that need to be reviewed otherwise an addition in some Firewall Rule would be necessary. Enterprises are always cautious in opening incoming connections to the firewall i.e. users/programs dialing in from outside the corporate network.

Does the Application Integrates with Firm's Authentication System

Multi-tier applications must be driven for integration with firm approved authentication systems that protect the enterprise with the universal enterprise policy like Netegrity SiteMinder Authentication for web applications.

Does the Application have Auto-update Feature

The auto-update feature must be disabled as they can invite malicious program from invading the corporate network. Patching and updating must be done by the IT Operations team on scheduled days.

Is there any Remote Vendor Access to the Application for Operational/Service Support

Vendor sometimes connect to the internal corporate network for application trouble-shooting which can be risk as they can then have un-authorized data exposures. Virtual Private Networks (VPN) may tunnel directly into the server and provide the service avoiding any traces on the gateways and perimeter firewalls. Incoming vendor VPNs from the Internet must to be totally avoided. Vendor should provide onsite support or use the firm approved remote computing plants that are available.

Remote Desktop normally runs on port 3389. This is the port the Remote Desktop client connects to on default and this is the port hackers scan to find open Remote Desktop connections. By changing this port number, Remote Desktop connection can be hidden from hackers who scan port 3389 and no one will be able to connect your computer through Remote Desktop unless they know the port it runs on [Nick Diel, 2008].

The results of the above security area must determine whether the application should be deployed. Applications that do "dangerous things" must ONLY be deployed in isolated environments like stand-alone PCs for business usage.

Externally Facing Applications

Applications that face the Internet and have their databases deep inside the corporate network are externally facing internal applications. These applications are generally web applications used for clients or "nomadic" employees who access the corporate resources remotely. These applications accept traffic using a SSL encrypted connection along with a RSA SecurID token or equivalent. The connection hit a web service located in the DMZ (De-Militarized Zone). A proxy service, then connect the legitimate requests to the internal service.

Deployment of these application involve rigorous vulnerability scanning and penetration test to plug any risks from the external network. These applications generally use a virtual platform where the entire infrastructure has strict audit/logging of all incoming/outgoing traffic pairs.

Special Sections of Externally Facing Applications Security Assessment

Assessment of Externally facing Applications are entrusted applications and thus requires certain aspects to be assessed and audited categorically. These are:

What is the Data Exposure for the External Clients and whether the Data is Authorized for Offsite Storage/Access by Infosec Guidelines/Assessment

External clients and other users have exposure to data that should be tightly bound by entitlements and Infosec guidelines as data compromise may have reputational risks or legal restrictions.

Has the Application Undergone a Vulnerability Test Each Version Deployment

Every externally facing application must be scanned and patched for vulnerabilities on regular schedules and audit logs analyzed for any anomaly in access.

Enterprise applications accessed through a mobile device like Blackberry also follow a similar architecture where a Blackberry server directly authenticates the device, then open the remote computing plat of the enterprise for access.

Vendor Hosted Services

These applications are conceptually reverse of externally facing in-house applications. These applications are accessed using the client UI (User Interface) from the enterprise network and the service actually resides at the vendor site. The request generally involves an enterprise-to-vendor data transfer along with request parameters, which is through an encrypted SSL channel that hit the vendor server. Role-based security and logical segmentation of data determines which user/account has access to which data.

Some vendor hosted services are like an exchange terminal like Bloomberg or Reuters, Research Analyzers, Medical/Insurance data providers, Payroll calculators etc. These applications require site reviews which require vendor involvements in order to incorporate vendor level security.

Assessments must involve in areas of access control, data security and retention, physical security controls in-place for data security.

For confidential and highly restricted data sent out of the enterprise, data dumps may be scrutinized by Infosec before a security signoff.

OFFSHORING ARCHITECTURES

Instances of applications accessed by an Offshore team must meet a different set of requirements to meet data security. Applications accessed by an Offshored team must have an "Offshore" access role profile implemented in the application that would restrict data exposure. Legal restrictions like cross-border Swiss client data access are fully restricted. The offshore profile thus incorporate filtering logics like masking that would mask CIDs (Client Identifiable Data). Offshore access is also regulated and logged generally through a virtual plat access like nfuse.

Application testing team must ensure proper data exposure as per Infosec guidelines.

CONCLUSION

As now it is evident that consumerization of IT has really blurred the perimeters of the enterprise, organizations now forced to focus on Information Security and then build controls over it rather than network/infrastructure security. Enterprises now focus not on protecting "everything" but build controls based on data sensitive levels and associated risks.

ISO 27001 is a good standard that can pave the path to a data centric security where distributive mobility remains the essence of a new computing era.

The security architectures covered in this research paper provide an insight into the new trends of evolving patterns in security assurance. Modern enterprises can now build their business models with an integrated security stand. This becomes the key to cyber survival.

ADDITIONAL REFERENCES

[1] Dmitri Alperovitch, Toralv Dirro, Paula Greve, Rahul Kashyap, David Marcus, Sam Masiello, François Paget, and Craig Schmugar, McAfee Labs- 2010 Threat Predictions- www.mcafee.com

[2] Mandeep Khera, Cenzic Enterprise Application Security: Web Application Security Trends Reports- *www.cenzic.com*

[3] OWASP-Top Ten (The Ten Most critical Application Security Risks)- http://owasptop10.googlecode.com/files/OWASP%20Top%2010%20-%202010.pdf

[4] JD Meler, Alex Mackman, Srinath Vasireddy, Michael Dunner, Ray Escamilla, Anandha Murukan- Improving Web Application Security- Threats and Countermeasures

[5] Roberta Bragg. Mark Phodes-Ousley and Keith Strassberg- Complete Reference Network Security

[6] GRAND Project: http://www.jisc.ac.uk/whatwedo/programmes/aim/grand.aspx

[7] SiteMinder Authentication-

[8] http://www.ibm.com/developerworks/lotus/library/siteminder-authentication/

[9] *http://www.cisco.com/en/US/docs/net_mgmt/cisco_transport_manager/9.0/application_note/developer/guide/90_extau.html*

On Mobile Payment Technology Adoption Issues in India: Case of Airtel Money

Parijat Upadhyay, Saikat Ghosh Roy and Abhishek Sharma

IMT Ghaziabad

ABSTRACT

Technology adoption issues have always been subject of extensive research in various countries. Researchers are always in search of theories to explain the consumers' perception about the acceptance of a technology and the benefit accrued by that technology. A KPMG survey (March 2012) revealed that 64 per cent Indians were 'at least somewhat likely' to conduct banking through a mobile device in the next 12 months (2012-13). The most profound impact of mobile banking and payment services is that they provide the non-banking population with access to modern financial services, giving them tools to improve their living standards. Innovative mobile banking (m-banking) services are fast arriving in the market. Mobile money has strong potential to become a catalytic platform. This study focuses on the technology diffusion issues amongst Indian consumers with reference to the launch of Airtel Money by India's leading cellular service provider, Airtel. The study is exploratory in nature, seeks to identify the issues affecting adoption of mobile money transfer applications by subscribers. The results of a survey undertaken by the authors in metro and non-metro cities in India analyses the issues worth highlighting if the operators wish to have higher adoption rates resulting in more financial inclusion for the country as a whole in near future.

INTRODUCTION

India has the world's second largest cell phone subscribers with over 903 million(as per a TRAI report 'Highlights of Telecom Subscription Data as on December 31, 2011').The figure implies that the number of mobile users may have already exceeded the number of banked people in India. The banking subscriber base is barely crossing 200 million (taking into consideration the number of multiple accounts), implies that 83% of the population does not have access to bank accounts. On the brighter side, this shows the scope for banks and banking solutions in future. Mobile phones can offer a communications channel for initiating and executing financial transactions. This channel may not only reduce the cost of financial transactions for provider and customer, but also allow new entrants to the financial sectorand new relationships to be formed for distributing services. The growth trend in the mobile channel is global, as research firm Gartner recently reported the number of people around the world using mobile phones to make payments is expected approaching 200 million by end of 2012.Innovative mobile-banking(m-banking) services are fast arriving in the market. This study in particular, seeks to explore the issues of adoption of mobile money transfer applications by subscribers in India with reference to Airtel Money.

LITERATURE REVIEW

After credit and debit card, mobile payment is the new thing that is emerging in India. Cell phones have the highest penetration amongst any technical devices and it creates immense opportunity for the business to market its products and services through mobile (Tomi Dahlberg et al., 2007). Previous researchers have focussed on mainly four features that influence different mobile services like m-payments, they are – Usefulness, Price, Ease of use and Speed of use. Among them 'usefulness' and 'ease of use' are the two most important parameters but it varies according to age groups (PaganiMargherita, 2004).Demographic characteristics have impact on consumers' payment method (Yoris A. Au et al., 2007). Like in USA people use credit cards heavily as their payment methods (Yaobin Lu et al, 2011) but countries like India and China have cash-centric payment cultures where people are more likely to use hard cash as payment method. The factors that affect m-payments or more generally e-Commerce are technological, cultural, social, commercial and legal factors. But how the social and cultural factors impact mobile payments is still an unexplored area (Tomi Dahlberg et al., 2007). Payment behaviour of consumer is very rigid to change unless any reason involved. The reason can be anything like convenience of use, low cost or reward system etc. So, Mobile payment can take on credit card if reward system started (J. Jette, 2005). Mobile services can be accessed independent of time and location, which is the key advantage of mobile commerce (Jarvenpaa S.L. et al., 2005). This advantage has to be leveraged by the mobile payment service companies. The cost is a very important factor for mobile payments. The cost of item purchased through mobile payment is higher as the cost of transaction is included in the price of the item (MallatNiina, 2007). This could be a deterrent factor for mobile payments. Short message services (SMS) and near field communications (NFC) are the two technologies that are leveraged by the m-payment companies. Companies like PayPal, TextPayMe adopted SMS technology. Service providers prefer SMS to deliver m-payments service despite it's inappropriate and outdated technology (Yoris A. Au et al., 2007). The main reason is that use of uncomplicated services like SMS are easily acceptable (PaganiMargherita, 2004). As mentioned earlier, the 'ease of use' is one of the important features that influence mobile payments the service providers have to keep the payment process simpler. Another reason for using SMS as delivery medium for mobile payment is that it avoids regulatory problems in many countries and also gives the service provider 30-70% margin level, but it is not suitable for mature markets as security is compromised (Yoris A. Au et al., 2007). Customer's trust on Internet payment services may influence one's trust on m-payment services (Yaobin Lu et al, 2011).Though earlier studies shows inclination of consumers towards m-payments applications, service providers see consumer acceptance as a big hurdle to overcome (MallatNiina, 2007). The degree of interest in the new technology or service is directly related to the degree of knowledge (PaganiMargherita, 2004). Change in payment behaviour of the consumers, as mentioned earlier is also a barrier in acceptance of the new mobile payment technology. Different Mobile Network Operators (MNO) and third party vendors (e.g. PayPal, AliPay) provide mobile payment service. M-payments can be linked to existing bank account or a new account can be opened for debit and credit of m-payments. So, the main stakeholders in the mobile payment are the customers, MNOs, Banks or financial institutions and third party vendors.

Several theories and models have tried to explain or predict a person's technology acceptance, e.g. the theory of planned behaviour (TPB, Ajzen, 1985), the technology acceptance model (TAM, Davis, 1989), and the unified theory of acceptance and use of Technology (UTAUT)(Venkatesh et al., 2003). Among them, the TPB and the TAM are generic and have been used to study various technology acceptance phenomena that differ in terms of technology, target users, and context. According to the TPB, an individual's acceptance of a technology can be explained by his or her intention, which is jointly determined by attitude, subjective norms, and perceived behavioural control. The TPB is good at explaining a person's behaviour in a social setting. This theory has been tested in a wide variety of settings; e.g., health care (Conner and Sparks, 1996), consumer decision making (Fortin, 2000), and technology acceptance/adoption (e.g., Chau and Hu, 2001). The existing empirical evidence reveals the theory's explanatory power and predictive ability (Venkatesh et al., 2007).

The TAM argues that perceived usefulness and perceived ease of use are critical determinants of an individual's technology acceptance (Davis, 1989; Taylor and Todd, 1995; Chau and Hu, 2001). The TAM has been empirically examined across a variety of technology acceptance scenarios that include email (e.g., Gefen and Straub, 1997), office automation software (e.g., Mathieson, 1991), online consumer decision making (e.g., Koufaris, 2002), and enterprise systems (Venkatesh et al., 2003). This model has shown high predictive power of technology adoption across different technologies, user groups, and organizational contexts (Davis et al., 1989; Venkatesh and Davis, 2000).

Several researchers have replicated Davis's original study (Davis 1989) to provide empirical evidence on the relationships that exist between usefulness, ease of use and system use (Adams, Nelson & Todd 1992; Davis 1989; Hendrickson, Massey &Cronan 1993; Segars& Grover 1993; Subramanian 1994; Szajna 1994).

METHODOLOGY

The data for this study has been obtained from cell phone users through a primary survey. The respondents have been using cell phone for not less than 2 years and who uses more than 60% of features which comes in a mobile handset. The respondents for the survey have been users in the age bracket of 18-35years.

Survey Instrument Development

A review of the literature found very few survey instruments with measures corresponding to technology adoption, service quality, and impact of advertisement and security issues. Those few found were applicable to the context of technology adoption only. The researcher therefore created items to measure the constructs. Questionnaire based survey method was adopted following the previous study to evaluate the importance of issues found from the literature review. Multiple-item scales from pre-validated measures in ICT TAM studies were used in the questionnaire designing to ensure the validity of the content. The item scales were engineered to suit the context of the study. The survey used five point Likert type scales where "1" means strongly disagree and "5" means strongly agree. The items were empirically tested and validated.

Pilot Study

Since we could not found previous literature and some of the items were introduced by the authors, a pre-test was conducted with 15 faculty members and management students who were experienced mobile phone customers and presently using other m-banking options; they were required to list items. All of the pilot participants completed the survey in the presence of the investigator. The pilot test resulted in several small revisions to the primary instrument that included rewording of a few items, the addition of a few demographic questions, and alterations to the instructions to make them easier to understand. No scaled item was dropped or added as a result of the pilot study. The scaling method we used was 5 point Likert scale, for this categorical multivariate data analysis .The scale was ranging from "strongly agree" to "strongly disagree". This small scale pilot survey was conducted to curb the possibility of ambiguity in the questionnaire items. After certain modifications we have prepared the final version of the questionnaire. With the survey result, the items (the questions in the questionnaire) with high factor loading for each factor were included in the instrument.

DATA ANALYSIS

The objective of this study was to understand these customers' choice criteria for a value added service of money transferring and to recommend some suggestions to make future strategy.

We have administered structured questionnaire in the different locations of Delhi and Kolkata mega polis and we got 70 valid responses and results were thoroughly analyzed and the output of the results clearly explained in this section. Applying SPSS, the principal component analysis (PCA) was carried out to explore the underlying factors.The construct's validity was tested applying Bartlett's Test of Sphericity and The Kaiser–Mayer–Olkin (KMO) Measure of Sampling adequacy analyzing the strength of association among variables. The Kaiser–Mayer–Olkin measures of sampling adequacy (KMO) were first computed to determine the suitability of using factor analysis. The results reveal that the value of KMO is .508 which is above 0.5. The results for Barlett's Test of Sphericity and KMO both were highly significant (Table

1) and so it is concluded that factor analysis is suitable. The output of factor analysis has been provided in the annexure.

KMO and Bartlett's Test

Kaiser-Meyer-Olkin Measure of Sampling Adequacy.		.508
Bartlett's Test of Sphericity	Approx. Chi-Square	197.957
	df	28
	Sig.	.000

DISCUSSION

A detail analysis of the data bring into focus some interesting obseravtions.The exploratory factor analysis has identified 3 important factors for metro and non-metro customers, namely

Tariff, Payment Plans and Service Quality

Tariff plans along with payment terms is one of the prominent issues that has emerged out of this study.Coupled with this is the service quality dimension that must be taken into consideration. In other words, service quality will determine the level of acceptability by the users.In context to this study, service quality assessment includes two aspects: concerns regarding signal coverage and quality and perception regarding provider's service stability. Since m-transfer is predominantly SMS based transaction processing model, network congestion problem may occur and there may be interruptions while processing the transaction and delivering the confirmation to both the parties.

User Friendliness, Upgradation and Security Assurance

Complexity is determined as the 'degree to which an innovation is perceived as difficult to understand and use'(Rogers,1995).Limitations in mobile devices features(like limited transmission speed, memory, short battery life, etc.) diminish the use of mobile technologies (Siau et al., 2004). Operators should emphasise on security and ease of use for the mass.The end users can identify the perceived benefits of the service even if they are not that tech savvy. Around 70% of the respondents seem to have concerns regarding data and transaction security and the assurance by the service provider in this regard will help to popularize the service.

Branding and Promotion

Brand image can be loosely summarized as customer's net extract from the 'brand'. It basically implies value perception for the product or the service. In this context end users' must have a feeling that they are getting value of their money as around 80% of the respondents have expressed their willingness to pay extra charges in order to avail such facility. An established service provider can capitalize on this factor if they have been successful in projecting positive brand image through various brand building exercises.

CASE STUDY: AIRTEL MONEY

Bharti Tele-Ventures was incorporated on July 7, 1995 as a company with limited liability under the Companies Act, for promoting telecommunications services.In India, the company's product offerings include 2G, 3G and 4G services, fixed line, high speed broadband through DSL, IPTV, DTH, enterprise services including national and international long distance services to carriers. Bharti Airtel had over 246 million customers across its operations at the end of February 2012.

Success of Airtel Money in other countries

Before its launch in India, Airtel's mobile phone based money transfer system has been launched in other countries like Ghana, Uganda, Kenya, Nigeria, Sierra Leone, Zambia, Tanzania etc. In these countries, Airtel's money transfer has been widely accepted and very much successful so far. The success of Airtel's mobile funds transfer in these countries has also been attributed by the favorable Telecom governance. The 'Openness' and 'Certainty' factors of the African market have largely instrumental behind the success of this system in African countries.

Airtel Money in India

Airtel launched first mobile payment service in India on April 5, 2012 in the name of 'Airtel Money'. It is still in its early stage and Airtel is promoting it aggressively. The national availability of Airtel money follows the success of service's first phase of launch in Delhi NCR and Chennai in 2011.

Airtel Money allows the convenience of paying bills or recharge as per users convenience. No need to remember the last date or go to physical locations for paying bills. Saves a lot of time, effort and money.It keeps track how much cash is in left in the account. Know where what amount have been spent and when.There is no need to store or carry cash. Reduce the risk of theft or loss. The money is completely secure on the phone. Even if the phone gets lost or stolen the m-PIN and details remain inaccessible.Usingairtel money is as easy as making a call. Airtel money gives exclusive value on Airtel payments. Not only that, there are also a lot of other discounts with merchant partners.

The Challenges of Airtel Money in India

Although so far there is no m-money product launched by any other service provider, may be in future someone can come up with such service offering and be a potential competitor of Airtel, which would possess a threat to Airtel Money.Whileit is expected that the growth of

Airtel Money is not going to be as explosive in a short period of time compared to some countries in Africa, it is still a numbers game. If the population of India is compared to that of Kenya (with the most successful mobile money system), we can see that it is just a matter of time, but India's user base will eventually dwarf that of Kenya. The key is getting the Reserve Bank of India to allow some relaxation on regulations.

LIMITATIONS AND FUTURE PERSPECTIVE

The study attempted to explore the issues that are likely to affect the adoption of m-transfer mechanism in India. However,the researchers feel that there is ample scope for improvement of the paper.To start with,the sample size should be increased so as to make the results more meaningful by performing a confirmatory study. Also the sample groups, as data have been collected from the city of Delhi and Kolkata and its adjoining districts only. For further generalization cross validation in different cities should be conducted.

In this study we confined ourselves to the identification of the factors only. With these factors a structural model can be built to test influence of these factors on the actual use of this data transferring service.

REFERENCES

[1] Adams, D.A., Todd, P.A. & Nelson, R.R. (1993) A comparative evaluation of the impact of electronic and voice mail on organizational communication. Information and Management, 24, 9–21.

[2] Adoption-Implementation: A Meta-Analysis of Findings." IEEE Transactions on Engineering Management Vol. EM-29, No.1: 28-45.

[3] Ajzen, I., & Fishbein, M.(1980). Understanding attitudes and predicting social behavior. New Jersey: Prentice-Hall.

[4] Alain Yee-Loong Chong, Felix T.S. Chan, Keng-Boon Ooi (2011), Predicting consumer decisions to adopt mobile commerce: Cross country empirical examination between China and Malaysia.

[5] Antoine, P.(2004). Understanding the mobile phone market drivers. Alcatel Telecommunications review, 4th Quarter 2003/1st Quarter 2004, pp.2–5.

[6] Chau, P.Y.K., & Hu, P.J. (2001). Information Technology Acceptance by Individual Professionals: A Model Comparison Approach, Decision Sciences, 32(4), 699-719.

[7] Conner & P. Norman (Eds.), Predicting health behavior (pp. 121-162). Buckingham, UK: Open University Press.

[8] Conner, M., & Sparks, P. (1996). The theory of planned behavior and health behaviors. In M.

[9] Davis,F.D.(1989).Perceived use fulness, perceived ease of use, and user acceptance of information technology. MIS Quarterly, 13, 319–340.

[10] Davis,F.D.,Bagozzi,R.P.,&Warshaw,P.R.(1992).Extrinsic and intrinsic motivation to use computers in the workplace. Journal of Applied Social Psychology, 22, 1111–1132.

[11] Fortin, D. R. (2000). Clipping coupons in cyberspace: A proposed model of behavior for deal-prone consumers. Psychology & Marketing, 17, 515-534.

[12] Gefen, D. & Straub, D. (1997) Gender difference in the perception and use of e-mail: an extension to the technology acceptance model. MIS Quarterly, 21, 389–400.

[13] J. Jette (2005), Ka-ching! Mobile commerce gets closer, Working Knowledge for Business Leaders, Harvard Business School, Cambridge.

[14] Jarvenpaa S.L., Lang K.R., (2005), Managing the paradoxes of mobile technology. Information Systems Management 22 (4), 7–23.

[15] Koufaris, M. (2002). Applying the Technology Acceptance Model and Flow Theory to Online Consumer Behavior. Information Systems Research, 13(2), 205-223.

[16] Lu, J., Liu, C., Yu, C.-S., & Wang, K. (2008). Determinants of accepting wireless mobile data services in China.Information & Management, 45(1), 52–64.

[17] M. Baddeley (2004), Using e-cash in the new economy: an economic analysis of micropayment systems, Journal of Electronic Commerce Research.

[18] MallatNiina (2007), Exploring consumer adoption of mobile payments – A qualitative study, Helsinki School of Economics.

[19] Mathieson, K. (1991). Predicting user intentions: comparing the technology acceptance model with the theory of planned behavior, Information Systems Research, 2(3), 173-191.

[20] PaganiMargherita (2004), Determinants Of Adoption Of Third Generation Mobile Multimedia Services, Journal Of Intekactive Marketing Volume 18/Number 3/Summer 2004.

[21] S. Karnouskos, A. Vilmos, P. Hoepner, A. Ramfos, N. Venetakis (2003), Secure mobile payment: architecture and business model of SEM-OPS, EURESCOM Summit 2003, Heidelberg, Germany.

[22] S. Okazaki (2006), What do we know about mobile Internet adopters? A cluster analysis Information & Management 43 (2).

[23] Taylor, S. and Todd, P. A. (1995a). Assessing IT usage: The role of prior experience. MIS Quarterly, 19(4), 561-570.

[24 [Tomi Dahlberg, NiinaMallat, Jan Ondrus,AgnieszkaZmijewska (2007), Past, present and future of mobile payments research: A literature review.

[25] Tornatzky, Louis G. and Katherine J. Klein. 1982. "Innovation Characteristics and Innovation

[26] Venkatesh, V., Morris, M.G., & Ackerman, P.L. (2000). A longitudinal field investigation of gender differences in individual technology adoption decision making processes.Organizational Behavior and Human Decision Processes, 83, 33–60.

[27] Venkatesh,V., & Brown, S.A. (2001). A longitudinal l investigation of personal computers in homes: Adoption determinants and emerging challenges. MIS Quarterly, 25(1), 71–102.

[28] Wixom, B.H. & Watson, H.J. (2001) An empirical investigation of the factors affecting data warehousing success. MIS Quarterly, 25, 17–41.

[29] Y.S. Wang, H.H. Lin, P. Luarn (2006), Predicting consumer intention to use mobile service, Information Systems Journal.

[30] Yaobin Lu, Shuiqing Yang a, Patrick Y.K. Chau, Yuzhi Cao (2011), Dynamics between the trust transfer process and intention to use mobile payment services: A cross-environment perspective.

[31] Yoris A. Au, Robert J. Kauffman (2007), The economics of mobile payments: Understanding stakeholder issues for an emerging financial technology application.

ANNEXURE

Results

Eigenvalues of the Correlation Matrix: Total = 19

	[Eigenvalue	*[Difference*	*[Proportion*	*[Cumulative*
1.	4.68140234	1.65255153	0.2464	0.2464
2.	3.02885081	0.79166748	0.1594	0.4058
3.	2.23718333	0.49703289	0.1177	0.5235
4.	1.74015044	0.25882108	0.0916	0.6151
5.	1.48132937	0.30370030	0.0780	0.6931
6.	1.17762907	0.16041249	0.0620	0.7551
7.	1.01721658	0.19135269	0.0535	0.8086
8.	0.82586388	0.04923452	0.0435	0.8521
9.	0.77662936	0.23319254	0.0409	0.8930
10.	0.54343682	0.10310513	0.0286	0.9216
11.	0.44033169	0.06138374	0.0232	0.9447
12.	0.37894795	0.12418524	0.0199	0.9647
13.	0.25476271	0.09866058	0.0134	0.9781
14.	0.15610213	0.02319794	0.0082	0.9863
15.	0.13290419	0.07392198	0.0070	0.9933
16.	0.05898222	0.01615990	0.0031	0.9964
17.	0.04282231	0.02496091	0.0023	0.9987
18.	0.01786140	0.01026803	0.0009	0.9996
19.	0.00759338		0.0004	1.0000

4 factors will be retained by the NFACTOR criterion.

Performance Management System and Multisource Feedback: A Comparative Study of Software Organizations

Geeta Mishra

ACCF, Amity University, Noida

ABSTRACT

The purpose of this paper is to discuss the significance of employee's satisfaction from performance management system in two software organisations in NCR. The paper attempts to compare the perceived satisfaction of employee's from their performance management system in two software organizations under study in which one organization supplements the Performance Management System with a 360 degree feedback mechanism while other organisation does not implement 360 degree feedback process. The paper also discusses the significance of 360 degree feedback in the development of employees and in the synchronisation of organisation goals with that of the employees creating a synergistic effect for both the stakeholders. Also the paper discusses the process of 360 degree feedback used in the organization under study.

INTRODUCTION

Since decades Performance Appraisal is considered to be one of the most significant HR Practices which has always attracted the attention of organizations irrespective of their size and structure. The focus in thenew economy is undoubtedly on performance with the slogan 'Perform or Perish' Hindustan Times (2001). In the light of increasing complexities, focus of organizations is on gaining sustainable competitive advantage through the skill set and competencies of human capital. In such a changing scenario there is a paradigm shift from performance appraisal to performance management which is considered to be one of the most significant process having the potential to significantly contribute to organizational success and effectiveness.Nankervis and Compton (2006). With the knowledge based economy and ever increasing emphasis on performance, Performance Management System is considered to be one of the key deliverables for HR Department.

Performance Management is an integrated process in which managers work with their employees to set expectations, measure and review results and reward performance in order to improve employee performance with the ultimate aim of positively affecting organizational success Armstrong and Baron (1998); Mondy et al.(2002). Performance Management is not just about evaluating but managing the performance of employees in the interest of both the employees as well as the organization. Also in a knowledge intensive industry where performance outcomes are not in terms of units produced or sales targets achieved and the organizations compete on the basis of services and key skills embedded in its human capital, performance management has a special significance. In the wake of ever increasing competition an employee is not only required to be competent enough to fulfill the expectations of his supervisor but needs to be competitive enough to meet the requirements of anyone and everyone who falls within his/her exposure area including his subordinates, peers, , supervisors,internal and external customers.All this requires sensitivity on the part of management to support an employee in the fulfillment of his commitment to various stakeholders. Since software industry capitalizes on its intellectual capital and various researchers have suggested that appraise satisfaction determines the organizational effectiveness and success, it becomes quite inevitable to understand the perceived satisfaction of employees from the Performance Management System of their organizations.

Performance Management System (PMS) comprises of four key components:

Performance Planning: It provides a framework for performing the role and outlines the activities that an employee is expected to undertake during a specified period of time.

Feedback and Coaching: It is an important process whereby an employee is continuously communicated about his/her strengths and weaknesses at regular intervals and training sessions are organized to improve the weak areas identified.

Performance Review: It is a process whereby an employee is evaluated against a set of pre-established standards and relevant inputs are provided to him/her for the preparation of development plans.

Outcome: It comprises ofrewarding employees with monetary and non-monetary rewards and acknowledging their contribution individually and as members of the group towards accomplishment of organizational goals.

Employee's perceived satisfaction has been assessed on each of these four dimensions of PMS.

OBJECTIVE

In the light of the above, the following two key objectives were formed for the study:

- To compare the perceived satisfaction of employees from the PMS across two software organizations in NCR where one of the organization supplements the PMS with a 360 degree feedback mechanism while other does not implement a multi-source feedback mechanism.

- To explore and understand the implementation of 360 degree feedback in organization under study which implements it.

HYPOTHESIS

Null Hypothesis: There is no significant difference in the perceived satisfaction of employees pertaining to performance planning, feedback and coaching, performance review and outcome across the organizations under study.

Alternate Hypothesis: There is a significant difference in the perceived satisfaction of employees pertaining to performance planning, feedback and coaching, performance review and outcome across the organizations under study.

RATIONALE OF THE STUDY BACKED BY REVIEW OF LITERATURE

Ilgen et al. (1979) argue that dissatisfied employees would be much less motivated to use the evaluation information to improve performance. Therefore it becomes essential to ascertain the perceived satisfaction of employees with the performance management system since the utilisation of feedback that they get is to a large extent determined by the level of their satisfaction.

Mount (1983) reflect that there is greater possibility that positive outcomes would occur if employees are satisfied with the appraisal process and perceive it to be fair and support the system. Since the true ownership of the performance management system lies with the Line Managers, the success of the process depend on how satisfied they are with the appraisal process and to what extent they support its implementation.

Bernardin and Beatty (1984) and Dobbins et al. (1990) suggest that an important link exists between satisfaction with appraisal process and an appraisal's potential as an effective force for change and improved performance. Since the objective of any performance management system would be improved performance and behaviour of its employees, it is essential that they are satisfied with the mechanism so that the purpose of the process is achieved.

Hellervik, Hazucha, & Schneider(1992) also reflect that obtaining information on an individual's performance from multiple sources enhance the credibility of the information and therefore presumably the individual's motivation to change his or her behaviour.

Hazucha et al (1993) argue that 360-degree feedback as compared to feedback from a single person usually the supervisor is associated with greater reliability, fairness, and the person's acceptance of performance appraisal feedback.

Cawley et al. (1998) argue thatappraisal satisfaction has broader impact on factors like motivation, productivity.

RESEARCH DESIGN AND METHODOLOGY

To meet the above mentioned objectives it was essential that the organizations under study had an established Performance Management System. Two organizations agreed to participate in the facilitation of research, one with a 360 degree feedback mechanism and other without a multi-source feedback mechanism.The sample size comprised of 100 employees, 50 employees from each organization. Purposive sampling was used since the study required collection of data from employees who had undergone at-least one appraisal cycle in the organization. The questionnaire was developed after review of relevant literature in this area. The insights for the development of questionnaire have been taken from the dimensions used by DDI and SHRM (1994) in their study on Performance Management Practices. The dimensions are namely performance planning, feedback and coaching, performance review and outcomes. Also relevant inputs were taken from academic experts and practitioners in the area of Performance Management.The Final Questionnaire comprised of 19 items.Responses were obtained on a five point scale ranging from 1 to 5 where one implied strongly disagree and 5 implied strongly agree. The content validity was affirmed by theexperts and reliability was tested through cronbach alpha which was .874 which confirmed the reliability of the instrument.

Data was analysedusing SPSS 16.A semi structured interview was also conducted with the appraisee's (N=6) to understand the implementation process of 360 degree feedback in the organization which was implementing it.

RESULTS AND FINDINGS

The data collected on various performance management dimensions namely performance planning, feedback and coaching, performance review and outcome was analyzed through SPSS 16. Independent T test was applied to compare the perceived satisfaction of employees across two software organizations in NCR under study. Organization 1 is using a multi-source feedback mechanism while organization 2 is not utilizing 360 degree feedback mechanism. The results are as follows:

Table 1. Descriptive Statistics of Employee's Perceived Satisfaction from PMS

PMS	*Organisation*	*N*	*Mean*	*Std. Deviation*
PP	Organization 1	50	3.83	.43
	Organization 2	50	3.16	.44
F&C	Organization 1	50	3.79	.44
	Organization 2	50	3.21	.53
PR	Organization 1	50	3.72	.42
	Organization 2	50	3.11	.51
Out	Organization 1	50	3.66	.58
	Organization 2	50	2.86	.69

The Table 1 shows the descriptive statistics of the perceived satisfaction of employees from PMSin the two organizations under study. The mean score of 3.83onperformance planning (PP) suggests that employees were fairly satisfied with the performance planning dimension in organisation 1as compared to organisation 2 where the mean score is 3.16. This suggests that organisation 1 entails better practices when it comes to planning the performance of its employees such as employees have a clear idea of what is expected from them, goals are set in partnership with employees, organisation values are reflected in performance plan and employees have strong ownership of the plan. The mean score of 3.79 on Feedback and Coaching (F&C)in organization suggests that employees are relatively more satisfied in organisation 1 as compared to organization 2 where the mean score on Feedback and Coaching is 3.21. The employees in organisation 1 were comparatively more satisfied on items such as continuity of feedback, employee gets required training throughout the year, feedback is given pertaining to both strengths as well as weaknesses. Similarly the mean score of Performance Review (PR) in Organisation 1 is 3.72 as compared to the mean score of 3.11 in organization 2 reflecting that the perceived satisfaction of employees in organisation 1 is relatively higher in terms of how their performance is being reviewed as compared to their perceived satisfaction in organisation 2. The mean score on Outcome (Out) in organisation 1 is 3.66 as against 2.86 in organisation 2 again reflecting that employees in organisation 1 perceived the reward system to be more fair and were more satisfied on items like they are satisfied and motivated after the review process and the pay and rewards are linked to performance. PMS is a process which creates a vicious circle as can be seen from the mean scores mentioned in the table above. An effective planning process backed by continuous and timely feedback provides enhanced satisfaction from the entire appraisal process in terms of review and outcomes. It is quite evidentthat employee's perceived satisfaction on all the dimensions was relatively high in organisation 1 as compared to organisation 2. The Next table shows the results of the Independent T test which also supports the findings from table 1.1.The results are shown in Table 2 below:

The Table 2 above shows the results of the Independent T test. The Levene's test signifies that the two groups of organisations have approximately equal variance on the dependent variable as the significance value is greater than 0.05.The t value is 7.625, $p< 0.05$ for performance planning, it is 5.946, $p<0.05$for feedback and coaching, the t value for performance review is 6.497, $p<0.05$ and for outcome it is 6.251, $p<005$. Thus the results imply that there are significant differences in the perceived satisfaction of employees on all the dimensions of PMS namely performance planning, feedback and coaching, performance review and outcome across the two organizations under study.On the basis of the results, Null Hypothesis can be safely rejected.

The results from the descriptive statistics and independent t test support that the perceived satisfaction of employees in organization 1 which is using a multi source mechanism as a supplement to Performance Management System are more satisfied as compared to the organization which does not implement the mechanism of 360 degree feedback supporting the contributions of researchers who argued that 360 DF can lead to enhanced employee satisfaction.

Table 2. Independent T test Results

		Levene's Test for Equality of Variances		*t-test for Equality of Means*						
		F	*Sig.*	*t*	*df*	*Sig. (2-tailed)*	*Mean Difference*	*Std. Error Difference*	*95% Confidence Interval of the Difference*	
									Lower	*Upper*
PP	Equal variances assumed	.001	.977	7.625	98	.000	.67333	.08831	.49809	.84858
	Equal variances not assumed			7.625	97.980	.000	.67333	.08831	.49809	.84858
F&C	Equal variances assumed	.962	.329	5.946	98	.000	.58000	.09754	.38643	.77357
	Equal variances not assumed			5.946	94.575	.000	.58000	.09754	.38635	.77365
PR	Equal variances assumed	3.403	.068	6.497	98	.000	.61000	.09390	.42367	.79633
	Equal variances not assumed			6.497	94.844	.000	.61000	.09390	.42359	.79641
Out	Equal variances assumed	.476	.492	6.251	98	.000	.80000	.12797	.54605	1.05395
	Equal variances not assumed			6.251	94.776	.000	80000	.12797	.54594	1.05406

360 Degree Feedback

360 DF or multi-source feedback facilitates performance feedback from various sources & hence deserve attention at an academic and practitioner level.Kane and Lawler (1978, p-584) state that "rather than having any one level do the entire assessment of a person's performance, it is better to have each level contribute to the assessment of the portion that it is able to perform more effectively than any other level" . Various researchers have documented that 360 degree feedback helps in improved employee relationships, reduced grievances, opportunity for employee involvement and a demonstration of partnering employees and respecting their opinions on the part of top management. They also support that an effective 360 degree process can lead to enhanced satisfaction and increased self awareness amongst employees since it incorporates feedback from significant multiple sources.

The 360 DF process in this organization is applicable to all employees in the organization who have completed minimum one yearsof service in the organization. The organization started the process in 1996 and became web enabled in the year 2000. It is used as a purely developmental tool and is not used for making decisions like promotion, compensation changes, etc.

One of the Line manager remarked that *360 DF eliminates any bias as the views are taken from the entire exposure area. The rater's team is made on the basis of work related interactions. The feedback is based on critical work related behavioral competencies. Each competency is broken down into statements known as behavioral indicators and the behavioral indicators for the same attribute differs according to the level of competency mapped for a role.* The purpose of the process is to provide information as to how the behavior of employees is affecting or influencing others in the organization.

The organization also collaborates with leading B-Schools such as XLRI, IIM, MDI to facilitate training programs in the area of developing managerial and behavioral competencies in employees. It also facilitates courses in the area of leadership skills development, courses for first time managers, conflict management, communication skills, project management.The feedback is used for developmental purposes only. The 360 DFmechanismcomprises of the seven attributes on which an employee is rated by supervisor, subordinate, self and peers namely Analytical and Conceptual Ability, Customer Orientation, Impact and Influence, Initiative, Integrity, Result Orientation and Team Work and Cooperation. The rating is done on a four point scale where 1 implies never observed and 4 impliesalways observedbehavior.

Yet another Line manager remarked *that the organization also encourages employees to speak to people in confidence and gather personal feedback to validate the assessment. The supervisors, mentors and HR also assist employees to understand the feedback and make more focused action plans.*The entire process is a self developmental tool focused towards building key competencies for the role that he/she is performing and does not impact his/her performance assessment.

The Line Managers also reflected that 360 DF leads to enhanced awareness, building healthy relationship with peers, supervisors and subordinates, fosters trust in the organization and leads to enhanced performance and improved behavior of employees.

CONCLUSION

Performance Management System is significant in any industry but software service industry being knowledge intensive and dynamic industry makes PMS even more critical. Also since the success of any process to a large extent depends on the human capital which implements it, understanding their perceived satisfaction from the process becomes even more significant. Research has also supported the belief that the feedback from Performance Management System will be effectively utilized only when they deem the process to be fair and support it in its true spirit. The research findings make it clear that the employee's perceived satisfaction from the PMS was higher in organization 1 as compared to organization 2. It was clear from the semi structured interviews conducted in organization 2 that a multi source feedback process enables employees to make development plans in consultation with their managers and enhances their self awareness by gathering the feedback from all the relevant sources. It also enables organizations to organize training program as per the grey areas identified and encourages employees to meet their career goals in the attainment of organization goals. Thus it can be said that 360 degree feedback mechanism has potential to improve the satisfaction level of employees and result in enhanced motivation and improvement in performance and behavior.

REFERENCES

[1] Armstrong, Michael, & Baron, Angela. (1998). *Performance management: The new realities*. London: Institute ofPersonnel and Develcpment.

[2] Bernardin.H.John and Richard W.Beatty (1984). Performance Appraisal:Assessinghuman performance at work. *Boston*: Kent.

[3] Cawley. Brian D., Lisa M. Keeping., and Paul E. Levy.(1998). Participation in the Performance Appraisal Process and Employee Reactions. A Meta AnalyticReview of Field Investigations. *Journal of Applied Psychology*, *83*, 615-33.

[6] Development Dimensions International (DDI) and Society for Human Resource Management (SHRM). (1994). Performance Management: What's hot-What's not. Compensation and benefits Review, 26, (May-June), 71-75.

[7] Dobbins, Gregory.H.,Robert. L.Cardy., Stephanie J. Platz Vieno.(1990). AApproach to Appraisal Satisfaction : An initial Investigation of the jointeffects of organisationalvariables [and appraisal characteristics. *Journal ofManagement, 16*(3), 619-32.

[8] Hazucha, J.F., Hezlett, S.A., & Schneider, R.J. (1993). The impact of 360-degreefeedbackon [management skills development. *Human Resource Management, 32* (2-3),325-351.

[9] Hellervik, L.W., Hazucha, J.F., & Schneider, R.J. (1992). Behaviour change: Models, methods, and a review of evidence. In M D. Dunnette & L. Hough (Eds.), *Handbookofindustrial and organizational psychology,* 3 (2), 823-895,Palo Alto, CA: Consulting Psychologist Press.

[10] Hindustan Times (2001). Hindustan Times Survey *28,* December, 1–15

[11] Ilgen, Daniel. R., Cynthia, D. Fisher., and M. Susan., Taylor. (1979).Consequences ofIndividual [Feedback on Behavior in organisations. *Journal of Applied Psychology,64*,349-71.

[12] Mondy, R.W., Noe, R.M., &Premeaux, S.R. (2002).*Human resource management* (8th edn). Upper Saddle River, NewJersey: Prentice-Hall

[13] Mount, M.K. (1983). Comparisons of managerial and employee satisfaction with a performance appraisal system. *Personnel Psychology, 36*(1), 99-110.

[14] Nankervis, A.R., & Compton, R.L. (2006). Performance management: Theory in practice? *Asia Pacific Journal of HumanResources*, *44*(1), 83–101

Problems in Existing RFID Systems: User-Centered Design Methods

Manjeet

IT Department, NIILM CMS, Greater Noida

ABSTRACT

RFID (Radio Frequency Identification) is an emerging identification technology having greater capability than bar codes. But, the use of these systems is being discouraged by certain practical problems associated with them. Such as, high costs, tag reader sensitivity, limited transmission distances etc. End users participation and designers expertise when combined, form the key ingredients of igniting improvements and innovation in any system. This paper proposes some user-centered approaches for the improvement in the existing RFID systems.

INTRODUCTION

The magic of RFID is everywhere. The pace with which this technology is expanding its wings, as of now, it may sound futuristic but within next 10 years, we might witness fully automated homes, offices and markets and so on. Radio Frequency Identification (RFID) is an automated identification technology with greater identification capabilities than bar codes. This technology offers promising advantages like: (1) Read through obstacles (2) Read in hostile environment (3) Read in real-time by the RFID Reader [1]. Due to this attractive package, this technology is making its way into the bodies of consumers [4], and even introducing itself to the newly born ones by tagging mothers and their new borne babies to prevent mismatching later [3]. In the past, there have been several obstacles that have kept RFID from gaining full acceptance in consumer applications as well as in enterprises. Some of these obstacles included tag reader sensitivity, RF transmission distance, and the high cost of implementing RFID. It was observed that the end users feedback played an extremely important role in finding these obstacles and to some extent removing them [5].

Conceptual mapping is a structured conceptualization technique used to stimulate the generation of ideas. More often concept maps are used to communicate complex ideas. For example, it combines group processes with a sequence of multivariate statistical analysis in multidisciplinary research teams (Maize, Soya beans and Swine) investigating market opportunities within the Global food system [2].

USER PARTICIPATION IN RFID SYSTEMS

User participation becomes obvious in a world where day to day objects like garments, food and home appliances and so on carry RFID tags. By exploiting RFID tags, home appliances could operate in more sophisticated ways [6]. Some of these ways are very much suggested by users of these products like your refrigerator might warn you when a particular item in it has been expired and so on. Thus user needs may lead to creative innovations and of course may lead to improvements in the existing system. Hence user centered design demands for user engagement in the various design processes, ranging across the wide spectrum of requirement analysis to the working model with desired functionalities.

RFID are mostly used at Wall Mart Stores and Department of Defense. They demand from the supplier that goods should be attached with RFID tags so that they can uniquely identify and trace the goods when required. If some problem occurs with the quality then they can easily trace out the batch number, supplier and even the precise assembly line which held that flaw. The problems of tag reader sensitivity, RF transmission distances, high cost etc. discourages both customers and suppliers to adopt the RFID technology to a larger extent in spite of lucrative offers provided by the technology. The main focus of the paper is on describing these problems from the user's perspective and proposing their corresponding solutions. Since a picture is worth thousand words, concept maps have been used to communicate the idea.

PROBLEMS AND SOLUTIONS

Problem 1: Tag Reader Sensitivity

The RFID tag has no fixed location for pasting it on goods package. Hence a problem in determining where the tag is located relative to the RFID reader device. So if the RFID tag is not present in the main lobe of the Tag reader, then it can not be sensed by the reader or vice-versa. This problem is known as reader sensitivity. This is due to the fact that the antenna of tag reader or RFID tag itself comes in the dead zone. Also, since the RFID signal is not in the visible range of the user, the problem becomes more critical. The temporary solution suggested by the user is to rotate the goods, so that both the antennas should come out of the dead zone. But this leads to the inconvienence faced by the user in rotating the goods and especially the heavy ones. For example, when a user purchases a heavy item like a 20 kg floor packet and the RFID tag reader antenna comes in the dead zone of the RFID tag antenna, then it is not readable by the RFID Reader. Then it becomes difficult for the user to rotate the packet, so that it gets scanned by the RFID reader. Similarly the situations may become worse when we talk of more heavy and unmanageable items.

Solution: These reader sensitivity issues can be resolved by using a dual dipole antenna in the RFID Tag. These antenna are placed such that one signal transmitted by one antenna will overcome the dead zone for the other antenna. It will enhance the use of RFID for a broader range of applications making life of the user a little more convenient. The idea is being illustrated with the help of the concept map.

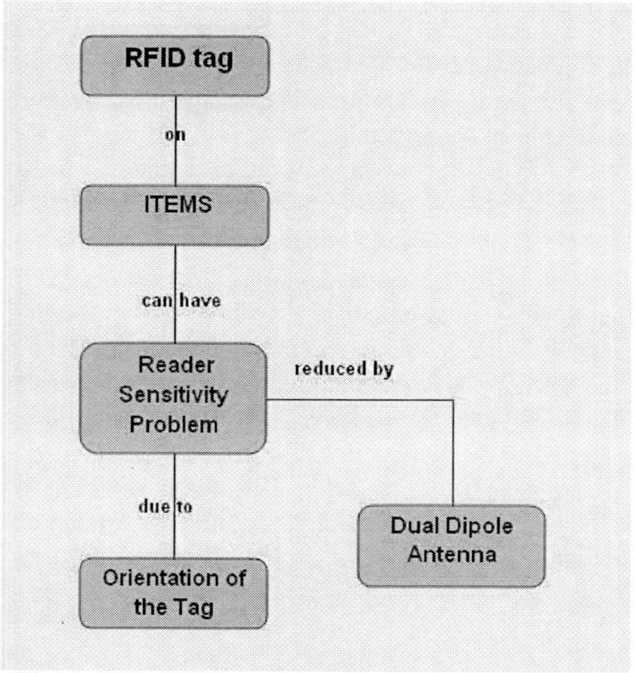

Fig. 1. RFID Tag Reader Sensitivity Resolving Model

Problem 2: RF Transmission Distance

There are two types of RFID tags Active and Passive. The problem associated with the users of both kinds of tags is with their transmission range. Their transmission ranges are very small. Mostly EPC class 4 type tags are used which have a very small transmission range capability [8]. The problems associated with it are many. For example, consider a big mall or showroom where each of the items is RFID Tagged and the customer wants to trace the goods with the help of sales person and sales person does not know the exact location of that product. Then he comes near to the tag reader, sends query signals to all RFID tags, receives acknowledgement and tries to find the location. But due to limited range capability of the RFID tag, he fails to locate it. One solution of the above problem is that he should have mobile tag reader, so that he walks and try to find the location of the product.

This problem of tracking goods which are kept at long distances is enhanced when a user of RFID wants to track a valuable entity like car, etc. For example, suppose user handed over the car to the parking staff to park the car in a highly crowded parking lot spreaded in big area. By the time user wants to get back to the car, then parking staff takes a lot of time to search it. Now, if the car were holding an RFID tag of higher range transmission capability, then it can be easily located with RFID Reader. When a user is interested in tracking mobile items, with existing RFID tag then the problem becomes even worse due to its limited range capability. A recent study says that 30% cars, laptops and mobiles are stolen every year. In most of the cases they are not traced at all and even if traced then also it becomes difficult for the police to find the actual owner of that item.

Solution: Noticing the above problem it is concluded that there is requirement of the RFID tag with the various range capabilities. The one solution is that we should have RFID tag with having a varying range capability. The designing of such RFID tags is highly complex and uneconomical. Another approach is that we can have separate RFID tags for the various range capability, so according to the need user can select it. For short range communication between RFID tag and RFID reader, RFID tags with HF waves are used. For medium range communication, RFID tags with UHF wave are required. Similarly for long distance (in few kilometers) communication, microwave can be used and more than that SAW can be used. The advantage of using SAW is that its signal does not deteriorate with the environmental changes. This quality of the RFID tags with SAW can be utilized in the seizing the gray market, because missed or stolen things can be easily located by the owner or police even over long distances.

The proposed idea is illustrated with the help of concept map.

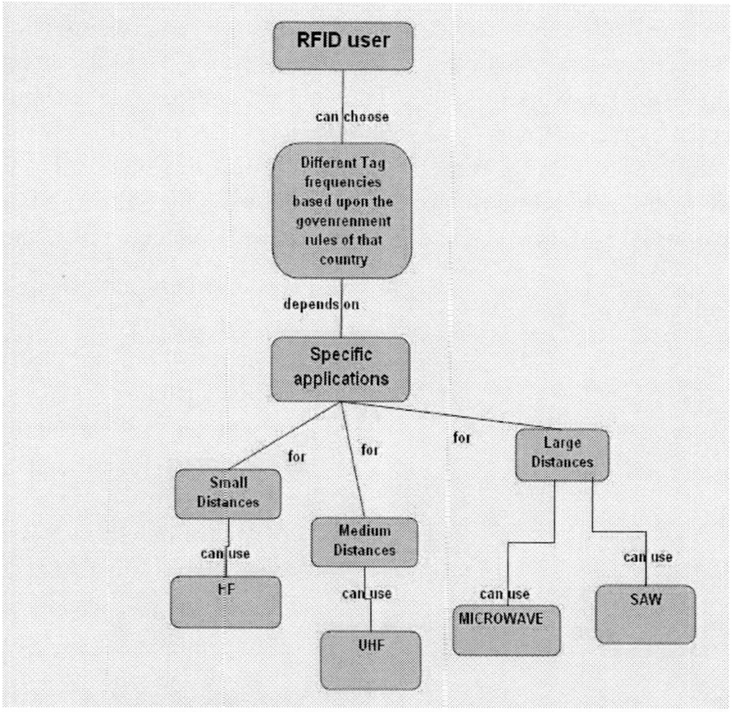

Fig. 2. RFID Long Transmission Distance Model

Problem 3: High RFID Cost

A recent study shows that the biggest users of RFID technology Wal-mart Stores and department of defense feel that the RFID cost is still a primary reason that RFID hasn't become common place [7]. A solution to this is to increase the manufacturing of the number of tags so that the cost should come down. But it further leads to upgrading the existing infrastructure to support RFID such as storage devices, new methods for searching database etc. To be precise, an RFID infrastructure needs a number of elements apart from the RFID Tag and Reader which includes additional servers, databases, middleware and applications. Further, the middleware and application layers need to support number of critical components such as device management, data collection data management and integration with the back–end system, collaboration with partners and customers and integration with data synchronization networks. And a result of doing all this will further increase cost and Risk.

Solution: The proposed solution is inspired by those products which are a part of daily needs of consumers, precisely, with small life span and disposable packets (with pasted RFID Tags) such as milk carton. After selling such products there is no need to store information for a long time in the RFID database, since it leads to unnecessary overloading of the information in the database, causing a penalty in terms of searching time for other items. Therefore, one of the possible solutions to reduce the cost factor in RFID systems is Tag recycling which includes reprogramming of the RFID chip and updating the database entries. This should be implemented with proper instructions being issued to the customers and if special bonus schemes are incorporated, this idea can work wonders. The empty goods packet containing RFID Tags should be collected by the customers and sold to RFID street vendors (to be introduced in the system) which further are sent for reuse. The advantage of this idea is that there will be no need to increase in the production rate of the tags and existing RFID infrastructure. Hence, this can bring cost of RFID tags considerably down without inducing risky complexities in the RFID systems.

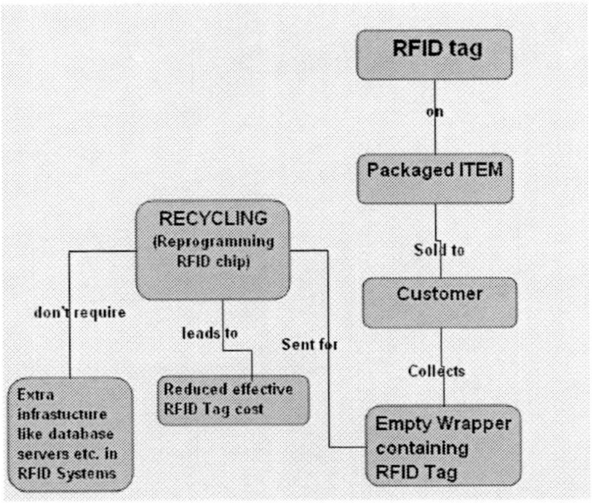

Fig. 3. RFID Cost Reduction Model

CONCLUSION

Recent research shows that user-centered design approach leads to great innovations in the existing systems. In the case of RFID systems also it has been observed that problem faced by the user works as catalyst in incorporating improvements. The advantage of using concept maps made the design procedure simple to illustrate and cost effective

REFERENCES

[1] Gaetano Borriello, RFID: Tagging the world, Communications of the ACM, Volume 48. No 9 September 2005, pp. 34-37.

[2] William Trochim and Mary Kane, Concept mapping: an introduction to structured conceptualization in health care, *International Journal for Quality in Health Care* 2005; Volume 17, Number 3: pp. 187–191.

[3] http://rfid.idtechex.com/knowledgebase/en/nologon.asp

[4] IEEE Spectrum, March 2007 Issue.

[5] James P. Zappen, Sibel Adali, Teresa M. Harrison, "Participatory design and mediation: Developing a youth – services information system for city and county government: experiments in user designer collaboration. Proceedings of the 2006 International Conference on Digital Government Research dg. o '06, ACM Press.

[6] "Merloni unveils RFID appliances," RFID J., Apr. 4,2003.[Online]. Available :http:// www.rfifjournal.com/article/articleview/369/1/1/.

[7] http://www.eweek.com/article2

[8] Jerry Banks and Les G. Thompson, RFID Applied *John Wiley, 2007.*

[9] Ying Liu, An-tao-Bu, En-she Li, De-min Fu, Liang-yong Xiao, "A New Dual Polarization Dipole Antenna", IEEE, International Conference on Microwave and Millimeter Wave Technology Proceedings, pp. 5-7, 2004.

Refined Coefficient Fixed Effects

Subrato Banerjee

Indian Statistical Institute, New Delhi

ABSTRACT

Instrumental variables are most often used to overcome to problems of endogeneity in regression. Good instruments, however, are very hard to find. Fixed effects estimators partially fill in this void by assuming that certain unobserved factors can be held fixed in the short to medium term and can hence be differenced out. For long panels, however, the assumption that unobserved effects are fixed is often questionable, and could lead to estimation biases when such effects actually vary with time. I drop this assumption and propose a two-stage fixed-effects estimator for long panels that relies on the law of conditional (iterated) expectations to overcome endogeneity in the absence of instruments. This will be helpful in today's world that already promotes massive data-keeping and will eventually maintain huge sets of data over many years. Alongside, I also develop tests for discrete changes in unobservables and present two (important) business applications.

INTRODUCTION

In this paper I propose a two stage fixed-effects estimator that seeks to mitigate the problem of biases in the estimates of parameters of interest (in the absence of instruments) caused by the existence of unobserved (and hence omitted) variables that change with time, but are believed to be fixed. For example, consider a data set of firms that have lasted for over 80 years. If the unit of observation is a firm, then assuming that the unobserved managerial quality, ability, and possibly structure for each firm has remained fixed during the entire period is indeed unreasonable. To add to the problem, they will, in most cases, be correlated with the observed regressors (such as size of workforce, etc.). Substantial research can be found on the area of fixed effects (see Angrist and Pischke (2008); Balestra and Krishnakumar (2008); Baltagi (2001) and Wooldridge (2010) that largely sum up most of the prominent research) and this area continues to see contributions (see for example, Wooldridge (2005); and Orne and Yamagata (2006) for some of the most recent developments).[1] The possibility that unobserved factors could themselves systematically evolve over time has received relatively limited attention. In

[1] For some of its applications it may be useful to look at Bundell and Bond (1998), Cameron and Trivedi (2005), and Chamberlain (1984).

this paper, I seek to fill this void. I make no assumption on the functional form, of the unobservables and simply require that it be non-stochastic. I look at the possibility that there may be an element of evolution that systematically governs important factors that we do not observe, which if ignored, can cause biases in regression estimates. This means, we can not rely on fixed-effects estimators that involve differencing from the mean and have to resort to those that involve adjustments in obtained standard errors to account for serial correlation (see for example Baltagi and Li (1991)). In this paper, I systematically eliminate the effects of these unobserved factors (that cause biases) in two stages (the data generation stage and the refined coefficients stage) to arrive at more 'refined' parameter coefficients. In section 2 that follows, I formalize the structure. Section 3 illustrates the stages involved in the estimation process and identifies a test to detect if unobserved effects are indeed fixed. Section 4 focuses on a test that I build for detecting discrete changes in unobservables and section 5 concludes with a discussion on business applications.

THE STRUCTURE

We start with the following regression equation

$$y_{it} = \alpha + \lambda(t) + \boldsymbol{X}_{it}\boldsymbol{\beta} + \boldsymbol{A}_i\gamma + \varepsilon_{it} \qquad \text{... (1)}$$

In the above equation (1), y_{it} ($i \in \{1, 2, \ldots, I\}$; t $\{1, 2, \ldots, T\}$) is our recorded outcome variable for an individual unit$i$ (could be an individual or a household, we will use the word 'individual' throughout this paper to denote a unit of observation) in time t. $\lambda(t)$ is just a (polynomial) trend component, to account for the possibility that y_{it} may be evolving in time, due to the very factors that are intrinsic to itself. $\boldsymbol{X}_{it}$ is a (*K-dimensional*) vector of observed (individual-specific) factors recorded overtime and believed to affect our outcome variable. $\boldsymbol{A}_i$ is a (*N-dimensional*) vector of unobserved (individual-specific) factors that are believed to be invariant across time but affect our outcome variable – these are theindividual(possibly fixed) effects with the coefficient vector $\boldsymbol{\gamma}$ (which we are not particularly interested in).$\boldsymbol{\beta}$ is the (*K-dimensional*) vector of parameters of interest. For short term data, certain factors in $\boldsymbol{A}_i$ can be held fixed, and a fixed-effects estimator $\widehat{\boldsymbol{\beta}}$ can consistently be obtained either by differencing, or by taking deviations from the mean (defined across time) characteristics $\boldsymbol{X}_i$. For long term data (say for T> 100, when t is measured in years), however, assuming that A_i is fixed is not reasonable. We should expect that

$$\boldsymbol{A}_i = \boldsymbol{A}_i(t) \qquad \text{... (2)}$$

In other words, what we believe to be fixed may not be fixed.[2] Formally, there exists $l \in \{1,2, \ldots ,(T-l)\}$ such that

$$\boldsymbol{A}_i(t) - \boldsymbol{A}_i(t-l) \neq \boldsymbol{0} \qquad \text{... (3)}$$

[2] Since ε_{it} is indexed by both, individual and time subscripts, we take $\boldsymbol{A}_i(t)$ to be a deterministic or non-stochastic (but unobserved) function of t.

which means that the difference shown in the left hand side (LHS) above is significantly different from the (*N-dimensional*) null vector (the right hand side). The difference $A_i(t) - A_i(t-l)$ does not 'vanish'. Note that we should expect l to be large enough. From the equation above, it directly follows that differencing (1) with l lags as shown below (ignoring at the moment for convenience, the differenced effects of the trend component $\lambda(t) - \lambda(t-l)$)

$$y_{it} - y_{i(t-l)} = [X_{it} - X_{i(t-l)}]\boldsymbol{\beta} + [A_i(t) - A_i(t-l)]\gamma + \varepsilon_{it} - \varepsilon_{i(t-l)} \qquad \ldots (4)$$

and running a fixed effects estimation process will lead us to a (omitted variable) bias in $\widehat{\boldsymbol{\beta}}$ because of unobserved (significant) covariance terms between our observed and unobserved variables of interest (this is where we deviate from the standard assumption of fixed and random effect models – that regressors are uncorrelated with unobserved factors). We define this biased fixed-effect estimate of β as $\widehat{\boldsymbol{\beta}}^{l}$. This is just to show that, since $A_i(t)$is changing with time, the fixed-effect estimate of β will change with the size l of lags (i.e. the extent of this bias is conditional on l), we are willing to take in (4). For ease of notation, we write our variables as

$$\Delta^{l} z_{it} = z_{it} - z_{i(t-l)}$$

so that (4) can be written as

$$\Delta^{l} y_{it} = (\Delta^{l} X_{it})\boldsymbol{\beta} + (\Delta^{l} A_i(t))\gamma + \Delta^{l}\varepsilon_{it}\,; \ \forall l \in \{1, 2, \ldots, (T-1)\}$$

The above regression(s) as very vary l from 1 to T – 1 (provided l is large enough, since otherwise, we will have to settle for regression estimates generated from a lesser number of lags) is the first stage of our estimation.

THE 'TRUE' ESTIMATOR – TESTING IF FIXED EFFECTS ARE INDEED FIXED

At this stage, we are in a position to test the hypothesis that what we believe to be fixed effects are indeed fixed. Note that the differenced relation (4) is defined for all l. The idea is that if $A_i(t)$ isindeed fixed (i.e. if $\Delta^{l} A_i(t) = 0\ ; \ \forall l \in \{1, 2, \ldots, (T-1)\}$), then our fixed effects estimator $\widehat{\boldsymbol{\beta}}$ should remain largely unchanged regardless of l, the number of lags we choose to difference over for our fixed effects regression. In particular suppose we are interested in the specific parameter $\beta_k \in \boldsymbol{\beta}$ (which is the coefficient of X_k), it must be the case that

$$Var(\widehat{\boldsymbol{\beta}}_k) = 0\ ; \widehat{\boldsymbol{\beta}}_k = \{\widehat{\beta}_k^{l} \mid l \in \{1, 2, \ldots, (T-1)\}\} \qquad \ldots (5)$$

Consequently, if we reject the above hypothesis against the alternative, i.e. if $Var(\widehat{\boldsymbol{\beta}}_k) > 0$, then it must be the case that what we believe to be fixed effects are not fixed. Then it directly follows that $\widehat{\beta}_k^{l}$ itself will vary with l, the number of lags we consider (the time lapse) – all factors in $A_i(t)$ that affect $\tilde{\beta}_k$ also change with time – fixed effects are no longer fixed. Formally,

$$\widehat{\beta}_k^l = E[\beta_k|\Delta^l A_i(t)] = E[\beta_k|A_i^*(l)] \qquad \dots (6)$$

where, $\Delta^l A_i(t) = A_i^*(l)$

since $\Delta^l A_i(t)$ will be a function of l which I am denoting as $A_i^*(l)$. That $\Delta^l A_i(t)$ is a function of t, implies that $A*i(l)$ will be a function of l.[3]Now, we use the law of conditional expectation (informally, that the smaller information set always dominates) in (6) above and immediately see that

$$\widehat{\beta}_k^l = E[\beta_k|A_i^*(l)] = E[E[\beta_k|A_i^*(l)]|l] \qquad \dots (7)$$

Note that our unit of observation is now of the form $(l, \widehat{\beta}_k^l)$, the data we have generated from our first stage, for our second stage regression implied by (7) above. We therefore define $E[E[\beta_k|A_i^*(l)]|l]$ to be a (say) cubic polynomial in l as below.

$$E[E[\beta_k|A_i^*(l)]|l] = \underbrace{\tilde{\beta}k0}_{\text{Fixed}} + \underbrace{\tilde{\beta}k2l + \tilde{\beta}k2l^2 + \tilde{\beta}k3l^3}_{\text{Bias conditional on the lags}} \qquad \dots (8)$$

In (8) above, our stage two regression, we have decomposed $\widehat{\beta}_k^l$ into two components – one that is variable with lags (or the part dependent on time via $A_i(t)$), and the other part $\tilde{\beta}_{k0}$, that remains uninfluenced by the biases caused because of time lapse (or lags) we consider. It is the latter, that we take to be our fixed-effects estimator. We similarly obtain estimates for the other elements of **β**. We call this $\tilde{\beta}_0$, our suitable parameter for X_{it} in (1). [4]The true model can thus be written as

---

[3] This follows immediately from the fact that $A_i(t)$ is non-stochastic (see Footnote 1) and can be better explained with a slight change of notation. One can, for instance, immediately see this by observing data in points intime t_0, t_1, t_2, etc. with a gap of time period l between each of them, thereby making them equally spaced. Thus, $t_1 = t_0 + l$, $t_2 = t_1 + l = t_0 + 2l$ ... etc.So what we index as t_0, t_1, t_2, etc. can also be indexed as t_0, $t_0 + l$,$t_0 + 2l$etc. Since for any data, $t_0$will be fixed and given, we could write our unobservablesA(t_0), A(t_1), A(t_2), explicitly as functions of l ‹A(t_0), A($t_0 + l$), A($t_0 +2l$) etc.). Thus, any differencing between them will also lead us to functions of l.

[4] In doing so, we have to take a call on whether we want simultaneous determination of elements of $\hat{a}$, or we want to individually run the two stages for each element (the latter is the simpler of the two). While this question is largely out of scope of this paper, the former is attainable provided that there is some external information on marginal effects of interest in our model. Conditional on that effect (which could be called M), I recommend a three-stage least squares method of estimation across our units of observation $(l,m,\widehat{\beta}_k^l)$ to account for possible significant covariances between the errors of equations with $\widehat{\beta}_k^l$ and $\widehat{\beta}_j^l$ as the dependent variables. Just as before, we use the constant terms as elements of our final fixed effects estimator $\boldsymbol{\beta}$.

$$y_{it} = \alpha + \lambda(t) + \boldsymbol{X}_{it}\tilde{\boldsymbol{\beta}}_0 + \boldsymbol{A}_i(t)\tilde{\boldsymbol{Y}} + \varepsilon_{it} \quad \ldots (9)$$

Note that the very process of differencing leads us to get observation pairs (l, $\tilde{\beta}_k^l$) in a way that the sample sizes diminish as l increases. Thus, it is recommended that we use Generalised Least Squares (GLS) to address the possible issue of heteroskedasticity to estimate (8) above. Another test to ascertain if fixed effects are indeed fixed is to simply test for significance of the GLS regression coefficients of (8). For example, if even one of $\tilde{\beta}_{k1}$, $\tilde{\beta}_{k2}$, or $\tilde{\beta}_{k3}$, is significant, we could rest assured that what we believed to be fixed in (1) was actually varying with time.

A TEST FOR DISCRETE CHANGES IN UNOBSERVABLES

A possible concern with the fixed effects estimator above may be the possibility that there may have been a discrete change in our unobserved fixed-effects somewhere within the time period under consideration (polynomials are too gradual and well-behaved). For example, suppose we want to estimate the effects of some known factors on sports performances of local athletes over time, and that a few of them start using steroids somewhere in between – obviously without disclosing this to us.[1] Controlling for other (observed) factors, there will be a significant jump in our dependent variable (some measure of performance). Although, we will immediately observe discrete jumps in some individuals' performances, we will never know what caused it. In order to account for the same, I propose an alternative specification in stage two (stage one remains exactly the same) instead of the one represented by (8). Formally, let us assume that such a discrete change in the unobservable variable happens at time t^* then it must be true that

$$A_i(t) - A_i(t-l) \neq 0\ ;\ \forall\, l > t^*$$

$$A_i(t) - A_i(t-l) \cong 0\ ;\ \forall\, l\, t^*, \text{ provided that } T < 2t^* \text{ and } t \neq t^*$$

Instead of a polynomial specification in the lags (which we call $B(l)$,which, in our case is a polynomial of degree three, specified by (8) – we retain the constant separately), I propose Padé's rational specification $P(l)$,to exploit the asymptotic properties that mimic discrete changes. Formally, we compare the root mean square errors (RMSEs) of the two models

$$\tilde{\beta}_k^l = \tilde{\beta}_{k0} + B(l) + \varepsilon_l$$

and

$$\tilde{\beta}_k^l = \tilde{\beta}_{k0} + P(l) + \varepsilon_l$$

and pick the model with the (significantly) lower RMSE. For instance, a significant fall in the RMSE from a polynomial specification to a Padé's specification, should ideally effectively detect a discrete change in our unobserved effects.

5 Let us just assume, for convenience, that they do not get caught.

CONCLUDING REMARKS ON APPLICATIONS

When there is tremendous business investment in sports activities, there is an implicit pressure on sportspeople to perform well. Many succumb to the same in a negative manner by (say) resorting to drugs. In the light of the example discussed in the previous section, we could think of a (unobserved) dummy variable '*Steroid-Intake*' to be included in our $A_i(t)$ vector. Clearly, if in a group of sportspeople, some measure of performance (say number of goals for a footballer, number of runs for a cricket batsman etc.) is recorded over several time periods, and if some performers in this group start taking drugs sometime during the time period under observation, then this may be interpreted as the variable *Steroid-Intake* switching from zero to unity (for some individuals) – our unobserved effects are not fixed. What is worse? The effect of steroid intake on performance measures interacts with observables (for example, steroids may have stronger effects with women than men, or may have different reactions for tall and short people), and thus, are observables get correlated with unobservables absorbed in the errors. The econometric detection of such forms of conduct on the part of sportspersons simply amounts to the testing of the significance of regression coefficients in (8) as discussed in Section 3. Fraudulent activities in business leading to financial scams could also now be econometrically detected with such an algorithm which involves considering ones personal wealth as the outcome variable measured overtime.

It is interesting that we can consistently arrive at fixed effects estimates even without making any assumption on the functional form of $A_i(t)$. This paper seeks to eradicate the effects of endogeneity stemming from all possible sources to kill potential biases caused due to the often wrong assumption that all unobservables are fixed across time. In the first stage, we worked out fixed-effects estimators that accounted for evolving trends in y_{it} through $\lambda\ (t)$ itself. Thus, after the first stage, the only potential biases that remain in our parameter estimates will be due to potential nonzero covariances between X and A conditional on the number of lags we choose to difference over – this is what I seek to eliminate in stage two.

I must point out that a few known problems of fixed-effects estimators still remain. To put it in the words of Angrist and Pischke (2008), "Although they control for a certain type of omitted variable, fixed-effects estimates are notoriously susceptible to attenuation bias from measurement error. On one hand, economic variables …tend to be persistent …On the other hand,measurement error often changes from year-to-year. Therefore, while union status may be misreported or miscodedfor only a few workers in any single year, the observed year-to-year changes in union status may be mostlynoise. In other words, there is more measurement error in the regressors … than in the levels of the regressors. This fact may account for smaller fixed-effects estimates. A variant on the measurement-error problem arises from that fact that the differencing and deviations-from-means estimators used to control for fixed effects typically remove both good and bad variation. Inother words, these transformations may kill some of the omitted-variables-bias bathwater, but they alsoremove much of the useful information in the baby - the variable of interest."

REFERENCES

[1] Angrist, J. and J. Pischke (2009), Mostly harmless econometrics: An empiricist's companion, Princeton University Press, New Jersey.

[2] Balestra, P. and J. Krishnakumar (2008), Fixed effects models and fixed coefficients models, in: L. Mátyás and P. Sevestre (eds.), The econometrics of panel data, Springer, Netherlands.

[3] Baltagi, B.H. (2001), Econometric analysis of panel data, Wiley, West Sussex, UK.

[4] Baltagi, B.H. and Q. Li (1991), A joint test for serial correlation and random individual effects, Statistics and Probability Letters, 11, 277-280.

[5] Blundell, R. and S. Bond (1998), Initial conditions and moment restrictions in dynamic panel data models, Journal of Econometrics, 87, 115–143.

[6] Cameron, A.C. and P.K. Trivedi (2005), Microeconometrics, methods and applications, Cambridge University Press, New York.

[7] Chamberlain, G. (1984), Panel data, in: Z. Griliches and M.D. Intriligator (eds.), Handbook of econometrics, Elsevier, Amsterdam, North Holland.

[8] Hausman, J.A. (1978), Specification tests in econometrics, Econometrica, 46 (6), 1251—1271.

[9] Orne, C.D. and T. Yamagata (2006), The asymptotic distribution of the F-test statistic for individual effects, Econometrics Journal, 9, 404-422.

[10] Wooldridge, J. (2005), Fixed-effects and related estimators for correlated random-coefficient and treatment-effect panel data models, Review of Economics and Statistics, 87, 385-390.

[11] Wooldridge, J. (2010), Econometric analysis of cross section and panel data, MIT Press, Massachusetts.

Steganography: An Approach for Invisible Communication

Nidhi Gupta, Rashmi Upadhyay and Thirunavukkarasu K.

Department of Computer Science and Engineering, Galgotias University, Greater Noida

ABSTRACT

Steganography, camouflages the secret information to conceal its presence from unauthenticated users.Many different carrier file formats can be used, but digital images are the mostpopular because of their frequency on the Internet.For hiding secret information in images, there exists alarge variety of steganographic techniques some are more complex than others and all of them have respective strong and weak points.The purpose of this paper is to discuss on this technology bydescribing various concepts of steganography, and a look at some of the steganographic techniques, how digital images can be used as a carrier to hide messages using these techniques.

INTRODUCTION

The word steganography comes from the Greek word *Steganos*, which mean covered or secret and *graphy*means writing or drawing. Therefore, steganography means, literally, covered writing. Steganography is the art and science of hiding information such that its presence cannot be detected [1] and a communication is happening [2, 6]. Secret information is encoded in a manner such that the very existence of the information is concealed.Paired with existing communication methods, steganography can be used to carry out hidden exchanges.The main goal of steganography is to communicate securely in a completely undetectable manner [3] and to avoid drawing suspicion to the transmission of a hidden data [4]. It is not to keep others from knowing the hidden information, but it is to keep others from thinking that the information even exists.The main goal or steganography is to communicate securely in a completely undetectable manner and to avoid drawing suspicion to the transmission of a hidden data [5]. During the process, characteristics of these methods are to change in the structure and features so as not toimages, videos, sound files, and other computer files that contain perceptually irrelevant or redundant information can be used as "covers" or carriers to hide secret messages[19]. After embedding a secret message into the cover-image, a so-called stego-image is obtained. The basic model of steganography consists of Carrier, Message, Embedding algorithm and Stego key. The model for steganography is shown in Figure 1. Carrier is also known as a cover-object, which embeds the message and serves to hide its presence.

Steganography_medium=hidden_message +carrier+stego_key

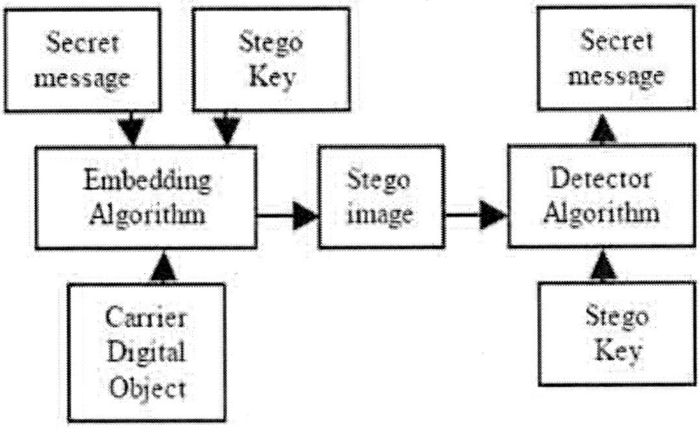

Fig. 1. Basic Model of Stegnography

Information hiding is an emerging research area, which encompasses applications such as copyright protection for digital media, watermarking, fingerprinting, and steganography [7]. All these applications of information hiding are quite diverse [7].

In watermarking all of the instances of an object are "marked" in the same way. The kind of informationhidden in objects when using watermarking is usually a signature to signify origin or ownership for the purposeof copyright protection [10]. With fingerprinting on the other hand, different, unique marks are embedded indistinct copies of the carrier object that are supplied to different customers. This enables the intellectual propertyowner to identify customers who break their licensing agreement by supplying the property to third parties [9].

In watermarking and fingerprinting the fact that information is hidden inside the files may be public knowledgesometimes it may even be visible – while in steganography the imperceptibility of the information is crucial[8]. A successful attack on a steganographic system consists of an adversary observing that there is informationhidden inside a file, while a successful attack on a watermarking or fingerprinting system would not be to detectthe mark, but to remove it [9].

In those applications, information is hidden within a host data set and is to be reliably communicated to a receiver. The host data set is purposely corrupted, but in a covert way, designed to be invisible to an informal analysis. However, this paper will only focus on information hiding using image steganography approach.

BACKGROUND AND SCOPE

Security is the important issue in communication from last decades. It is believed that steganography was first practiced during the Golden Age in Greece. An ancient Greek record describes the practice of melting wax off wax tablets used for writing messages and then inscribing a message in the underlying wood. The wax was then reapplied to the wood, giving the appearance of a new, unused tablet. The resulting tablets could be innocently transported without anyone suspecting the presence of a message beneath the wax[4].

Another common form of invisible writing is through the use of Invisible inks[20]. Such inks were used with much success as recently as WW-II. An innocent letter may contain a very different message written between the lines. Early in WW-II steganographic technology consisted almost exclusively of invisible inks. Common sources forinvisible inks are milk, vinegar, fruit juices and urine. All of these darken when heated.

The scope of the project as follow:

- Overview of steganographyand various concepts for hiding information in image files.
- Different approaches being explored which are least significant bit, masking and filtering and modern steganographic techniques.

OVERVIEW OF STEGANOGRAPHY

To provide an overview of steganography, terms and concepts should first be explained. An overview of thedifferent kinds of steganography is given at a later stage.

Steganography Concepts

Although steganography is an ancient subject, the modern formulation of it is often given in terms of the*prisoner's problem* proposed by Simmons [11], where two inmates wish to communicate in secret to hatch anescape plan. All of their communication passes through a warden who will throw them in solitary confinement should she suspect any covert communication [12].The warden, who is free to examine all communication exchanged between the inmates, can either be passive oractive. A *passive* warden simply examines the communication to try and determine if it potentially containssecret information. If she suspects a communication to contain hidden information, a passive warden takes noteof the detected covert communication, reports this to some outside party and lets the message through withoutblocking it. An *active* warden, on the other hand, will try to alter the communication with the suspected hiddeninformation deliberately, in order to remove the information [9].

Different Kinds of Steganography

Almost all digital file formats can be used for steganography, but the formats that are more suitable are thosewith a high degree of redundancy. Redundancy can be defined as the bits of an object that provide accuracy fargreater than necessary for the object's use and display [13]. The redundant bits of an object are those bits thatcan be altered without the alteration being detected easily [9]. Image and audio files especially uncovered other file formats that can be used for information hiding.

Figure 2 Shows the four main Categories of file formats that can be used for steganography.

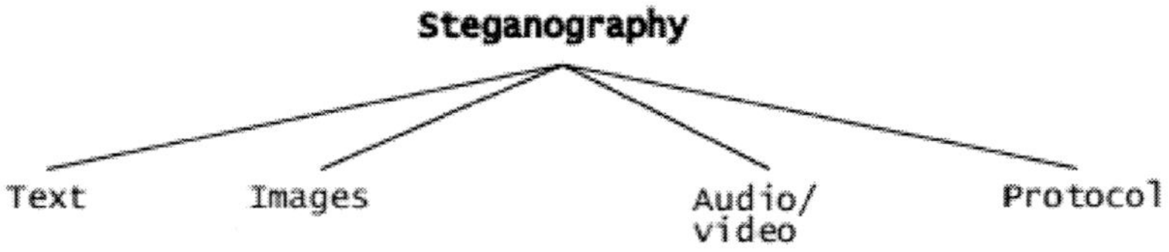

Fig. 2. Categories of Steganography

Hiding information in text is historically the most important method of steganography. An obvious method wasto hide a secret message in every *nth* letter of every word of a text message. It is only since the beginning of theInternet and all the different digital file formats that is has decreased in importance [14]. Text steganographyusing digital files is not used very often since text files have a very small amount of redundant data.Given the proliferation of digital images, especially on the Internet, and given the large amount of redundant bitspresent in the digital representation of an image, images are the most popular cover objects for steganography.This paper will focus on hiding information in images in the next sections.

To hide information in audio files similar techniques are used as for image files. One different technique uniqueto audio steganography is masking, which exploits the properties of the human ear to hide informationunnoticeably. A faint, but audible, sound becomes inaudible in the presence of another louder audible sound [14].This property creates a channel in which to hide information. Although nearly equal to images in steganographicpotential, the larger size of meaningful audio files makes them less popular to use than images [15].The term protocol steganography refers to the technique of embedding information within messages and networkcontrol protocols used in network transmission [17]. In the layers of the OSI network model there exist covertchannels where steganography can be used [16]. An example of where information can be hidden is in theheader of a TCP/IP packet in some fields that are either optional or are never used. A paper by Ahsan andKundur provides more information on this [17].

Steganograpy Approaches

The steganography approaches can be divided into three types [18]:

Pure Steganography: This technique simply uses the steganography approach only without combining other methods. It is working on hiding information within cover carrier.

Secret Key Steganography: The secret key steganography use the combination of the secret key cryptography technique and the steganography approach.The idea of this type is to encrypt the secret message or data by secret key approach and to hide the encrypted data within cover carrier.

Public Key Steganography: The last type of steganography is to combine the public key cryptography approach and the steganography approach. The idea of this type is to encrypt the secret data using the public key approach and then hide the encrypted data within cover carrier.

STEGANOGRAPHY AND CRYPTOGRAPHY

Comparison of Steganography and Cryptography

Steganography is a technique of hiding information in digital media. In contrast to cryptography, it is not to keep others from knowing the hidden information but it is to keep others from thinking that the information even exists.Cryptography and steganography achieve separate goals. Cryptography concealsonly the meaning or contents of a secret message from an eavesdropper. However,steganography conceals even the existence of the message.Furthermore, steganography provides more confidentiality and informationsecurity than cryptography since it conceals the mere existence of secret messagerather than only protecting the message contents. Therefore, one of the majorweaknesses of cryptosystems is that even though the message has been encrypted,it still exists.

Combination of Steganography and Cryptography

In some situations, sending an encrypted message will acrosssuspicion while an invisible message will not do so. Both methodscan be combined to produce better protection of the message. In case,when the steganography fails and the message can be detected, it isstill of no use as it is encrypted using cryptography techniques.Since steganography adds an extra layer of protection to cryptography, combiningsteganography and encryption gives the ultimate in private communication.Therefore, the purpose of steganography is to complement cryptography and toavoid raising the suspicion of system attackers but not to replace cryptography.

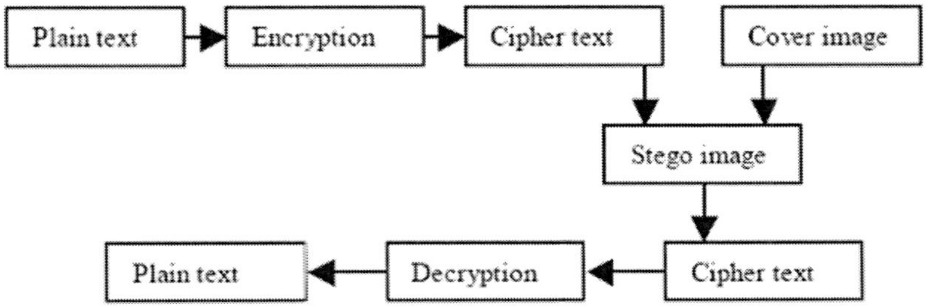

Fig. 3. Combination of Cryptography and Steganography

In figure 3, both the methods are combined by encrypting message using cryptography and then hiding the encrypted message using steganography. The resulting stego-image can be transmitted without revealing that secret information is being exchanged. Furthermore, even if an attacker were to defeat the steganographic technique to detect the message from the stego-object, he would still require the cryptographic decoding key to decipher the encrypted message.

IMAGE STEGANOGRAPHY

People often transmit digital images over E-mail and other Internet communication.For sending files of enormous size, a number of compression schemes have been developed over time, notably Bitmap (BMP), Graphic Interchange Format (GIF), and Joint Photographic Experts Group (JPEG) file types. Not all are equally suited to steganography. However, GIF and 8-bit BMP files employ what is known as lossless compression, a scheme that allows the software to exactly reconstruct the original image. JPEG, on the other hand, uses lossy compression, which means that the expanded image is very nearly the same as the original but not an exact duplicate. While both methods allow computers to save storage space, lossless compression is much better suited to applications where the integrity of the original information must be maintained, such as steganography. While JPEG can be used for stego applications, it is more common to embed data in GIF or BMP files.

JPEG format seems more interesting because the system operate in a transform space and are not affected by visual attacks (visual attacks means that you can see steganographic messages on the low bit planes often images because they overwrite visual structures this usually happen in BMP images).

Concealment in Digital Images

Information can be hidden many different ways inimages. To hide information, straight message insertionmay encode every bit of information in the imageor selectively embed the message in "noisy" areas thatdraw less attention—those areas where there is a greatdeal of natural color variation. The message may alsobe scattered randomly throughout the image.Redundant pattern encoding "wallpapers" the coverimage with the message. A number of ways exist to hide information in digitalimages. Common approaches include

- Least significant bit insertion, and
- Masking and filtering

Each of these techniques can be applied, with varyingdegrees of success, to different image files.

Least Significant Bit Insertion

First we will investigate least significant bit insertion, where youliterally put the information in the least significant bits of an image. This is one of the most commontechniques used today in steganography where you pack the hidden messages into insignificant bits in image data. This is a simple technique but the down side is that the message is very susceptible toinformation loss when using lossy compression techniques. A 1,024 by 768 image has the potential tohide a total of 2,359,296 bits (294,912 bytes) of information. If you compress the message to be hidden before you embed it, you can hide a large amount of information. To the human eye, the resultingstego-image will look identical to the cover image.LSB insertion requires on average that only half the bits in an image bechanged. For example since the 8-bit letter A only requires eight bytes to hide it in, the ninth byte of the three pixels can be used to hide the next character of the hidden message. Here is the original raster data:

(00100111 11101001 11001000)

(00100111 11001000 11101001)

(11001000 00100111 11101001)

The binary value of A is 10000011 and encoding A into the last bits of this 3 pixel sequence willchange the above sequence to:

(00100111 11101000 11001000)

(00100110 11001000 11101000)

(11001000 00100111 11101001).

Notice that only the underlined bits had to be changed in order to createthe A. A slight variation of this technique allows for embedding the message in two or more of theleast significant bits per byte. This increases the hidden information capacity of the cover-object, butthe cover-object degrades more statistically, and it is more detectable.For example, using LSB (Least Significant Bit) technique, in the imagein Figure 4 (Saint Olga planting Christianity in Russia symbolized as a tree) on the left below each pixel is encoded in 24 bits, 8 each for the red, green, and blue intensity of that pixel. In the image onthe right the least significant bit for each color of some number of pixels was used to encode a hidden message which is the Gospel of Judas in its English translation by Kasser, Meyer, and Wurst. Theoriginal image size was 500 × 320 pixels, giving 961,000 bits or about 120,000 bytes for a hiddenmessage and quite more than enough for the short difference between the full 24-bit color of the image on the left from the slightly modified imageon the right.

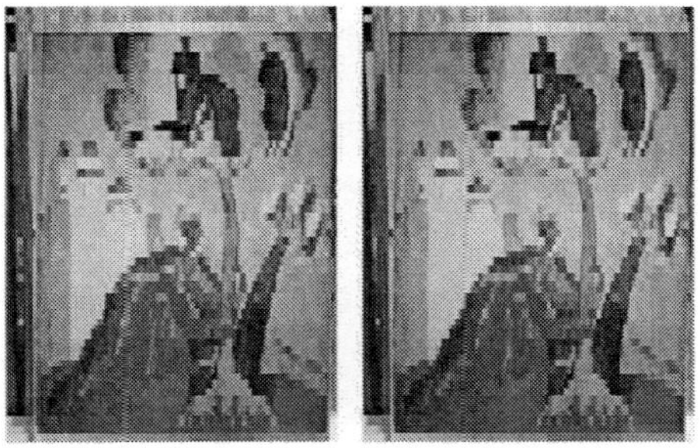

Fig. 4. A Message is Embedded in the Right Image using LSB Technique in Steganography

Steganography software processes LSB insertion to make the hiddeninformation less detectable. For example, the EzStego tool arranges the palette to reduce the occurrenceof adjacent index colors that contrast too much—before it inserts the message. This approach worksquite well in gray-scale images and in images with related colors.S-Tools, another steganography tool,takes a different approach by closely approximating the cover image,which may mean radical palettechanges. As with 24-bit images, hanging the pixels' LSB may create new colors. (New colors may not be added to an 8-bit image due to the palette limit.) Instead, S-Tools reduce the number of colorswhile maintaining the image quality, so that the LSB changes do not drastically change color values.For example, eight color values are required for each color if values 000through 111 are to be stored. Reducing the number of unique colors to 32 ensures that these values canbe used and that the number of colors will not exceed 256 (256/8 = 32). Each of the 32 unique colors inthe palette may be expanded to eight colors having LSB values of the red, green, blue (RGB) triplesranging from 000 to 111. This results in multiple colors in the palette that look the same visually butthat may vary by one bit.

Some of the advantages of this technique of least significant bit insertion aregiven below:

- Major advantage of LSB algorithm is that it's quick and easy.
- LSB insertion also works well with grey scale images.

On the average only half of the bits would have to be changed in an LSBencoding scheme.With such small variation in the colors it would be verydifficult for the human eye to discern the difference.

Implementing LSB

Steganography software processes LSB insertion to make the hidden information less detectable. For example, EzStego tool arranges the palette to reduce the occurrence of adjacent index colors that contrast too much—before it inserts the message. This approach works quite well in grayscale images and may work well in images with related colors. S-Tools, another steganography tool, takes a different approach by closely approximating the cover image, which may mean radical palette changes. As with 24-bit images, changing the pixels' LSB may create new colors. (New colors may not be added to an 8-bit image due to the palette limit.) Instead, S-Tools reduce the number of colors while maintaining the image quality, so that the LSB changes do not drastically change color values. For example, eight color values are required for each color if values 000 through 111 are to be stored. Reducing the number of unique colors to 32 ensures that these values can be used and that the number of colors will not exceed 256 (256/8 = 32). Each of the 32 unique colors in the palette may be expanded to eight colors having LSB values of the red, green, blue (RGB) triples ranging from 000 to 111. This results in multiple colors in the palette that look the same visually but that may vary by one bit.5 These tools take a similar approach with gray-scale images. However, the resulting stego-images as applied with S-Tools are no longer gray-scale. Instead of simply going with adjacent colors as EzStego does, S-Tools manipulate the palette to produce colors that have a difference of one bit. For example, in a normal gray-scale image, white will move to black with the following RGB triples

(255 255 255), (254 254 254), ...,

(1 1 1), (0 0 0)

After processing with S-Tools, the value for white will be spread over a range of up to eight colors such as

(255 255 255), (255 255 254), and

Visually, the stego-image may look the same as the gray-scale cover image, but it has actually become an 8-bit color image.

Masking and Filtering

Masking and filtering techniques are mostly used on 24 bit and greyscaleimages. They hide information in a way similar to watermarks on actual paper and are sometimes used asdigital watermarks. Masking images entails changing the luminance of the masked area. The smaller the luminance change, the less of a chance it can be detected. Observe that luminance in figure.5 is at15% in the mask region if it was decreased then it would nearly be invisible.

Fig. 5. Masking

Because watermarking techniques are more integrated into the image,they may be applied without fear of image destruction from lossy compression. By covering, or masking a faint but perceptible signal with another to make the first non-perceptible, we exploit thefact that the human visual system cannot detect slight changes in certain temporal domains of theimage.Technically, watermarking is not a steganographic form. Strictly,steganography conceals data in the image; watermarking extends the image information and becomesan attribute of the cover image, providing license, ownership or copyright details. Masking techniquesare more suitable for use in lossy JPEG images than LSB insertion because of their relative immunityto image operations such as compression cropping.Stego-images (images that have been manipulated by steganographicmethods) that are masked will keep a higher fidelity than LSB through compression, cropping and some image processing. The reason that a stego image encoded with masking, degrades less under JPEG compression is that the secret message is hid in the significant areas of the picture. There is a toolcalled JPEG – J steg that takes advantage of the compression of JPEG while trying to keep a highmessage fidelity. The program takes a secret message and a lossless cover image as input and outputs astego image in JPEG format.

MODERN STEGANOGRAPHIC TECHNIQUES

- *Thumbnail steganography:* It is a new type of steganography designed to increase the complexity required when attempting to automate steganography detection. It requires the original image (jpg, gif, etc) as well as the thumbnail to extract the file from the thumbnail.
- Embedded pictures in video material (optionally played at slower or faster speed).
- *Blog steganography:* Messages are fractionalyzed and the (encrypted) pieces are added as comments of orphaned web-logs (or pin boards on social network platforms). In this case the selection of blogs is the symmetric key that sender and recipient are using. The carrier of the hidden message is the whole blogosphere.
- A new steganographic technique involves injecting imperceptible delays to packets sent over the network from the keyboard. Delays in key presses in some applications can mean a delay in packets, and the delays in the packets can be used to encode data.

CONCLUSION AND FUTURE SCOPE

Steganography become more important as more people join the cyberspace revolution. Steganography is the art of concealing information in ways that prevent the detection of hidden messages. Steganography include an array of secret communication methods that hide the message from being seen or discovered. We pointed out the enhancement of the image steganographic system using JPEG approach to provide a means of secure communication. A *stego-key* has been applied to the system during embedment of the message into the cover-image.

Although steganography is applicable to all data objects that contain redundancy, but JPEG images are best because people often transmit digital picture over E-mail and other Internet communication. JPEG is one of the most common format for images. Moreover, steganographic system for JPEG format seems more interesting because the system operates in a transform space and is not affected by visual attacks.

In the near future, the most important use of steganographic techniques will probably be lying in the field of digital watermarking. Content providers are eager to protect their copyrighted works against illegal distribution and digital watermarks provide a way of tracking the owners of these materials. Steganography might also become limited under laws, since governments already claimed that criminals use these techniques to communicate.

REFERENCES

[1] H. T. Sencar, M. Ramkumar and A.N. Akansu, "Data Hiding Fundamentals and Applications": Content Security in Digital Multimedia. Elsevier-Academic Press, 2004.

[2] N.F. Johnson, S. Jajodia, "Staganalysis: The Investigation of Hiding Information", IEEE, pp. 113-116, 2004.

[3] N.F. Johnson & S. Jajodia, "Steganalysis of Images Created Using Current Steganography Software", in Proceeding for the Second Information Hiding Workshop, Portland Oregon, USA, April 1998, pp. 273-289.

[4] N.F. Johnson and S. Jajodia. (1998, Feb.). "Exploring steganography: seeing the unseen." IEEE Computer Journal.[On line]. 31(2), pp. 26-34. Available:http://www.jjtc.com/pub/r2026.pdf [Jun. 2011].

[5] F.A.P Peticolas, R.J. Anderson and M.G. Kuhn, "Information Hiding – A Survey", in proceeding of IEEE, pp. 1062-1078, July 2009.

[6] R.Popa,"An Analysis of Steganographic System", The "Politehnica" University of Timisoara, Faculty ofAutomatics and Computers, Department of Computer Science and Software Engineering, May 25, 2008.

[7] R A Isbell, "Steganography: Hidden Menace or Hidden Saviour", Steganography White Paper, 10 May 2002.

[8] H. Wang and S. Wang.(2004, Oct.). "Cyber Warfare: steganography vs. steganalysis." Communications of the ACM. [On line]. 47(10), pp. 76-82. Available: www.csc.liv.ac.uk/~leszek/COMP526/week4/comp526-3.pdf [Mar., 2011].

[9] I.J. Cox, M.L. Bloom, J.A. Fridrich, and T. Kalkert.Digital watermarking and steganography.USA: Morgan Kaufman Publishers, 2008, pp. 1-591.

[10] Marvel, L.M., Boncelet Jr., C.G. &Retter, C., "Spread Spectrum Steganography", IEEE Transactions on image processing, 8:08, 2009.

[11] Simmons, G., "The prisoners problem and the subliminal channel", CRYPTO, 1983.

[12] Chandramouli, R., Kharrazi, M. &Memon, N., "Image steganography and steganalysis: Concepts and Practice", Proceedings of the 2 ndInternational Workshop on Digital Watermarking, October 2003.

[13] Currie, D.L. & Irvine, C.E., "Surmounting the effects of lossy compression on Steganography", 19thNational Information Systems Security Conference, 2006.

[14] Moerland, T., "Steganography and Steganalysis", Leiden Institute of Advanced Computing Science,www.liacs.nl/home/ tmoerl/privtech.pdf

[15] Artz, D., "Digital Steganography: Hiding Data within Data", IEEE Internet Computing Journal, June 2001.

[16] Handel, T. & Sandford, M., "Hiding data in the OSI network model", Proceedings of the 1StInternational Workshop on Information Hiding, June 1996.

[17] Ahsan, K. & Kundur, D., "Practical Data hiding in TCP/IP", Proceedings of the Workshop on Multimedia Security at ACM Multimedia, 2002.

[18] B BZaidan, A.A Zaidan, A.K. Al-Frajat and H.A. Jalab, "On the Differences between Hiding Information and Cryptography Techniques: An Overview", Journal of Applied Sciences 10(15): 1650-1655, 2010.

[19] N. Provos and P. Honeyman. (2003, Jun.). "Hide and seek: An introduction tosteganography." IEEE Security and Privacy Journal. [On line], 1(3), pp. 32-44. Available: http://niels.xtdnet.nl/papers/practical.pdf [Jul., 2011].

To Be or Not to Be: Challenges and PLanning for Embracing Cloud Computing

Sanjiva Shankar Dubey

Asia Pacific Executive IBM Service Delivery, Internal IT (CIO)

ABSTRACT

Planning and implementation of cloud computing model is a serious activity that requires careful considerations. Unlike other computing models where the failure would at best mean delayed accrual of benefits, in this case the failure may also mean losing out vital competitive data and exposing the organization to serious risk. According to a KPMG study[2] 81% of businesses are either planning their initial forays, are in early or advanced stages of experimentation or have full implementations. However, Cloud adoption is fraught with business and operational challenges surrounding technology, security, total cost of ownership, and the intersection with business strategy and operations.

In this paper we will present various stages of cloud implementation planning and precautions to be taken while going ahead with cloud computing model. This paper describes a practice oriented approach that mitigates the risk of adopting this highly promising technology.

INTRODUCTION

According to a KPMG study[3] 81% of businesses are either planning their initial forays, are in early or advanced stages of experimentation or have full implementations. However, Cloud adoption is fraught with business and operational challenges surrounding technology, security, total cost of ownership, and the intersection with business strategy and operations. Planning

---

[2] http://www.kpmg.com/Global/en/IssuesAndInsights/ArticlesPublications/Documents/cloud-clarity.pdf accessed 11112012 Titled Clarity in the Cloud -A global study of the business adoption of Cloud kpmg.com

[3] http://www.kpmg.com/Global/en/IssuesAndInsights/ArticlesPublications/Documents/cloud-clarity.pdf accessed 11112012 Titled Clarity in the Cloud -A global study of the business adoption of Cloud kpmg.com

and implementation of cloud computing model is a serious activity that requires careful considerations. Unlike other computing models where the failure would at best mean delayed accrual of benefits, in this case the failure may also mean losing out vital competitive data and exposing the organization to serious risk. In this paper we will present various stages of cloud implementation planning and precautions to be taken while going ahead with cloud computing model. This paper describes a practice oriented approach that mitigates the risk of adopting this highly promising technology.

WHAT IS CLOUD COMPUTING

Buyya et al.[4] define cloud computing as "*A Cloud is a type of parallel and distributed system consisting of a collection of inter-connected and virtualized computers that are dynamically provisioned and presented as one or more unified computing resources based on service level agreements established through negotiation between the service provider and consumer*". However the most standard definition from US NIST[5] states cloud computing as *"a model for enabling convenient, on-demand network access to a shared pool of configurable computing resources (e.g., networks, servers, storage, applications, and services) that can be rapidly provisioned and released with minimal management effort or service provider interaction"*.

Accordingly Cloud Computing is characterized by the following features:

(a) Computing power is available as needed automatically without having to seek any manual intervention

(b) Use of public (dedicated private) internet infrastructure to access data and other services using standard features through wide variety of devices such as laptop, smart phones, tablets etc.

(c) Computing Resources are not dedicated to one customer but comes from pool that is meant for multiple customers to balance load and make it cost effective through this model.

(d) Location Opaqueness: The end customer is neither informed nor is required to know how the services are being provisioned and from what location.

(e) Pay as you use: the charge out mechanism is the biggest differentiator of Cloud computing with traditional hosting where the customer pays based on usage characterized by number of users, duration, space consumed, etc.) as we do while consuming any utility such as electricity.

---

[4] Rajkumar Buyya, Chee Shin Yeo, and Srikumar Venugopal. 2008. Market Oriented Cloud Computing: Vision, Hype, and Reality for Delivering IT Services as Computing Utilities. In Proceedings of The 10th IEEE International Conference on High Performance Computing and Communication. Pages: 5-13, CS Press.

[5] P. Mell and T. Grance. Definition of cloud computing. Technical report, National Institute of Standard and Technology (NIST), July 2009.

(f) Ability to expand capability at short notice. Another important Cloud computing characterized is its expandability to give more computing power at short notice.

WHY PLAN FOR CLOUD ADOPTION

Contrary to popular belief, cloud adoption is not easy or risk free. Bad planning and poor execution can put the organization back by few years and also exposing it for data security, leakage and associated risks. Zardari and Bhasoon[6] suggest a goal-Oriented Requirements Engineering Approach for cloud adoption that will prevent many risks associated with cloud adoption. They propose the following steps for cloud adoption using a case study as:

- Requirement Elicitation
- Requirement Analysis and Negotiation
- Requirements Evaluation
- Requirements Documentation and Management

In another research[7] the City and County of San Francisco (CCSF) IT management took the approach of defining "people/process/technology/policy" when developing their Cloud Computing strategy. They first took ratification of their "Cloud First" policy followed by cloud certification training for designated IT personnel to re-skill their staff to support the cloud computing model. And finally, selected a technology solution that could offer an onpremise/ off-premise SaaS solution for maximum flexibility. Best practices such as QoS requirements verifications and validation of risk and mitigation plans along with selecting vendor-neutral "cloud middleware" to reduce technical architectural complexity were also suggested.

Another significant work[8] has been done by Oracle corporation who define a Cloud Computing Maturity Model covering sixty capabilities under eight domains that capture the best practices. These domains are Business & Strategy, Architecture, Infrastructure, Information, Projects, Portfolios & Services, Operations, Administration & Management, Organization and Governance.

---

6 Cloud Adoption: A Goal-Oriented Requirements Engineering Approach, Shehnila Zardari ,School of Computer Science University of Birmingham Birmingham B15 2TT, United Kingdom, sxz845@cs.bham.ac.uk and Rami Bahsoon, School of Computer Science University of Birmingham Birmingham B15 2TT, United Kingdom, r.bahsoon@cs.bham.ac.uk, SECLOUD'11, May 22, 2011, Waikiki, Honolulu, HI, USA Copyright 2011 ACM 978-1-4503-0582-2/11/05,

7 http://cloudslg.techamerica.org/wp-content/uploads/2012/02/TAF_SLG_CC_implementing_cloud.pdf accessed 11112012 Implementing the Cloud , The Cloud Imperative: Better Collaboration, Better Service, Better Cost, TechAmerica Foundation I SLG Cloud Commission

8 Cloud Computing Maturity Model – Guiding Success with Cloud Capabilities, An Oracle White Paper, December 2011. http://www.oracle.com/technetwork/topics/entarch/oracle-wp-cloud-maturity-model-r3-0-1434934.pdf accessed 11112012

However, upon close examination it is realised that all these approaches lack simplicity and comprehensiveness without giving end to end perspective and may not cover all the challenges that are required to manage the risk of cloud adoption.

STAGES OF CLOUD ADOPTION

According to an IBM study[9], cloud computing is a cost efficient model for service provisioning. However, it would be in the interest of enterprise to take a measured approach for cloud adoption. An individuals and small enterprise may adopt a trail and error approach to try out any cloud based services such as SaaS without much investigations but the same may not work for large enterprises to choose, public cloud model without making several considerations. Author with series of cloud adoption project over last few years while working with IBM projects and its clients projects has arrives a simple model which contains the following stages

- **Start with Business need**: In this step establish business justification and goals for adopting cloud computing covering priorities such as cost savings, scalability, flexibility etc and are prepared for , reliability, availability, security, control.
- **Enable organization preparation through technology Virtualization**: enterprise must understand and deploy virtualization technology at their own premises to understand how multi tenancy works in cloud environment. This will help them to understand the sue of Public cloud platform and prevent from making large risky investment of money, time and efforts.
- **Conduct thorough assessment:** Enterprise must make business justification for public, private and hybrid cloud models and develop enterprise integration and migration strategy towards cloud provisioning covering
  - (a) **Business needs by** identifying advantages disadvantages, possible risks and opportunities to define strategy for adopting cloud.
  - (b) **Target Cloud environment:** deciding cloud type and delivery model amongst private, public and hybrid and ISSS, PaaS and SaaS.
  - (c) **Security and control issues:** by evaluating Security and Regulatory concerns and how these will be met in cloud alternatives.
- **Experiment and create reference architecture**: enterprise must experiment with few options to build confidence in cloud adoption. Enterprise also should do Solutions planning, budget the investment required and then acquire cloud capabilities. A reference architecture of its cloud adoption which must co-exist with the on-premises applications and how these together will provide necessary service to the end users of IT is also needed.

---

9 IBM, "IBM Perspective on Cloud Computing", Whitepaper Published on the Web, ftp://ftp.software.ibm.com/software/tivoli/brochures/IBM_Perspective_on_Cloud_Computing.pdf , accessed 11112012

- **Monitor:** having achieved success with experimental cloud adoption and created a cloud adoption roadmap and architecture, Enterprise must monitor the service levels and create a governance mechanism to ensure that the requisite parameters are maintained. This will help arrive at the true business benefits from cloud solutions.
- **Exploit and Scale** through broad based deployment, manual provisioning and load balancing.
- **Finally Reach Dynamic Cloud environment** where the end users will be able to self provision and the service provider will be able to do automatic scaling and load balancing.

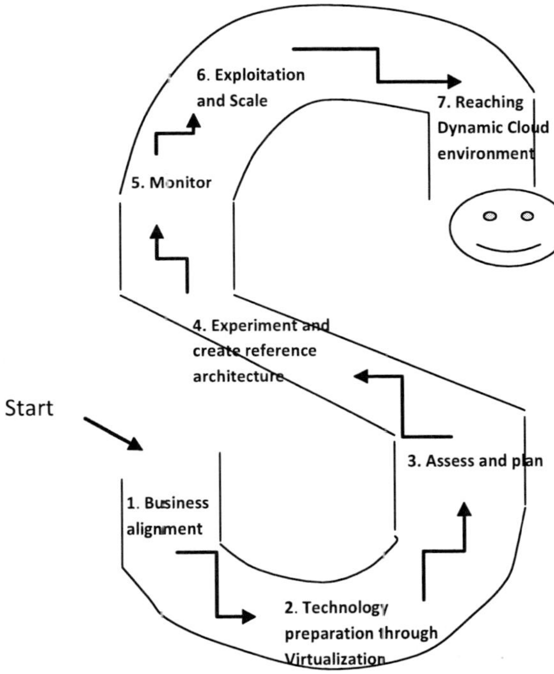

Fig. 1. Shows Various Stages of Adoption on the S-curve[10]

ISSUES TO BE CONSIDERED WHILE ADOPTING CLOUD MODEL

Before adopting cloud models of any type , IaaS, PaaS or SaaS, one must think about the possible questions:

1. *Data migration and management issues:* covering what enterprise data is suitable for Cloud migrations? Enterprise must think about what data to be migrated to the cloud

[10] Cloud Computing and Beyond By: Sanjiva Shankar Dubey Publisher: I K International Publishing House; First Edition edition (May 23, 2012)

environment what are not going to impact its risk profile. In addition the enterprise must ascertain other features for ensuring data security and control.

2. *Application issues:* What applications should be run from cloud environment? Since Cloud has too many elements in the delivery chain and not all can be said to be fully "fool-proofed' from security and vulnerability point of view, an enterprise must choose Cloud environments that provide secured application development set ups. However, highly confidential or private systems must not operate in cloud environment.
3. *Operational issues:* how will the continuity and reliability issues of the cloud environment will be addressed? It can be addressed through proper service level agreements (SLAs) and some through the penalty clauses in the event the services are not available. Performance parameters such as response time for interactive user applications and bulk data transfer rate must be sought, audited and benchmarked on regular basis
4. *Security, control and privacy issues:* What are the security and privacy challenges for the cloud environment and what is the best model to choose from? This is by far the most critical considerations for the cloud computing implementation which demands that enough security and control features are adopted by the cloud service provider and also is able to demonstrate its adherence.
5. *When Cloud Vendor fails to deliver:* In the cloud market place there is lot of hype and several players are coming up with rock bottom price and seductive features. There are multiple providers and they are also offering standardizations as well as security features such as encryption, firewalls and VLANs to instil confidence . However one should be aware of the challenges of data lock-in, availability, Data Condentiality and Auditability. Issues of service provider getting bankrupt[11], or getting into legal hassle has come to light in recent times.
6. *Is cloud a panacea of all IT Cost?:* Like any business proposition cloud computing also requires a through comparison of economics well before adopting the Cloud model. The cost of hosting may be low but it also brings in cost of network access and other associated cost such a lost productivity due to slow network response or long time required to down load or upload data. Dubey[12] defines an equation that may help to understand the economics of cloud adoption (Per user Cloud Cost * Number of users * user hours * network cost) + one time cost of data transportation and other cost such as training < Data centre cost.

---

[11] Coghead Failure Highlights Risks Of Cloud Computing http://www.informationweek.com/news/services/saas/214600083

[12] Cloud Computing and Beyond By: Sanjiva Shankar Dubey Publisher: I K International Publishing House; First Edition edition (May 23, 2012).

7. *Beware if you are a growing organisation:* For a SME using occasional Cloud based services and managing unpredictability may be fine but for a continuously growing enterprise will lead to ballooning cost involving large data transfer and growing user population, usage charges. Unless the cloud provider services provisioning are fast enough to beat competitive situations the cloud based system may put a drag on your growth aspirations. Cloud many also give Performance bottle neck issues and no one agency answerable when it arises due to several players involved. You may also have to redesign application for cloud readiness as not all applications would be ready for moving to cloud platform. For good success cloud application should be able to run on standard hardware, OS and associated middle ware and they should not violating and data protection, regulatory and legal considerations.
8. *Back out strategy:* All these considerations require that the organization must have a back out strategy in case it decides to withdraw its applications either by desire or due to forced events. Proper technical as well as administrative governance practices must be in place to implement the back out plan and bring the application back on n premises data centre.
9. *Conclusions:* It may be noted that planning and implementation of cloud computing model is a serious activity that requires careful considerations. Hence a careful crafted approach that mitigates the risk is needed for adopting this technology. While there have been several attempt to address this problems a comprehensive approach covering various stages of cloud adoption should be adopted. While doing the cloud adoption considerations such as:
   - Data migration and management issues
   - Application issues
   - Operational issues
   - Security, control and privacy , should be considered.

Care should be taken for the eventualities of vendor failure and if the organization requirement is likely to grow in future. A suitable back out strategy must be in place.

REFERENCES

[1] CIO Council, "Proposed Security Assessment and Authorization for U.S. Government Cloud Computing, Draft version 0.96, Nov. 2010. Online: *www.FedRAMP.gov*.

[2] Micheal Armburst, Armando Fox, Rean Griffith, Anthony D. Joseph, Randy Katz, Andy Konwinski, Gunho Lee, David Patterson, Ariel Rabkin, Ion Stoica, and Matei Zaharia. 2010. A View of Cloud Computing. In *Communications of ACM.* Volume 53, No. 4, Pages: 50-58.

[3} David Oppenheimer, Archana Ganapathi, and David A. Patterson, "Why do Internet services fail, and what can be done about it?" Proceedings of the 4th Usenix Symposium on Internet Technologies and Systems, 2003.

[4] Redhat, "RED HAT PaaS: Bringing open choice & application portability to the cloud," 2010, http://www.jboss.com/pdf/RedHatPaaSWhitepaper.pdf

[5} NIST Special Publication 800-146, DRAFT Cloud Computing Synopsis and Recommendations, Recommendations of the National Institute of Standards and Technology *http://csrc.nist.gov/*

[6] Lessons From The Demise Of A Cloud Startup, John Foley, Feb 2009.

[7] Cloud Control, InformationWeek Reports, 2009.

Use of VSAT Technology for Supplemental Education at School Level for Wider Accessibility

Nishal Joseph Thaikattil

Educomp Learning Hour Private Limited

ABSTRACT

Growth of internet over the past decade has lead to an exponential growth in its adoption in the education sector. Internet is being widely used for providing supplemental content for better learning experience. Conducting classes over internet has removed, to a great extent the boundaries of physical distances. Latest online tools like sharing of digital board have tremendously increased interactivity and improved the overall learning experience.

Internet penetration and bandwidth availability is good in metros and tier 1 cities. But these cities already have good options for supplemental educations in form of physical, face-to-face classes and good quality trainers. The real challenge lies in providing internet access in remote / far off areas where connectivity is still a major bottleneck.

VSAT technology provides a feasible alternative to this problem at hand and is being used extensively for executive education and other professional training. Adoption of VSAT technology at school level where the number of learners is larger is a relatively new concept. It poses huge opportunities but the challenges are equal. The education sector is closely watching the developments in the regards with bated breath. The paper aims to delve deeper into the adoption of VSAT for supplemental education among K-12 students – the opportunities, constrains, and other economic aspects of business.

SUPPLEMENTAL EDUCATION IN INDIA

'Supplemental Education' is a relatively new term, which gained ground with the introduction of No Child Left Behind Act of 2001 in USA. NCLB was a reauthorization of The Elementary And Secondary Education Act[1] (ESEA) and one of the provisions of NCLB was to provide supplemental education or additional academic resources to struggling students. These additional academic resources would help the child to be at par with the other students and perform well

[1] US Department of Education Website, http://www.ed.gov/esea

academically. Broadly, it refers to any extra classes a student attends apart from regular school, which help him/her to perform better academics. Mostly it is used for the K-12 Segment (Kindergarten – Class XII).

As a concept, this is not something new for India. Provision of additional academic resources has been prevalent here for a long time, being referred to as 'tuitions' or 'coaching'. This could be to augment what is being taught in the school or to prepare for specialized Exams. In India, Entrance Exams have been a popular method of screening and selecting meritorious students, for the limited number of seats available in prestigious institutions of higher education. The competition is fierce with the number of aspirants increasing at an exponential rate but the number of seats not increasing at a commensurate rate. A quick look at the number of aspirants for IITs, the premier institute for Engineering in India and the number of seats on offer across the 17 IITs, pretty much explains the situation.

Table 1: Number of IIT JEE Aspirants Over the Last three Year and IIT Seats on Offer

Year	*Number of Aspirants*[2]	*Seats Offered*	*Per Capita Seat Availability*	*% Increase in Aspirants*	*% Increase in Seats Offered*
2010	4,56,000	9509	48	–	–
2011	4,86,000	9618	51	6.58%	1.15%
2012	5,02,000	9647	52	3.29%	0.30%

With such high degree of competition, the studentsare left with no options but to seek help from institutes offering specialized coaching for such entrance exams.

Graduate Courses for Commerce and Humanities Stream largely depend on Class XII Marks for admissions and even if they have Admission Tests, preparation for these tests can be comfortably done in 2-3 months or the 'Crash Course' Mode.

For Science Stream students, the situation is different as most Engineering Colleges rely on such entrance exams for admissions. The most popular coaching course among the students is the Two Year Program and institutes have maximum enrolments for this program. This program starts when the student chooses Science stream as his specialization after completing Matriculation. The increasing competitiveness in Engineering Exams also has lead to creation of products of longer duration. Now-a-days programs of three, four or even more years are available in the market and students are thronging the coaching institutes for these courses. All this, to ensure that the students are in a position to give their best shot during the admission test as they would be competing with the best brains from across the nation for the limited seats. Earlier student would face multiple Entrance Tests like IIT JEE, AIEEE, Common Entrance Test organized by Different Sates (CETs), etc. But with the recent move of Human Resources Department, Government of India; to have a unified admission test for Engineering

[2] 'IIT-JEE: Over 5 lakh aspirants to appear in 2012' – *Times of India* – Mumbai Edition, 9 February 2012, http://articles.timesofindia.indiatimes.com/2012-02-09/education/31041115_1_madras-zone-jee-scores-iit-director.

courses competition is bound to increase manifold as the students have only one shot at getting admission in college of their choice.

The high degree of competition among students has also resulted in the 'coaching industry' evolving into an organized sector which was hitherto, a largely unorganized sector. The Market size of Private Coaching sector in India is considered to be approximately $6.4 billion.[3] The city of Kota in Rajasthan has over the past couple of years, evolved in to a Mecca for engineering aspirants. Nearly 1.2 lakh students from across the nation come to Kota and enrol for engineering preparation course. Indian majors like Vidyamandir Classes, FIITJEE, Educomp, Career Point, Resonance, Aakash Institute, Everonn, Sri Chaitanya, Career Launcher etc are present in multiple locations across the nation, offering courses of various durations to engineering aspirants. Career Point, which is exclusively into IIT JEE preparation, came out with an IPO of Rs 115 crores in September 2010.

The Indian coaching industry like any other Industry facing globalization,is not bereft of International presence either. International players like McGraw-Hill, Pearson, have also been present here for long. In 2011, Etoos Academy, South Korea's largest Coaching Conglomerate entered the Indian market in a big way and set up shop at Kota with an estimated investment of Rs. 300 million.

All these market developments are indicators of corporate sector's belief in the business potential of the private coaching industry.

QAC – THE THREE PRONGED PROBLEM

The Indian Supplemental Education system suffers from a three pronged problem of QAC - Quality, Access and Cost.

Quality

- Good Quality teachers are a scarce resource
- It is virtually impossible to replicate good teachers in large numbers. Training faculty members is an option but not a scalable one.
- Teachers are irreplaceable to the core process of teaching.

Access

- The best teachers are mostly based in bigger cities and hence students of these cities have an unfair advantage when it comes to competitive examinations like IIT JEE, AIEEE, etc.

---

[3] 'Cram schools boom widens India's class divide' – Reuters Report, 11 September 2012 - http://www.moneycontrol.com/news/wire-news/cram-schools-boom-widens-indias-class-divide_756118.html

- As the Entrance Exams are or national level, students from Tier 2 & 3 cities are not able to benchmark their preparation with students from Metropolitan and Tier 1 locations who have access to better resources for preparation.

Cost

- Remunerations of Faculty Members is the single biggest element among the Fixed Costs in the Coaching sector. According to Mr. A K Tiwari, Head HR-Bansal Tutorial, Kota; a good teacher with 3-4 years of experience can cost approximately Rs. 30-50 lakhs p.a.[4]
- Lease of premises and other operating expenses are rising across locations.

Metropolitan and Tier 1 cities have ample options for supplemental education in physical mode where good teachers are available and also the general paying capacity of households is higher. The QAC problemadversely affects students in Tier 2 & 3 cities and further widens the divide between students from metros and Tier 2 & 3 cities.

Thus a huge opportunity for the education industry lies in catering to these Tier 2 & 3 / remote locations where the options for good quality supplemental educationat school level are few and demand (in terms of number of students) is fairly high.

The challenge at hand is to provide high quality teaching cantered on the best faculty, to students in any part of the country, at economical costs.

THE SOLUTION – INFORMATION TECHNOLOGY

The solution to the three pronged problem of QAC faced by the Supplemental Education Industry,especially in Tier 2 & 3 cities/remote locations can be found using Information Technology. The quality (bandwidth) and availability (geographic coverage) of Internet & IT in the past decade has increase exponentially and has powered the growth of many sectors. Toady internet is easily available at broadband speeds and can be accessed using lesser expensive devices, as compared to the situation a decade ago. Reduction in cost of computer terminals, cost of internet access,cost of media (CDs, pen drives), availability of wide range of content, and overall increase in computer literacy has played a pivotal role in increasing the penetration of IT in the Indian household.

According to Internet World Stats, India has achieved 10.2% internet penetration as of December 2011[5] which is highly commendable. The sales for computer hardware is also bullish as per industry experts

---

4 'Korean firm invests in Kota's Education Sector' – Report by CNN IBN, 26 July 2011, http://ibnlive.in.com/news/korean-firm-invests-in-kotas-education-sector/170308-3.html

5 'India achieves a 10.2% Internet Penetration Rate' – Economic Times, 10 April 2012 http://articles.economictimes.indiatimes.com/2012-04-10/news/31318824_1_internet-users-penetration-number-of-facebook-users.

Table 2: Desktop & Laptop Sales, Source – Manufactures' Association for Information Technology Estimates

Device	*2010-11*	*2011-12*	*% Growth*
Desktops	6,030,418	6,711,911	11%
Notebooks	2,950,192	3,724,746	26%

IT can be used to as an enabler for Supplemental education in two broad ways:

- **Passive Mode**– One way communication – Teacher to student
  E.g. – Educational CDs, Software, E-Books, etc.
- **Interactive Mode** – Two way communication – Teacher to student and vice-versa, E.g. – Video Conferencing, Digital White Board, Streaming of Classes over IP, etc.

The biggest disadvantage of passive mode is the lack of interactivity; interactivity being an integral part of learning in our traditional learning methods. The limited or virtually nonexistent options for the students to ask questions or get their doubts clarified hamper thewidespread use of passive modes. Also the problem of piracy which is rampant in the Indian software content market reduces the financial viability for the content providers. The main advantage of passive modes is its low price (of both ownership and operation) which attracts customers who have access to limited IT resources and also the price sensitive customer.

The limitation of one-way communication in passive modes is overcome by the interactive modes. These modes provide more options for the feedback loop from student to the teacher and in many cases it is instantaneous feedback in the form of chat message/audio-visual feedback. This makes it quite close to the normal physical classroom teaching mode.

THE BOTTLENECK – LAST MILE CONNECTIVITY

Though IT has revolutionized the Education Sector, the main bottleneck in interactive modes is internet bandwidth at the users' end (both availability and cost). This is also referred to as 'The Last Mile Connectivity' issue. Market for internet access is divided into three parts or 'miles'

- First Mile – Global network of submarine cables
- Middle Mile – Inter-city and Intra-city networks of the network service provider
- Last Mile – Final connection to the consumer's location from the service provider's exchange/network operating centre, also known as retail mile.

The Last mile is what connects the user's device with the network operating centre of the Telephone Company/Cable Company/ISP. Normally it takes form of copper wire/ coaxial cable, leased line, wireless radio or even optical fibre (FTTH). Different modes of last mile connectivity have different bandwidth, cost, data loss, downtime etc. Moreover,

While metropolitan and tier 1 cities are better off in terms of Middle &Last Mile Connectivity with better internet speed, availability and lower cost; tier 2 & 3 cities and remote locations are disadvantage in this regards. For many of these tier 2 & 3 locations, broadband connectivity is an expensive proposition with low demand which makes it financially unviable for the service provider. Wireless mobile networks might be available but the bandwidth needed to stream two-way video might be an issue. 3G mobile networks which can support video data are not widely available across India yet and cannot be used to address the problem.

THE FEASIBLE SOLUTION – VSAT

VSAT (Very Small Aperture Terminal) is a two-way satellite ground station with a dish antenna that is smaller than 3 meters. Data rates typically range from 56 kbps to 4 Mbps. VSATs access satellites in geosynchronous orbit to relay data from small remote earth stations to other terminals or master earth station "hubs". VSATs are most commonly used to transmit narrowband data (point of sale transactions such as credit card, polling or RFID data), orbroadband data (for the provision of satellite Internet access to remote locations, VoIP or video). VSATs are also used for transportable, on-the-move or mobile maritime communications.

The VSAT is a good option of overcoming the 'Last Mile' bottle neck as it uses satellite communication rather than copper wire/fibre/ mobile or other mode of terrestrial network. VSATs need to be installed at the studio side (uplinking end) and the classroom side (downlinking end) for the classes to be conducted. This makes it possible to set up the class room in any part of the country, irrespective of it being a tier 1/tier 2 or tier 3 locations. VSAT also takes care of the Service Providers inability to provide connectivity in far off/geographically remote areas, where financial viability of a regular territorial network is not possible due to either high cost of over heads for Middle mile or low market demand.

The efficacy of the VSAT Technology is well proven and it is being used extensively in communications, banking (for ATM Machines), broadcast media (Outside Broadcast/ OB Vans of news channels), etc.

The main advantages of VSAT Technology can be enumerated as:

- **Last Mile Problem:** Service Provider might have reliable high-speed links between city exchanges, but the connections from the nearest exchange to customer location could be weak/unreliable could fail. VSATs located at customer's premises guarantee seamless communication even across the last mile.
- **Reach:** Terrestrial networks find it difficult to service remote/difficult locations due to the cost/technological challenges involved in laying cables, repeater, antenna etc. VSATs, on the other hand, offer unrestricted and unlimited reach.
- **Reliability:**Uptime of upto 99.5 percent is achievable on a VSAT network. This is significantly higher than the typical leased line uptime of approximately 80 to 85 percent.

- **Deployment Time:**VSAT deployment takes no more than 4-6 weeks as compared to 4 to 6 months for leased lines.
- **Network Management:**Network monitoring and control of the entire VSAT network is much simpler than a network of leased lines, involving multiple carriers at multiple locations. A much smaller number of elements need to be monitored incase of a VSAT network and also the number of vendors and carriers involved in between any two user terminals in a VSAT network is typically one. This results in a single point of contact for resolving all your VSAT networking issues.
- **Maintenance:**A single point contact for operation, maintenance, rapid fault isolation and trouble-shooting makes things very simple for a client, using VSAT services. VSATs also enjoy a low mean time to repair (MTTR) of a few hours, which extends upto a few days in the case of leased lines. Essentially, lesser elements imply lower MTTR.
- **Flexibility:**VSAT networks offer enormous expansion capabilities. This feature factors in changes in the business environment and traffic loads that can be easily accommodated on a technology migration path. Additional VSATs can be rapidly installed to support the network expansion to any site, no matter however remote.
- **Cost:** A comparison of costs between a VSAT network and a leased line network reveals that a VSAT network offers significant savings over a two to three years timeframe. This does not take into account the cost of downtime, inclusion of which would result in the VSAT network being much more cost-effective. Pay-by-mile concept in case of leased line sends the costs spiralling upwards. More so if the locations to be linked are dispersed all over the country. Compare this to VSATs where the distance has nothing to do with the cost.Additionally, in case of VSATs, the service charges depend on the bandwidth which is allocated to your network in line with your requirements. Whereas with a leased line you get a dedicated circuit in multiples of 64Kbps whether you need that amount of bandwidth or not.

VSAT TECHNOLOGY FOR SUPPLEMENTAL EDUCATION AT SCHOOL LEVEL

Now that the effectiveness of the VSAT technology has been discussed, let us see how it can be used in the Education Sector and specifically for Supplemental Education at School Level.

VSAT gained popularity among the teacher and students in 2010 with the overwhelming success of ETEN CA, a program which provided mentoring to CA Aspirants. The best of the teachers for the various subjects would teach from the Studio and the live class would be beamed to students across the nation. The student could also ask question and get their doubts clarified instantaneously. Several IIMs and other prestigious Institutes have also started using the VSAT platform for Executive Education where the teachers' lectures are beamed to various study centres where Mangers and other executive attend the classes.

How VSAT Classes Work?

Following is the process of teaching using the VSAT mode. The process may vary from firm to firm but more-or-less the following flow is followed.

- The Teachers teaches from a studio, where the audio-visual feed is captured and sent to the uplink antenna, routedtrough the exchange severs. This feed is live with minimum possible delay.
- The audio-visual feed is received by the satellite and bounced off to the antennas at the study centres.
- The visual feed is projected using a LCD projector while audio feed is sent to speakers in real time.
- Feedback Mechanism
  - Microphone Query – each classroom is provided with a microphone, which the student can use to ask question from the teacher. The question being asked is audible to the teachers and students across all study centres.
  - Computer Terminal with chat software – operatedby the class coordinator and is used to ask doubts, get clarifications. Students tell their doubt / question to the coordinator who types the sameinto the chat software.
  - IP camera – whichsends video feed from the classroom back to the teacher in the studio.
  - Students can also get their doubts resolved offline through phone/mail /discussion forums, etc.
- The teacher has three screens before him –
  - Output screen – showing what is being streamed to the classroom to adjust visual of the board, request for zoom in / zoom out on board, etc.
  - Chat software screen – all study centres are logged into this chatroom.
  - Video feeds form classes.

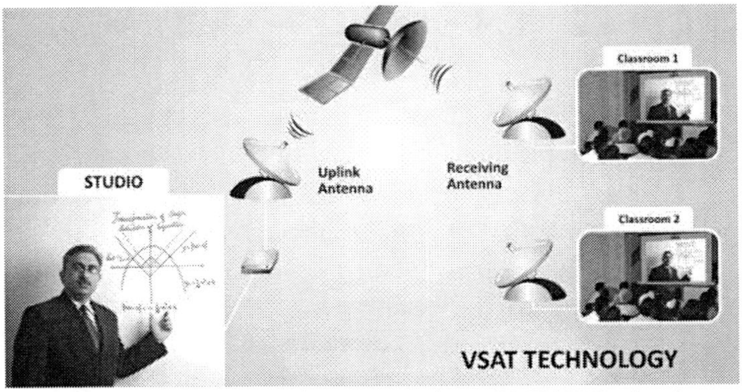

Illustration 1: Schematic Presentation of VSAT Technology

With advancements in technology the optimal number of study centres which can log in at the same time has improved. At present upto 50 study centre can comfortably log in for the same transmission without negatively affecting the performance. The monitor screen for feed form the centre changes in a sequential manner and the teacher can also request for feed from a specific centre. Additionally, associate faculty can assist the main teacher in monitoring the feed from the various classes. More centres can also login but the effectiveness of feedback loop through microphone requests/chat could be adversely affected

Advantages of VSAT Mode for Students

- Access to best of the teachers from metropolitan cities, which would not have been possible otherwise. Either the student would have to move out of their city to get better quality supplemental education or be content with whatever is available locally.
- Opportunity to study with student from across the nation. Though his class has only 30-35 students, there are several other classes logged in form different cities which provide excellent opportunities for peer-to-peer learning.
- Video recording for each lecture – Videos lectures are stored on the server and made available to the students in their online accounts for review and revision. So even if the student is absent for the class, he does not miss the lecture.
- Bane for shy students who hesitate to ask question in a normal physical classroom as they need not approach the teacher directly, all they need is a request through the chat software. Also it could possible that he need not even ask the question,given the large number of students logged in at the same time, it is quite possible that other students might ask the same question.
- Performance Benchmarking is possible with students from across the nation which is essential for a national level test like IIT JEE.
- Economical Pricing as compared to other physical classroom models.

Advantages of VSAT Mode for Test Prep Firms

- Firms can work withfewer 'Star Faculty' (qualified & experienced teachers with proven track record of mentoring top rankers), which is one of the biggest cost component for Engineering Test Prep Firms. If they are to expand using physical classroom mode, they need at least one set of teachers for each centre which increases the operating cost by a huge margin.VSAT implies lesser expenditure on training of teachers even if more centres are to be opened.
- Easier quality control on what is being taught to the students. Also synchronization of course covered across centres is easier as there are fewer teachers. Operationally speaking, this is an huge advantage.

- No need for good quality teachers (who are mostly located in Metropolitan/Tier 1 locations) to relocate to other Tier 2/3/remote locations
- Wider customer base – access to more number of students.
- Ease of scaling up operations across larger number of cities by opening new centres.
- Higher probability of students getting better rankers if more number of students are enrolled. Ranks achieved by students are advertised heavily to get more admissions.
- Geographically Remote locations such as industry townships with moderate demand which otherwise do not clear the financial feasibility criteria, can be profitably catered to using VSAT Mode.

COST ESTIMATES

The approximate fixed costs for setting up a VSAT Study centre with 1 Classroom for 35 students is given below:

Table 3. Approximate Cost of VSAT Classroom

Description	*Cost*
VSAT Equipment at Centre	1,00,000
Classroom Equipment like Projector, Computer, Amplifier, Router etc	1,50,000
TOTAL	2,50,000

Other costs at Study Centre like rent/lease for the premises, staffing cost, runningexpenses vary from location to location. Moreover these are more or less common to both physical classroom mode and VSAT Classroom mode

There are some other fixed costs at the Studio end like studio utilization expenses, VSAT at Studio, Bandwidth charges etc which depend on the service provider. Also, the average cost for each centre for these services reduces as more number of centres are operational.

The important cost saving in VSAT Mode for the firm is the Remuneration for Teacher at each centre as fewer teachers are required in VSAT Mode. In physical mode each centre successive centre would require more teachers, adding to the cost.

Hughes Communications India Limited and NELCO (Tatanet VSAT) are the two leading providers of VSAT services in India. Over the years, both capital expenditure and operating expenses for VSAT have seen decline.

Charting VSAT for Supplemental Education on Innovation Adoption Life Cycle

If we are to analyze the progress of VSAT for Supplemental Education on Rogers' Diffusion of Innovation Cycle, we can clearly see that it is has so far only been adopted by the **Innovators**.

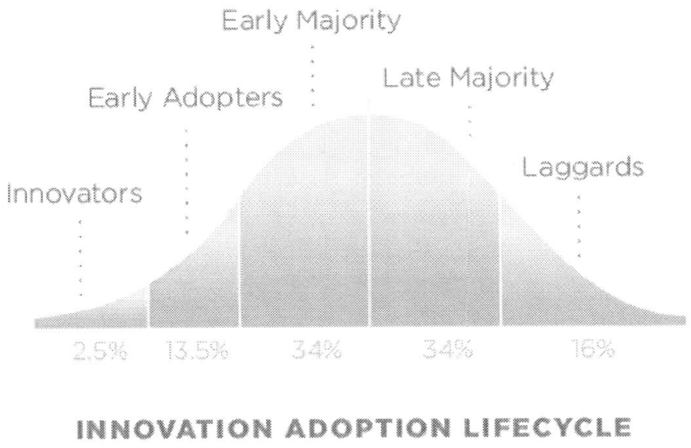

Illustration 2: Everett Rogers' Innovation Adoption Lifecycle.

The main reason which is slowing down the adoption of VSAT platform by students& parents is the rigidity of consumer mindset leading to consumer inertia. Since Vedic Ages,Teaching has been contact based activity in India and moving to a virtual classroom mode is bound to face resistance. But the progress achieved in a limited time span of 3-4 years has been promising.

Some of the common apprehension of parents and students hindering adoption of VSAT can be listed as below:

- The thought that a student would be 'studying from an LCD Screen' is difficult to assimilate for some parents.
- Stereotypes in the minds of people that any mode other than a physical teaching mode is just another correspondence course/distance learning program.
- Some parents presume that is just a recorded video lecture being show on an LCD screen, there by completely discounting the interactivity aspect of the VSAT mode.
- 'How would discipline be maintained in the class as there is no teacher in the class' – they are made to understand that the class coordinator acts as a representative of the teacher.
- 'What if more than one student have doubts at the same time? How will that Teacher answer them as the teacher is not physically present in the class' is another common question. The answer to which is – the same way it is done in physical class, students take turns in asking the questions.
- Parents assume watching a lecture on LCD is same as watching a TV and can put strain on eyes.

Most of these queries of parents & students are taken care of with demo classes. But motivating the parents to come to the study centre and attend demos is a challenge in some cases.

With students successfully completing the course and getting good sores in IIT JEE, the mindset is changing, but it is a slow process. Marketing and advertising is also being used as a catalyst to hasten the process.

Industry Scenario

Educomp Solutions Ltd. stared its pilotproject for the first VSAT based Engineering Test Prep Courses in 2010, close on the heels of its successful ETEN CA product. There were some apprehensions about replicating the success of ETEN CA model for Engineering Test Prep as the market and the kind of students are slightly different. CA students are more mature and require less monitoring/ disciplining as compared to the younger school students, the target market for Supplemental Education. Also CA courses are of shorter duration whereas Engineering Test prep the average duration of course is 2 years or more. But the pilot project was well received by the student community and since then, there has been no looking back.

Educomp's success inVSAT model for Supplemental Education at school level has lead to several other players entering the market for Engineering Test Prep on VSAT platform. Incumbent as well as new firm have joined the VSAT bandwagon. Vidyamandir Classes, Edurite, Bansal Tutorial/ IODL, Career Point, Resonance, BASE etc are now providing engineering test prep services through VSAT to students in tier 2/3 and other remote locations which were hitherto unavailable to them.

The cost advantages coupled with the opportunity to reach out to a wider student base are very strong incentives for incumbent and new firms to move into the VSAT Test prep space.

Thus it can be concluded that VSAT platform is strongly poised to change the scenario of for Supplemental Education at School Level. And this change is definitely going to be better, with more students getting access to better test prep at economical prices. This would help them in being prepared in a better way to take competitive exams and realize their dream of getting admission to premier institutes.

Web Data Mining: Emerging Challenges of a Technique and Its Significance

Nudrat Fatima, Iffat Ara Khanam and Thirunavukkarasu K.

Department of Computer Science and Engineering, Galgotias University, Greater Noida

ABSTRACT

This paper discusses about the concepts of web data mining which is one of the mining technologies and It is used to improve web services,its sources, the emerging challenges of today and the pros and cons regarding the web data mining. Italso discusses its classifications: web content mining, web structure mining and web usage mining's applications and the major purpose of each category of web data mining. The web usage mining pros and cons are also discussed further in this paper.

INTRODUCTION

Web Data mining is one of the applications of data mining techniques that finds interesting and potentially useful knowledge and information from the web data including the hyperlink structures of the web and web log data or both can be used. It collects information from various required information from different web resources that enables an individual or company to promote business,understanding marketing dynamics, new promotions floating on the internet.Web data mining technology is opening avenues on not just gathering data but it is also raising a lot of concerns related to data security. There is loads of personal information available on the internet and web data mining had helped to keep the idea of the need to secure that information at the forefront.Web data mining helps the visitors to get a lot of information in one location instead of reading information from different websites. People use this feature to build information listing, get information about different topics by searching in forums etc. Companies use this service to see what kind of service is floating in the World Wide Web for their products or services and take actions based on the data presented. Web mining aims to discover useful knowledge and information from web hyperlinks, usage data and page contents. Although web mining uses many conventional data mini g techniques but in a sense it is not purely an application of traditional data mining due to semi-structured and unstructured nature of the web data.

In general, the web data mining works in following manner:

1. Doing web mining efficiently by downloading information from the various websites.
2. Copying the useful website content.
3. Then extracting the text.

LITERATURE REVIEW

Web Data Mining is used to finding predictive information in large databases on the web. Also used for the automated discovery of previously unknown patterns. Web data mining has several tasks: resource finding: the task of retrieving intended web documents, information selection and preprocessing: automatically selecting and preprocessing specific information from retrieved web sources, generalization: automatically discovers general patterns at individual websites as well as across multiple sites, and Analysis: validation and interpretation of minded patterns.

EMERGING CHALLENGES

The web is a very huge and the distributed centre for the variety of the information services regarding the government, electronic commerce, news etc. It is also an important source for linkage and providing useful information and data for the data mining.However we are facing problems related to categorizing and collecting data for the data mining. The WWW is very huge and it's growing fast for effective data mining and data warehousing. There is a survey for the growth of the web from the year 1991 to 1997.

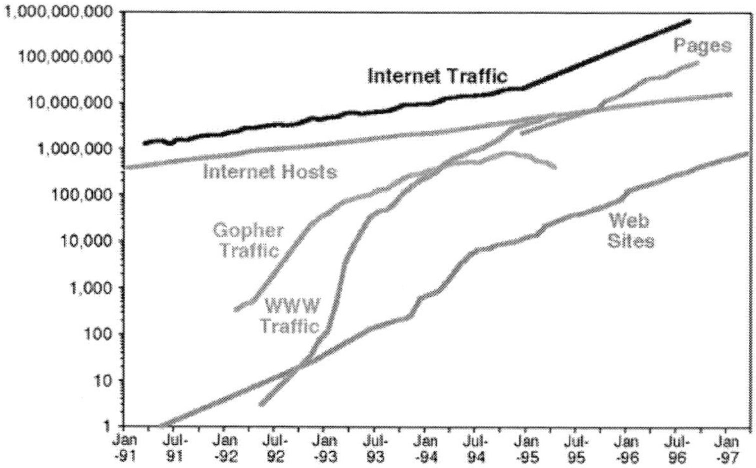

Fig. 1. Growth of Web Between 1991 and 1997

The search engines have only a part of information of the web. It is approximately assumed that the web is 500 times larger than the information any search engine represents and can measure. Because of the growing rate and mass of the web it is almost impossible tostore all the relevant data on the web. Complexity of the web pages is another main challenge.Some web pages are just text-based some of them contain multimedia data such as images and videos. There is no index bycategory, author, and title and so on. Extensible Markup Language (XML) is an attempt to reduce the complexity of the web pages. The complexity of web pages in general cannot be solved with the help of XML. For example in financial services there is an XML standard that is why structure of the information exchanged is in a format that is agreed upon by the communicating parties and that can be easily manipulated.

Since the users are from different culture and backgrounds having different data usage so the language issues are also one of the challenges of web data mining. Only certain information is of use to the users so keyword based search engines can be used but it also has certain deficiencies. Polysemy is one of the problems of data mining. For example the word "Turkey" contains the search for both the country Turkey and the animal Turkey. Synonymy is another problem for keyword-based search engines which means that two synonym words are similar in meaning but different in writing and search results don't contain its synonym.

One challenge is how to design classiers to handle ultra-high dimensional classication problems. There is a strong need now to build useful classiers with hundreds ofmillions or billions of features, for applications such as text mining and drug safetyanalysis. Some of the other problems and challenges include mining sequence data, time series data and mining of complex knowledge from complex data which is in the form of graphs.

CATEGORIES OF WEB DATA MINING

Web data mining task has been initially classified into two categories: Web content mining (getting patterns from Web data) and Web usage mining (getting Web logs). Then the

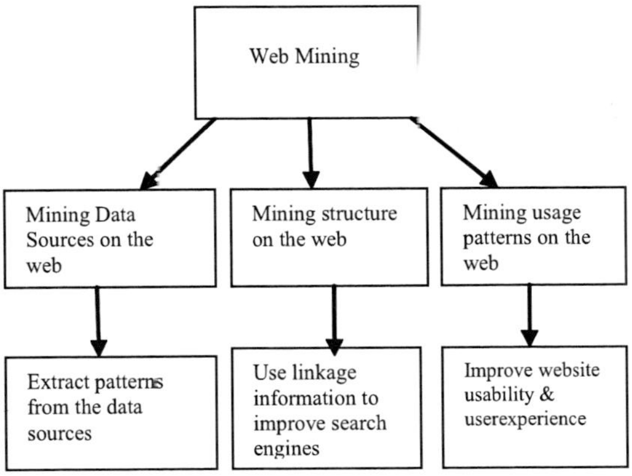

Fig. 2. Web Mining Categorization

classification is expanded to three partsthat are known as Web content mining, Web usage mining and WebStructure mining.Web content mining is mining the data including text, image, video, etc. on the Web. Web structure mining tries to discover the link structure of the hyperlinks. Based on the topology of the hyperlinks, Web structure mining will categorize the Web pages and generate the information, such as the similarity and relationship between different Web sites.

Web Content Mining

It deals with discovering useful information or knowledge from web page contents. It goes well beyond using keywords in a search engine. In contrast to web usage mining and web structure mining, web content mining focuses on web page content rather than the links. Web content is a very rich information resource consisting of many types of information. For example, unstructured free text, image, audio, video and metadata as well as hyperlinks. The content of web pages includes no machine readable semantic information. Search engines, subject directories, intelligent agents, cluster analysis and portals are employed to find what a user might be looking for. The unstructured data is the main challenge of content mining. There are two approaches for Web content mining: Information Retrieval Approach and Database Approach. It shows that most of the researchers use a bag of words, based on the statistics about single words in isolation, to represent unstructured text and take single words found in the training corpus as features. For the semi-structured data, all the works utilize the HTML structures insides the documents and some utilized the hyperlink structure between the documents for document representation. As for the database view, in order to have the better information management and querying on the Web, the mining always tries to infer the structure of the Web site to transform a Web site to become a database.

Web Structure Mining

It deals with discovering and modeling the link structure of the Web. Work has been carried out to model the Web- based on the topology of the hyperlinks. This can help in discovering similarity between sites for the particular topic or discipline or in discovering web communities. Kleinberg at Cornell has developed a connectivity analysis algorithm called Hyperlink- Induced Topic Search (HITS) based on the assumption that links represent human judgment. His algorithm also assumes that for any query topic, there are a set of authority sites that are relevant and popular focusing on the topic and there are hub sites that contain useful links to relevant sites on the topic including links to many related authorities.HITS uses two values for each page, the authority value and the hub value. Authority and hub values are defined in terms of one another in a mutual recursion. An authority value is computed as the sum of the scaled hub values that point to that page. A hub value is the sum of the scaled authority values of the pages it points to. Relevance of the linked pages is also considered in some implementations. A hub is one or a set of Web pages that provides collections of links to authorities. In general, a good hub is a page that points to many good authorities; a good authority is a page pointed to by many good hubs. This mutual releationship helps the mining of the authoritative Web pages and discovery of high quality Web structures and resources. Firstly, HITS uses the query terms to collect a starting set of, say, 200 pages from an index-based search engine. These pages form the root set. Since many of these pages are presumably relevant to the search topic, some of them should contain links to most of the prominent authorities. Therefore, the root set can be expanded into a base set by including all of the pages that the root-set pages link to, and all of the pages that link to a page in the root set such as 1000 to 5000 pages.

Second, authority weight and hub weight values are estimated numerically. We first associate a nonnegative authority weight ap and a nonnegative hub weight hp with each page p in the base set, and initialize all a and h values to a uniform constant. The weights are normalized and an invariant is maintained that the square of all weights sum to 1.

The main purpose for structure mining is to extract previously unknown relationships between Web pages. This structure data mining provides use for a business to link the information of its own Web site to enable navigation and cluster information into site maps. This allows its users the ability to access the desired information through keyword association and content mining. Hyperlink hierarchy is also determined to path the related information within the sites to the relationship of competitor links and connection through search engines and third party co-links. This enables clustering of connected Web pages to establish the relationship of these pages.

Therefore, Web mining and the use of structure mining can provide strategic results for marketing of a Web site for production of sale. The more traffic directed to the Web pages of a particular site increases the level of return visitation to the site and recall by search engines relating to the information or product provided by the company. This also enables marketing strategies to provide results that are more productive through navigation of the pages linking to the homepage of the site itself.

To truly utilize your website as a business tool web structure mining is a must.

Web Usage Mining

It deals with understanding human behavior in interacting with the Web or with the website. One of the aims is to obtain information that may assist website reorganization or assist site adaptation to better suit the user. The minded data often includes data logs of user's interactions with the Web. The logs include the web server logs, proxy server logs and browser logs. The logs include the information about the referring pages, user identification, time a user spends at a site and the sequence of web pages visited. While web structure mining shows that page A has a link to page B, Web usage mining shows how many people took that link, which site they came from and where they went when they left page B. It focuses on the techniques that could predict user behavior while the user interacts with the Web. E-commerce specialists have recently focused on this behavioral data to understand how users decide to buy something.

When comparing Web content mining and Web structure mining, Web usage mining is a considerably new research area and it has gained more attention in recent years. CGI scripts offer other useful information such as referrer logs, user subscription information and survey logs. This category is important to the overall use of data mining for companies and their internet/intranet based applications and information access.

Usage mining allows companies to produce productive information pertaining to the future of their business function ability. Some of this information can be derived from the collective information of lifetime user value, product cross marketing strategies and promotional campaign effectiveness. Usage mining is valuable not only to businesses using online marketing, but also to e-businesses whose business is based solely on the traffic provided through search engines. The use of this type of web mining helps to gather the important information from customers visiting the site. This enables an in-depth log to complete analysis of a company's productivity flow. E-businesses depend on this information to direct the company to the most effective Web server for promotion of their product or service.

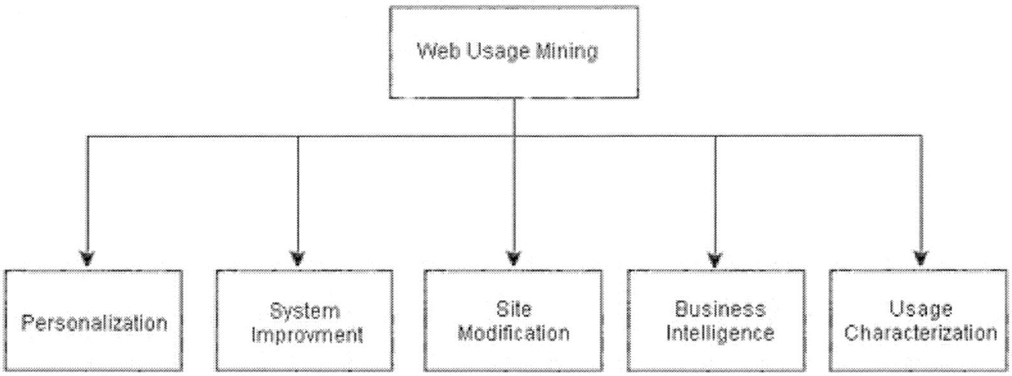

Fig. 3. Web Usage Mining

There are certain advantages and disadvantages of web usage mining.

This technology has enabled e-commerce to do personalized marketing, which eventually results in higher trade volumes. The governmentagencies are using this technology to classify threats and fight against terrorism. The predicting capability of the mining application can benefits the society by identifying criminal activities. The companies can establish better customer relationship by giving them exactly what they need. Companies can understand the needs of the customer better and they can react to customer needs faster. The disadvantages are also there in contrast to the advantages Privacy is considered lost when information concerning an individual is obtained, used, or disseminated, especially if this occurs without their knowledge or consent

SOURCES OF WEB DATA MINING

Devyani Sadh, Ph.D., president of Data Square, LLC, provides a detailed explanation of the many Web site data sources:

Every click on a Web site combines to generate a pattern for the organization to use in its business planning. A Web server, when properly configured, can record every click that users make on a Web site. For each click in the so called? Click stream? The Web server appends a line to a text file called a server log, recording information such as the user's identity, the page clicked, and the time stamp. At a very minimum, all Web servers record access logs and error logs. Web server can also be configured to append a type of file called the referrer log to the standard log.

The following list explains some sources of Web site data:

Application Server Logs

The drawbacks of the Web server logs are eliminated by using application server logging. The application server controls session, user registration, log in and log out data. It also logs click stream data and critical events such as? Add to cart? Change quantity? Etc. Web server logs have many deficiencies, which can be overcome if the site is architected properly and logging is done at the application layer.

Cookies

Cookies keep the information where visitors go while they are on a Web site. When the visitor returns to the same Web site, cookies which are stored in the user's local hard disk provide information about the user'spreferences and identity. Using cookie is privacy issue but Web sites utilized them for personalized Web pages.

Form/User Registration Data

Web sites have several kinds of forms which are used for gathering data from users. Membership required Web sites provide a user registration form including name, address, date of birth, gender, occupation, annual income, etc. Databases generated with this data are valuable sources for mining.

Web Purchase Data

Purchased data from non-Web environments and third party Internet data providers can be used together withWeb data available throughthe company Web site for data mining.

ADVANTAGES AND DISADVANTAGES OF DATA MINING

Advantages

There are several advantages of web data mining some of these we discuss.

It is helpful in marketing and retailing by providing aid to direct marketers with useful and accurate trends about their customer purchasing behavior. Based on this the marketers can direct their marketing attentions to customers with more precision. Likewise it is also helpful in banking/crediting, law enforcement, for researchers, etc.

Disadvantages

In contrast to advantages there certain disadvantages too that we are facing for the data mining. The major issues of web data mining are the privacy and the security issues. Personal privacy has been a major cause of concern and the security is also a major drawback of web data mining as the company has lot of information that is available on the internet. There is lot of misuse of the information.

CONCLUSION

Since large amount of data are available on the internet which may be structured, unstructured, multimedia and text so mining these complex data is important.

This paper explains and summarizes the sources, emerging challenges, the taxonomy of the web data mining which is a vast area in the field of neural networks, artificial intelligence and many more. We discuss the connection between the various categories of web data mining. It provides opportunities and ease to the users but still the privacy and the security are the major issues which are of concern to the users.

REFERENCES

[1] Han, J., & Kamber M. (2001). "Data Mining: Concepts and Techniques." San Diego, CA: Morgan Kaufmann Publisher.

[2] Rud, O.P. (2001). "Data Mining Cookbook: Modeling Data for Marketing, Risk, and Customer Relationship Management." Canada: Wiley Computer Publishing.

[3] Thuraisingham, B. (2003). "Web Data Mining and Applications in Business Intelligence and Counter-Terrorism." Florida: Crc Press.

[4] Kohavi, R. (2001). "Mining E-commerce Data: The Good, the Bad, and the Ugly". In Proc. of the seventh ACM SIGKDD international conference on Knowledge discovery and data mining.

[5] Kosala, R., & Blockeel, H. (2001)." Web Mining Research: A Survey." ACM Press.

[6] Man, L. (2002). "Hypertext, Information Retrieval and Data Mining: Behind Link There is Golden Mine." Retrieved November 6, 2006, from http://www.scholars.nus.edu.sg/cpace/ht/lanman/wm1.htm

[7] Ding, C., He, X., Husbands, P., Zha, H., & Simon, H. (2001)."Page Rank, HITS and a Unified Framework for Link Analysis." LBNL Tech Report 49372, (updated Sep 2002).

[8] Department of Computer Science and Engineering. "The Web SIFT Project Website." Retrieved November 6, 2006, from http://www.cs.umn.edu/research/websift/taxonomy.html

[9] Greening, D.R. (2000)." Data Mining on the Web: There is Gold in that Mountain of Data." RetrievedNovember 6, 2006, from http://www.webtechniques.com/archives/2000/01/greening

Author Index

Ahlawat, Vinay Kumar 101
Arora, Paras 24
Awasthy, Neeraj 81

Banerjee, Subrato 144
Bhatnagar, Vishal 1
Bhatnagarm Vishal 45
Bhusry, Mamta 54
Bhuyan, Prashanta K. 34

Chakraborty, Nirmalya 110
Chandrasekhar, S. 65
Dahiya, Naveen 1
Deshmukh, Vaishali T. 90
Dubey, Sanjiva Shankar 163

Gupta, Nidhi 151

Kaur, Prabhjot 74

Manjeet 138
Mishra, Geeta 130

Puri, Sandeep 24

Ranjan, Jayanthi 54, 101, 110
Rastogi, Aabhas 24
Rathi, Kavita M. 14
Routraym Susmi 34
Roy, Saikat Ghosh 120

Sahajwani, Mayank 24
Sawarkar, S.D. 14
Sharma, Abhishek 120
Sharma, Vandna 110
Singh, Manjit 1
Singh, Suvalaxmi 34
Sinham Sapna 45

Tayal, Sukriti 81
Thaikattil, Nishal Joseph 171
Thirunavukkarasu, K. 151

Upadhyay, Parijat 120
Upadhyay, Rashmi 151
Vaikole, Shubhangi 90